By the author

Labor in America

The Imperial Years

The Imperial Years

BY

FOSTER RHEA DULLES

THOMAS Y. CROWELL COMPANY · NEW YORK

MANUFACTURED IN THE UNITED STATES OF AMERICA

CONTENTS

1. Mr. Cleveland Takes Office   1

2. Pattern of the Past   5

3. Mr. Cleveland's Foreign Problems   17

4. Background of Adventure   32

5. The First Stirrings of Imperialism   50

6. Mr. Cleveland Returns   70

7. Behind the Scenes   91

8. The Rising Tide   107

9. "A Splendid Little War"   129

10. God, Destiny, and Mr. McKinley   148

11. The Great Debate   165

12. Establishing an Empire   183

13. The Open Door Policy   198

14. Theodore Roosevelt and World Power   219

15. Making Latin America Behave   241

16. War and Peace in Asia   266

17. An Even Keel in Europe   287

18. End of an Epoch   302

    Bibliographical Notes   314

    Index   327

FOREWORD

AT THE close of the 1890s the United States found itself—suddenly and dramatically—a great power. In the aftermath of war with Spain, the nation acquired distant overseas possessions, established an empire, and assumed a new role in international affairs. Becoming president soon after these epochal developments, Theodore Roosevelt was convinced that America was destined to exert a decisive influence on the future balance of world power. He sought to implement a positive and vigorous foreign policy in Latin America, in eastern Asia, and even in Europe, that would both compel full recognition of American influence and prestige and, at the same time, strengthen the forces making for global peace.

Yet the American people hardly realized the implications of what was taking place in their country's relations with the outside world. Their imagination had been fired by the movement for overseas expansion, a first and perhaps unavoidable expression of the nation's rising power in the context of the times, and for a time they were carried away by it almost in spite of themselves. How else could America play the great world role to which—they were told and firmly believed—she was destined? The acquisition of colonies, ironically enough, seemed somehow necessary in the process of seeking to realize the ancient dream of America's historic mission to promote liberty and justice.

There soon developed, however, doubts and misgivings as to whether the nation had set out on the right course. The imperialist fervor that swept the country at the turn of the century subsided as rapidly as it had arisen. The American people became confused and uncertain as to the future. Shaken loose from the comfortable isolationist moorings of the past, they were still reluctant to accept the responsibilities and obligations inescapably inherent in the country's new position of strength and power. In spite of the appeals of Theodore Roosevelt, they remained highly dubious of his thesis that American politics had become world politics.

The early 1900s were consequently marked by many contradictions in the realm of foreign policy. The United States made a first tentative assertion of international leadership, but any chance that it might play a truly decisive role in world issues was lost because there was no resolution of the basic conflict between isolationism and internationalism. Although the American people realized that any return to the past was impossible, they were unwilling to forego a traditional insistence upon complete freedom of action that rigidly barred any international commitments binding for the future.

During these years the perennial conflict between a realistic and idealistic approach to foreign affairs also became greatly accentuated. The more pragmatic demands of immediate national interest were set against the broad utopian goals of the mission to spread abroad American ideals. And conversely, there was much talk of moral responsibility and of the nation's duty, talk that bore little relation to the framework of power politics within which any foreign policy had to operate.

Expansion into the Caribbean and the Pacific, the Open Door policy in China, Roosevelt's amplification of the Monroe Doctrine, a mediating role during the Russo-Japanese war and at the Algeciras conference, the dispatch of the battleship fleet around the world—these events made the United States a conspicuous actor on the global stage. But while the public became periodically excited over such demonstrations of the nation's power and influence, there was still no sustained and lasting concern over the ultimate goals of foreign policy.

A popular feeling that the idealism leading to war with Spain was betrayed in its imperialistic consequences militated against further involvement in international politics. A totally unrealistic belief that the world had in fact entered upon a new age of settled peace and that the United States need have no fears for the future, created what was to prove a false sense of security. And a renewed absorption in domestic matters and progressive reform served to relegate still further into the background all international questions. At the very time that the United States appeared to be playing a more active role in world affairs, popular support for such a policy was dwindling away.

When a decade later the nation found itself involved in a world war in which it originally believed it had no stake, and was then catapulted into a position of acknowledged world leadership, the American people were consequently still unprepared for responsibility. The chance to develop a cohesive foreign policy at once realistic in terms of national interest and in keeping with basic American ideals was lost. Only the dreadful experience of not one but two world wars was able to drive home the lessons that had not been learned in the opening years of the century.

In the perspective of fifty years and more, popular attitudes in the 1890s and early 1900s toward foreign involvements take on a new significance. They have an unexpected relevancy for a day in which the United States has assumed the obligations and made the commitments it so long refused. These 'imperial years' marked the adolescence of a nation that only today is slowly and painfully attaining a maturity that holds out the promise of an effective world leadership built out of the experience of the past and embracing an idealism practically grounded in reality.

CHAPTER I

MR. CLEVELAND TAKES OFFICE

MARCH 4, 1885, WAS A BRIGHT SUNNY DAY, AND WASHINGTON was crowded with the throngs that had gathered to celebrate the Democrats' return to political power after the harsh days of Civil War and Reconstruction. Grover Cleveland, the party's triumphant standard bearer, was to be inaugurated as the twenty-second President of the United States.

The thirty to fifty-thousand partisans and admirers who were massed on the Capitol grounds saw a solid, powerfully built man—Cleveland weighed some 250 pounds—with a rather immobile face, pale gray-blue eyes, and a brown mustache. He wore a conventional double-breasted Prince Albert, but beside the sartorially perfect Chester A. Arthur, the outgoing President, he did not make a very impressive appearance. A young representative from Wisconsin, Robert La Follette, commented disparagingly on the new President's "coarse face, his heavy inert body, his great shapeless hands."

As Cleveland began to speak in a strong, penetrating voice, the first thing observed was that he had neither manuscript nor notes. "My God, what a man!" exclaimed Senator John J. Ingalls of Kansas. "What a gambler!"

The characterization was not very apt. Cautious, conservative, unimaginative, Cleveland was anything but a gambler; and the inaugural address itself—"solid and earnest—yet calm" —reflected the man far more than his disregard of manuscript or notes. It was a clearcut expression of his political philosophy with strong emphasis upon the need for administrative reform and the importance of introducing business principles into government.

As the first Democratic president since the Civil War, Cleveland was determined to give the nation an honest and efficient administration that would still further cement national unity. Except on the issue of the tariff, where he was later to fight valiantly, if unsuccessfully, in favor of downward revision, his views did not greatly differ from those of his Republican predecessors. He accepted with little questioning the prevailing laissez-faire philosophy and showed slight understanding of the deepening problems of farmers and industrial workers. Aggressively honest, conscientious, industrious—"it was work, work, work, all the time," wrote one member of his official household —and as stubbornly independent as any man in public life, Cleveland wanted above all else to preserve and strengthen existing American institutions. All this was plain in his inaugural address, an occasional eloquent affirmation of constitutional ideals, but no radical innovations, no fireworks.

On foreign policy, as opposed to domestic issues, he had very little to say. That little, however, was again an explicit restatement of the conservative traditions of the past.

The genius of the American people, their domestic needs, and the attention demanded for the development of the nation's vast resources, Cleveland declared, dictated the scrupulous avoidance of any departure from the foreign policy that the United States had always pursued. What was this policy? It was a policy of independence, favored by geographical circumstance and defended by justice and power; a policy of peace suitable to the national interest; and a policy of neutrality that rejected any share in foreign broils, harbored no ambitions for overseas expansion, and was at the same time prepared to repel any intrusion of European powers in the affairs of the New World. This policy, the new President concluded with words echoing those of all his predecessors in the White House, "is the policy of Monroe and of Washington and of Jefferson— 'Peace, commerce, and honest friendship with all nations; entangling alliances with none.' "

The inaugural address, enthusiastically applauded by his audience, largely reflected the views of his countrymen on domestic matters and, even more particularly, on foreign affairs. Few there would have been, in 1885, to dispute so succinct an analysis of the position of the United States in the nineteenth-century world.

The country was stable and prosperous when Cleveland took office. The years of his first administration have been characterized as an interlude between the hungry 1870s and the stormy 1890s. Although discontent was already developing in some farming areas as a consequence of crop failures, drought and falling prices, and although what was to become an angry spirit of revolt among industrial workers was foreshadowed by railroad strikes and the sensational Haymarket Square bombing, the American people as a whole were not unduly disturbed. They felt assured that there would be no serious interruption of the spectacular economic progress that had been made in the two preceding decades. The South was recovering from the ravages of war; settlement of the West was nearing completion; and the North was consolidating its new industrial economy.

An air of well-being pervaded most of the land. The cities, especially, were booming and beginning to enjoy some of the exciting new developments of the coming age of technology. Cable cars and elevated railways were revolutionizing urban transportation. Electric lighting and telephones, although still startling innovations, held out new promise for the future. In scores of ways other inventions and labor-saving devices were changing home life—furnaces, gas stoves, ice boxes, modern plumbing, new-fangled kitchen appliances. "Housekeeping," declared one commentator as early as 1887, "is getting to be ready-made as well as clothing."

The comfortable life of the wealthy and well-to-do was counterbalanced by dire poverty among some elements of the population. However basically conservative his views, Cleveland would note in terms that might have been borrowed from

Henry George that the gulf between classes appeared to be widening—"one comprising the very rich and powerful, while in another are found the toiling poor." He recognized that, while trusts and other combinations of capital were growing, the ordinary citizen was often "struggling far in the rear or is trampled to death beneath an iron heel." Every city showed these sharp contrasts in living conditions, with the great and costly mansions of the wealthy neighbored by crowded and ugly slums. This was especially true in the new metropolitan centers that had to absorb the yearly influx of European immigrants who flocked to the New World with hopes not always realized. Hordes of foreign-born, ignorant and penniless, worked and lived under well-nigh intolerable circumstances in such cities as New York, Philadelphia, and Chicago.

Yet in spite of such shadows over the American dream, it was still generally believed that the road to success and ultimate riches was open to every one. Opportunity beckoned; even the lowliest could aspire to the heights. It was not only Horatio Alger, with his hundred-odd books, who reflected the universality of the "rags to riches" theme and the prevailing idea that great fortunes were to be made by those who had pluck and at least a modicum of luck. Andrew Carnegie, one-time bobbin boy in a textile factory, was building an empire of steel; John D. Rockefeller, who started as a clerk in a commission house, an empire of oil.

The country was not only becoming richer. James Bryce, British author and the most observant of foreign visitors, wrote that "the sadness of Puritanism seems to have been shed off." The American people were increasingly enjoying themselves and discovering new means of entertainment and amusement. The one-time sacred Sunday, to the discomfiture of the godly, appeared to have become a day "for labor meetings; for excursions; for saloons, beer gardens, baseball games, and carousels." Big league baseball and college football were becoming popular spectator sports; John L. Sullivan, the "Strong Boy of Boston," was a hero throughout the land; bicycling was replacing roller skating as an almost universal craze. The huge playhouses of the cities were staging gorgeous blood-and-thunder melodrama to the delight of their audiences, and hundreds of traveling road companies brought such entertainment to the opera houses of the small towns. Barnum and Bailey was only the first among the many circus troupes that set up their magical tents at village crossroads to rival Chautauqua meetings and country fairs in the rural sections of the nation.

With its new industries, expanding production, broadening interests, and diversified cultural background, the United States was a vital, dynamic nation. Its people were superbly confident that theirs was the only first-class civilization in the world. "The old nations of the earth creep on at a snail's pace; the Republic thunders past with the rush of the express," cried an exuberant Carnegie the year after Cleveland's inauguration; ". . . America already leads the civilized world."

Still, for all its progress and complex urban culture, the country retained something of the simplicity, the slower tempo, and above all, the sense of security of an earlier age. Here was an America innocent of moving pictures, radio, and television; of automobiles and airplanes—and also of income taxes, vast armament expenditures, conscription, foreign alliances, and atomic bombs.

CHAPTER II

PATTERN OF THE PAST

IN CALLING FOR A POLICY BASED UPON PEACE, INDEPENDENCE, and neutrality, President Cleveland in his inaugural address accepted a pattern of the past that, as he himself stated, stemmed directly from principles enunciated by Washington, Jefferson, and Monroe. From the earliest days of the Republic there had been an implicit assumption that the United States would not engage in the quarrels of Europe or in any way intervene in the affairs of other nations. While he was the American minister at the Court of St. James's immediately after the Revolution, that staunch patriot John Adams had a conversation with the Swedish ambassador in London. "Sir," said the Swedish envoy in Adams's account of the incident, "I take it for granted that you will have sense enough to see us in Europe cut each other's throats with a philosophic tranquillity." Such advice was thoroughly congenial to John Adams. He had already emphatically gone on record—in 1776—as believing that, come what might, the United States should separate itself as far as possible and as long as possible from all European politics and European wars.

The warnings subsequently given by Washington and Jefferson against any entanglement in European affairs no more than emphasized the convictions of almost all Americans of their day. Complete freedom of action was essential to the United States if it were fully to establish its independence. This was not isolationism in the sense of withdrawal from the world. That the United States could never do. But it was an isolationist policy in that it embraced an adamant refusal to make any foreign political commitments or to enter upon any entangling alliances. If the purport of the Monroe Doctrine was to warn Europe to keep its hands off the American continents, this famous message also reaffirmed in traditional terms the intention of the United States to refrain from any interference in the affairs of the European powers.

There were occasions when this policy was challenged. When revolutionary struggles broke out in Europe in 1830 and 1848, a few voices were raised suggesting that the United States should throw its moral and even its physical support to the republican cause. They found little backing. There was to be no such deviation from the doctrine laid down by the Founders.

America was the well-wisher to the freedom and independence of all nations, John Quincy Adams declared, but "she goes not abroad in search of monsters to destroy." It was his firm belief —and would remain throughout the century the belief of the American people—that if the nation enlisted under the banners of foreign independence it would soon find itself involved "in all the wars of interest and intrigue, of individual avarice, envy, and ambition, which assume the colors and usurp the standards of freedom." This country's contribution to freedom, as Henry Clay was further to state on a later occasion, was to keep the "lamp burning brightly on this western shore, as a light to all nations."

Such conceptions of the nation's role in respect to Europe were never interpreted, however, as circumscribing American expansionist policies even if they risked collision with foreign powers. The United States was not to be hemmed in and confined within its original boundaries. The purchase of Louisiana and the acquisition of Florida, the annexation of Texas, the conquest of California, and the assertion of American rights in Oregon—these successive steps in establishing the continental domain reflected a determination that the United States should be free to build up an American empire.

The expansionist drive was older than the Republic. As early as 1771 the young poet Philip Freneau, still a student at Nassau Hall, glowingly envisioned a youthful people "warm in liberty and freedom's cause," spreading out over the entire continent:

"I see, I see
A thousand kingdoms rais'd, citizens and men
Numerous as sand upon the ocean shore;
Th' Ohio then shall glide by many a town
Of note; and where the Mississippi stream
By forests shaded now runs weeping on,
Nations shall grow and states not less in fame
Than Greece and Rome of old."

Here was "The Rising Glory of America"; and if there was for a time little idea that the entire continent could be welded into a single nation, the westward advance—across the Alleghenies, the rich valley of the Mississippi, the wide Missouri, the Great Plains, the Rockies themselves—was ultimately to give reality to the conception of a United States stretching magnificently from the Atlantic to the Pacific. This was the fulfillment of a manifest destiny. It was the inherent right of the nation, a contemporary editorial declared in 1845, "to overspread and possess the whole of the continent which Providence has given us for the development of the great experiment of liberty and federated self-government entrusted to us."

Did the conquest of the greater part of a continent mark the limits of national expansion? There were those in the exuberant days of the mid-nineteenth century who looked ambitiously beyond the boundaries resulting from war with Mexico and settlement of the Oregon dispute with Great Britain. The rich islands of the Caribbean and even more distant regions in the Pacific beckoned invitingly. Coming into office in 1853, President Pierce declared that his administration would not be controlled "by any timid forebodings of evil from expansion."

The Caribbean prize which most attracted the early imperialists was Cuba. The desire to attain control of this island may in fact be traced back to the first days of the Republic. John Quincy Adams declared in 1825 that its annexation "will be indispensable to the continuance and integrity of the Union." The movement to secure Cuba in the 1850s, however, became deeply entangled in politics and was widely interpreted in the North as no more than a southern effort to extend slave territory. The attempt on the part of the Pierce administration either to purchase the island or otherwise "detach" it from Spain could not command popular support.

The idea of possible expansion into the Pacific had quite different origins. It grew out of the search for new riches and new markets in the Orient—a significant factor in the westward movement itself—and was actively promoted in and out of

Congress. The influence of American missionaries was also to have a part in this movement, but commercial ambitions were paramount. The United States had long since initiated trade with China; its whaling ships every year scoured the North Pacific, and its merchantmen well knew Hawaii as a port of call and often visited the distant islands of the South Seas. Here, in the dreams of some statesmen, was a vast area where American commerce, American influence, and American power might well be extended.

Such ambitions inspired, in the mid-century, the expedition under Commodore Perry that opened up Japan to the Western world, negotiations with China wherein the United States insisted upon its right to share all commercial privileges granted other nations, and the conclusion of a treaty of annexation with Hawaii. This latter project collapsed—ironically enough because it contemplated the admission of Hawaii to the Union as a state—but on every hand there was a mounting interest in the Pacific. This ocean, its islands, and the vast regions beyond, William H. Seward prophesied in an often quoted speech before the Senate, were fated to become "the chief theater of events in the world's great hereafter." He declared enthusiastically that America "must command the empire of the seas, which alone is real empire."

Commodore Perry voiced even more significantly the dreams of the imperialists of his day. Reporting on his expedition to Japan, he stated that "the course of coming events will ere long make it necessary for the United States to extend its territorial jurisdiction beyond the limits of the western continent." He favored not only the annexation of Hawaii but that of additional naval stations off the Asiatic coast.

Perry specifically urged the establishment of an American outpost in what were then known as the Lew Chew Islands—today the Ryukyu Islands, where, a century after Perry's visit, the United States has built up its tremendous naval and air base at Okinawa—and in still more unexpected foreshadowing of the future, he also proposed an American protectorate over

Formosa. "I assume the responsibility," he wrote in a long dispatch to the State Department, "of urging the expediency of establishing a foothold in this quarter of the globe, as a measure of positive necessity to the sustainment of our maritime rights in the east."

Secretary Marcy did not give Commodore Perry any encouragement for his grandiose schemes in spite of the interest of the Pierce administration in promoting American commerce in the Pacific. He advised the naval commander—again in somewhat ironical foreshadowing of the future—that if resistance to American occupation of one of the Lew Chew Islands should develop, it would be "mortifying" to have to surrender it and yet "inconvenient and expensive" to maintain the forces necessary for its retention. "It is considered sounder policy," the Secretary of State said, "not to seize the island as suggested in your dispatch."

The country as a whole was not yet ready for overseas expansion, whether in the Caribbean or the Pacific. President Pierce's successor, James Buchanan, often appeared imperialist-minded, but no action whatsoever was taken to acquire new territory during his administration. Moreover, on the more general aspects of foreign policy, Buchanan reaffirmed the traditional isolationism in the relations of the United States with the outside world. In taking this stand, he said, in 1857, that no one could attempt to dispute the wisdom of the maxim prevailing since Washington's day that the United States should avoid all foreign entanglements. Certainly other issues were far more important at this time than territorial expansion. Over the nation hung the dread shadow of sectional conflict. Whatever possibility there might have been of acquiring new possessions during this decade—some fifty years before the imperialist explosion of the century's close—approaching Civil War ended it completely.

There was, it is true, another brief and ephemeral flare-up of imperialism in the years immediately following the struggle which finally cemented the Union. Some few Americans again looked toward the Caribbean and the Pacific as areas where the United States should seek island outposts. They urged the acquisition of Santo Domingo and the Danish West Indies, the purchase of Alaska, the annexation of Hawaii, and even the establishment of some sort of a foothold off the coast of China. President Johnson swung into the expansionist camp and told Congress in 1868 that national policy appeared to sanction the acquisition "of the several adjacent continental and insular communities" as speedily as it could be done peacefully and lawfully.

Yet there was even less popular interest in such ambitious projects than there had been in the 1850s. Seward, now Secretary of State, succeeded almost singlehandedly in purchasing Alaska from Russia in 1867; but it was with the greatest difficulty that he secured the necessary authorization and appropriation from a critical and reluctant Congress. "Have the people desired it?" Representative Williams of Pennsylvania inquired caustically. "Not a sensible man among them had ever suggested it. The whole country exclaimed at once, when it was made known to it, against the ineffable folly, if not the wanton profligacy, of the whole transaction." Only the powerful influence of Senator Sumner, more concerned with maintaining friendly relations with Russia than with overseas expansion, enabled the Administration to win approval of its treaty. And in supporting the purchase of Alaska, Sumner strongly emphasized that it should not be considered in any way as a precedent for further annexations.

Seward had to recognize that his other plans, except for assertion of American title to the little island of Midway, had no chance of acceptance. The domestic problems growing out of the Civil War—southern reconstruction, greenbackism, the corruption in high circles—absorbed all popular interest. Under such circumstances, he wrote somewhat despairingly, "the public mind refuses to dismiss these questions, even so far as to entertain the higher, but more remote, questions of national extension."

Seward's ideas, as those of Commodore Perry and other mid-century imperialists, were harbingers of the future. The interest shown in Cuba and the Danish West Indies, in Hawaii and other possible Pacific possessions, foreshadowed in a measure hardly realizable at the time the imperialism of the close of the century which this account will seek to chronicle. There was in almost every instance a half-forgotten precedent for the overseas expansion of 1898. In general terms, however, the post-Civil War years marked the complete submergence of all imperialist ambitions. Close commercial ties were maintained with the various regions into which American trade and commerce had penetrated, but all thought of new territorial acquisitions was seemingly abandoned. The American people were concerned with pushing the frontier of westward settlement across the Great Plains rather than with securing new territory.

This significant westward movement, together with the consolidation of that new industrial society to whose growth the Civil War itself had given such tremendous impetus, was indeed to relegate all matters of foreign policy into the background of public consciousness. There has perhaps never been a period in which national energy found a more complete outlet within existing political borders. The first half of the nineteenth century emphasized foreign relations because the very process of continental expansion brought the nation into contact—sometimes potential conflict—with other countries. The years at the century's close and the continuing history of the twentieth century were to be marked by ever greater involvement in international politics. The post-Civil War decades, however, found the United States more than content to stay at home and largely ignore the rest of the world.

There were no really significant foreign issues in any quarter to command the interest of either the government or the people. Without the urge for further expansion, the United States did not come into collision with other powers; in a general era of world peace, the nation had no fears for its own security. The traditional isolationist spirit was greatly strengthened.

One extreme example of this attitude was the refusal to accept even so innocuous an international agreement as the convention establishing the International Red Cross. It had always been deemed questionable, if not unwise, the Secretary of State declared in 1868 when a first invitation was extended to sign this convention, for the United States to become a party to any international agreement, and "nothing but the most urgent necessity should lead to a departure from this rule." Ultimately the State Department relented on this issue, but the isolationist spirit was again reflected in the criticism voiced when American delegates attended an international conference held in 1884 on African affairs and signed the Berlin General Act providing for the establishment of the Congo Free State. One of Cleveland's first moves was to withdraw this treaty from Senate consideration on the ground that the American delegates had exceeded their authority and there was no warrant for any such departure from traditional policy.

Throughout these years, with perhaps one exception, the secretaries of state had no previous experience with foreign affairs and were solely political appointees. Henry Adams was later to state that their only apparent function was to recognize the existence of a world that Congress would rather have ignored altogether. The problem created by Chinese immigration, with treaty agreements completely overruled by Congress, and minor issues arising in respect to Latin American affairs, were the State Department's principal concerns. Its general inactivity was reflected in the actual size of the diplomatic staff. There were only some sixty officers and clerks on the rolls of the State Department when Cleveland entered upon the presidency, and three years later the total personnel of all foreign legations (the rank of ambassador had not yet been created) and consulates was something under twelve hundred.

Even so limited a staff evoked some criticism on the ground of needless extravagance; and before Cleveland's first term ended, the New York *Sun* was attacking the diplomatic corps as a costly humbug and sham. "It is a nurse of snobs," the *Sun* declared irritably. "It spoils a few Americans every year, and does no good to anybody. Instead of making ambassadors, Congress should wipe out the whole service."

A further sign and symbol of popular disregard of the position of the United States in the world community was the general apathy toward the sad state into which the navy had been allowed to fall. While other nations had long since built modern, steel-armored vessels, it was not until the 1880s that the United States took even the first tentative steps in new naval construction. The existing fleet was no more than a handful of obsolescent, wooden ships, still relying primarily upon sail rather than steam power. It was not only inferior to the fleets of all the European naval powers, but even to those of a number of Latin American countries. Rudyard Kipling was to advise readers of his *American Notes* in 1891:

"China's fleet today, if properly manned, could waft the entire American navy out of the water and into the blue. The big, fat Republic that is afraid of nothing, because nothing up to the present has happened to make her afraid, is as unprotected as a jelly-fish."

The advocates of a stronger navy drew harrowing pictures of British, Brazilian, Chilean, and even Chinese warships shelling American ports and linked what they considered the ineptitude of foreign policy with the lack of any really effective navy. Senator John T. Morgan of Alabama, later to be an outspoken imperialist, stated that the policy of the United States had been "hesitating and lame . . . because we were known not to possess the available power that a great fleet would give us."

Among both American and foreign observers there was wide agreement on the indifferent complacency with which the people as a whole viewed international affairs. Henry Cabot Lodge, that astute and calculating politician who was later to have something of an influence in such matters, might sadly regret that foreign issues had "but a slight place in American politics, and excite generally only a languid interest"; but it did not trouble most of his contemporaries. They were content to ignore Europe and Asia in their very natural concentration on the domestic problems that so much more directly affected a nation still aloof from international rivalries and the struggle for colonies and power.

James Bryce stated authoritatively in the *American Commonwealth* that "the one principle to which people have learnt to cling in foreign policy is, that the less they have of it the better." He found in many instances an attitude of "pure and undisguised contempt" toward other countries, but he also noted that the development of the nation's resources left little time for any consideration of what might happen elsewhere in the world. "And into the mind of the whole people," Bryce added, "there has sunk deep the idea that . . . . the true way for the model Republic to influence . . . . [the] world is to avoid its errors, and set an example of pacific industrialism."

Cecil Spring-Rice, the brilliant young secretary of the British legation who a quarter of a century later would return as ambassador, also spoke of the condescending way in which Americans liked to refer to "the serfs of Europe" and discussed the popular notion which led Americans to consider themselves the only people to enjoy real political liberty. As a career diplomat, he regretted his Washington assignment in the 1880s—"it seems so far off the line." He wrote home on one occasion during Cleveland's administration that there was "very little experience of foreign politics here—in fact none."

Why should the American people have looked abroad? They firmly believed that everything they could possibly desire was to be found in the United States. In the great wheat-growing areas of the Midwest were being produced those bumper crops that made the United States the granary of all the world. Europe had to look to America, not America to Europe. The Myth of the Garden—the idea of an agricultural utopia entirely secure from all outside influences—had a powerful appeal to men's minds. And as other resources were discovered and de-

veloped in the vast continental domain that was the United
States, the well-being and happiness of the American people
seemed ever more assured.

Secure in its rich possessions, there was nothing the nation
wanted from the outside world. With no idea of interfering
with other countries' concerns, it asked only to be left alone.
The old image of Europe prevailed—a corrupt, decadent, and
dying continent in sharp contrast to the young, progressive,
virtuous Republic. Europe represented oppression, militarism,
and war; America represented opportunity, freedom, and peace.
The roots of isolationism remained deep and strong.

When Cleveland came into office he was not as wholly oblivi-
ous of the potential importance of foreign policy as the attitude
of the country and many contemporary statements would perhaps suggest. He was prepared to uphold American interests in
Latin America and the Pacific with a strong assertion of national rights wherever he thought those rights were under attack. Yet, at the same time, he remained convinced that the
United States should not under any circumstances allow itself
either to become involved in European affairs or to embark on
any expansionist program that might bring the country into possible conflict with other nations. The support that he was prepared to give to the nascent movement for a stronger navy was
limited by his feeling that the navy should have no other purpose than continental defense. His reaction to what was to become a rising demand for construction of an isthmian canal
was that any such project "must be for the world's benefit—a
trust for mankind, to be removed from the chance of domination by any single power." He believed that "the intimacy of
our relations with Hawaii should be emphasized" and was prepared to uphold American interests even in distant Samoa; but
in neither case did he countenance for a moment any idea of
territorial expansion.

"Maintaining, as I do," Cleveland stated in his first annual
message to Congress in 1885, "the tenets of a line of precedents
from Washington's day, which proscribe entangling alliances

with foreign states, I do not favor a policy of acquisition of new and distant territory or the incorporation of remote interests with our own."

Clinging firmly to the isolationist pattern of the past—once again asking in effect Washington's nearly century-old questions: "Why forego the advantages of so peculiar a situation? Why quit our own to stand upon foreign ground? Why, by interweaving our destiny with that of any part of Europe, entangle our peace and prosperity in the toils of European ambition, rivalship, interest, humor, or caprice?"—Cleveland was in full accord with the temper of the times. Yet his inaugural address was, in a sense, the swan song of the old tradition of foreign policy. He did not realize that America stood at the threshold of a new period in her history that would lead to far-flung overseas empire and rapidly—unavoidably—plunge the nation into the whirling vortex of world affairs.

CHAPTER III

MR. CLEVELAND'S FOREIGN PROBLEMS

IN SPITE OF THE COUNTRY'S GENERAL ABSORPTION IN DOMESTIC affairs, Cleveland was to be confronted with two significant problems in foreign policy during his first administration. They were quite different problems, and so were their implications. A vehement dispute with Great Britain over the North Atlantic fisheries was a heritage of the past; an incipient quarrel with Germany over the distant Samoan Islands was a harbinger of the future. The country became briefly excited over both of these problems. While it might remain true, as Bryce had suggested, that the one principle to which the American people clung was to have as little as possible to do with foreign affairs, even in the 1880s they could never be completely ignored.

For the United States to find itself petulantly bickering with England was a natural phenomenon. The relations between the two countries had been marked by a succession of disputes ever since the colonies had won their independence, and a latent antagonism toward everything British was still a national characteristic. There was no happier sport than that of "twisting the lion's tail." The problem of the fisheries had considerable economic importance, especially for the people of New England, but the blustering terms in which it was popularly discussed, as if the issue actually involved peace or war, bore little relation to the major interests of the country. Nothing could have more clearly demonstrated that the American people still had no conception of the realities of international politics.

This was further emphasized by the degree to which the quarrel became a football of domestic politics. Throughout the entire controversy, popular alignments were based upon what seemed to be partisan advantage. The approach of both politicians and newspapers was completely irresponsible. And if this did no real harm, it was only because partisanship in foreign policy was still a luxury that could be enjoyed without too much risk.

The Samoan episode involved a matter in which the public had far less interest than the fisheries dispute, even when the American position appeared to be challenged by Germany, yet it had a long-range significance hardly perceived at the time. For in insisting upon its rights in this group of South Pacific islands and refusing to allow them to fall into Germany's hands, the United States was suggesting a sphere of influence which stretched out far beyond its own borders. And for the first time it was engaged in rivalry with a new and aggressive European continental power.

President Cleveland's attitude in coping with the Samoan issue also had interesting implications. He emphatically stood for the principle that the United States should not become involved in foreign broils, as he had stated in his inaugural address, and remained no less forthright in his opposition to acquiring new territory. Nonetheless, he clearly demonstrated that these views in no way precluded his taking a determined stand in defense of what he considered national rights, even in so remote a part of the world as the South Pacific. And in so doing he encouraged the American people, in spite of isolationism, to take a broader view of their interests. His refusal to back down in the face of German pretensions to greater control over Samoa pointed the way to later developments in overseas expansion that Cleveland himself was obdurately to oppose.

The immediate cause for the fisheries dispute was the termination of the existing Anglo-American agreement which governed the rights of American and Canadian fishermen in the coastal waters of the North Atlantic. There was strong opposition in this country to the claims being put forward by England in behalf of Canadian fishermen, and comparable resistance on the part of England to what the United States asserted were the rights of American fishermen. Patriotic feeling began to run high when, in the summer of 1888, the Canadian authorities arbitrarily boarded and seized a number of New England fishing schooners off the Newfoundland Banks.

Cleveland's Secretary of State, the distinguished, courteous, pacific-minded Thomas F. Bayard, tried to deal rationally with the dispute. He was very friendly toward England—an attitude that would later lead to his being called "the most popular Englishman ever born in the United States"—and more than ready to negotiate a new fisheries agreement. The Republicans in Congress, however, had no idea of letting him handle a matter from which they might make political capital. They demanded immediate retaliation against Great Britain and heatedly debated a bill that would have peremptorily closed American ports to all Canadian vessels and prohibited the import of any Canadian fish. The moderation of President Cleveland— for he fully supported Bayard, in whose ability and patriotism he had great confidence—gave them an eagerly seized-upon chance to accuse the President of truckling under to the nation's ancient foe.

The most extreme Anglophobe was Senator Ingalls of Kansas. He had no hesitation in declaring that England—"the ruffian, the coward, the bully among the nations of the earth"—had, in the seizure of American fishing vessels, offered an affront to national honor that could not be allowed to go by default. His diatribes were loudly echoed in the Republican press. The New York *Tribune,* while conventionally deploring the idea of possible hostilities, declared that the United States was better prepared for war than Great Britain. To admit helplessness in the face of national insult, as the Cleveland administration seemed willing to do, the *Tribune* stated editorially, would be "a craven and pusillanimous policy." The Detroit *News* more belligerently suggested that if war should come from the fisheries disputes, the result would be one flag floating from the Rio Grande to the north pole—"the Canadian provinces will make elegant States in the Union." And the Columbus *Dispatch* stated bluntly that if England did not back down, war would be in order and the "continent will be ours."

Democratic papers rallied to the Administration's support. The *New York Times* took the moderate stand that American policy need not consider either concessions or war and vigorously criticized any idea of attacking Canada. "The war talk of the Senators is mostly bosh," said the Atlanta *Constitution,* while the Nashville *American* bluntly declared that the country was not going to fight "for the sake of a few hundred Yankee fishermen and a few stinking codfish."

Cleveland was not influenced by newspaper sensationalism or partisan attacks. He had no idea of enforcing the retaliatory measures proposed by Congress or of making any hostile demonstration against Great Britain. The negotiations with England were continued; and as the excitement gradually died down—in spite of Henry Cabot Lodge's fervid exhortation that "whenever the American flag on an American fishing smack is touched, the great American heart is touched"—Secretary Bayard was able to report encouraging progress. Finally, in February 1888, the United States and Great Britain concluded a new Anglo-American treaty with mutual satisfaction.

This was an election year, however. The Republicans in control of the Senate still had no idea of accepting the leadership of a Democratic president, and it was generally realized in Washington, as Spring-Rice reported to his government, that the treaty was "sure to be squashed . . . . not because the Senate disapproves of it, but because it disapproves of the present government." Indeed, one Republican senator inadvertently disclosed his hand. "We cannot allow the Democrats," he said, "to take credit for settling so important a dispute."

When the issue came up for debate in the Senate, Riddleberger of Virginia led off the new attack by asking why the United States wanted a treaty: "England has never kept a treaty; she had never made one that she did not violate." His avowed position was that the United States had defeated Great Britain in war on two occasions, and it was high time it whipped her again. These views were echoed by Senator Teller, who declared that in past wars England had proved herself among all nations to be "the most aggressive, the most bloodthirsty, the most destructive of the human race." While Senator Hoar of Massachusetts showed himself to be somewhat less anti-British, he nevertheless stated that the treaty negotiations had been "feeble, spiritless, ignoble, and timid." When consideration of the pact came to a final vote, party lines were solid. Twenty-seven ballots in favor of the treaty were cast by Democrats, but thirty Republican votes effectively killed it.

President Cleveland, who had been accused during the controversy of pigheadedness (and, somewhat irrelevantly and altogether falsely, of beating his wife), struck back promptly at his foes. He now proposed enforcement of the retaliatory measures against Canada that he had formerly opposed. This, too, was a political maneuver. For the consequences of carrying out such a policy would have placed the Republicans in a most awkward position, in this election year, because of the disrupting consequences of such a move on American trade and commerce. Their original plan had been devised only to put Cleveland in a hole. Unwilling to risk the adverse effects on American interests of a retaliatory policy against Canada, they now blocked authorization for the countermeasures they had once demanded.

Nevertheless the attacks upon the President as pro-British in no way let up. The Republican platform charged the Cleveland administration with being "conspicuously unpatriotic" on the fisheries dispute, and even more emphatically held it to account for playing into England's hands through its policy of downward tariff revision. This latter issue had become the paramount one in the presidential campaign; it was now cited as final proof of Cleveland's complete subserviency to British interests.

At this point, as charges and countercharges were hurled back and forth with all the happy abandon of partisan politics in a close election, the British minister, Sir Lionel Sackville-West, committed one of the most egregious of diplomatic blunders. This sad-eyed and most inept of foreign envoys, who had found friends in Washington, one of his secretaries acidly commented, only because he shared with Americans "a common taste for whiskey, poker, and business," let himself be caught in a transparent political trap. Asked by a correspondent what he believed to be Cleveland's real attitude toward England, he replied that in spite of the President's proposal for retaliatory action in the fisheries dispute, he was confident that Cleveland was basically a sincere Anglophile. The Republican high command, which had inspired the original letter, triumphantly published Sackville-West's reply as damning evidence of foreign interference in domestic politics. The anti-British sentiment was revived, and the Irish-American vote particularly was turned against a presidential candidate who stood so strongly in the good graces of England's envoy. As one sympathetic correspondent wrote Secretary Bayard, "the effect on our Irish Democracy is such as to utterly destroy all hope for us."

⚹ Cleveland was incensed and at once demanded that Great Britain recall her minister. When the British government hesitated, he took matters into his own hands and summarily dismissed Sackville-West. Possibly this move served to win back the Irish vote, which the Democratic National Committee believed to be "slipping out of our hands because of diplomatic shilly-shallying"; but it did not save Cleveland's candidacy. His party went down to defeat and the Republicans were returned to office under the leadership of Benjamin Harrison.

In spite of all the furor and excitement attending this Anglo-American quarrel, heightened by the exigencies of partisan politics, the American and British commissioners charged with reaching a new agreement on the fisheries did not let defeat of the proposed treaty end negotiations. They concluded a *modus vivendi* which did not need senatorial approval. Its provisions were supposedly to run only two years, but the reasonableness of its terms and the slackening of political interest made possible successive renewals until the fisheries issue was finally settled through its submission to arbitration at The Hague.

The maneuvering in 1888 did not reflect credit on any of those concerned. The contemporary significance of the controversy, apart from its effect upon the immediate economic interests involved, remained the irresponsible war talk in which the Republican foes of Cleveland so freely indulged themselves. The American people were only very briefly diverted from their continuing absorption in affairs at home.

The Samoan affair, providing the only other break in the quiet pattern of foreign relations during these years, grew out of a surprisingly long record of American interest in the South Pacific. Half a century earlier an American naval officer, Commodore Charles Wilkes, had chanced to visit Samoa and liked what he saw. He was cordially received by the natives, to whom English missionaries had introduced the happy benefits of church-going, calico clothing, and cricket, and he found a lively trade underway in copra and coconut oil. Far more important, he discovered at Pago Pago, on the island of Tutuila, a broad and beautiful bay which has been characterized as "the most perfectly landlocked harbor that exists in the Pacific Ocean."

While his visit led to the appointment of an American consul, nothing further was done to promote American interests in Samoa until the 1870s. The possibility of developing a steamship line between San Francisco and Australia then renewed interest in the islands; and in 1872 another naval officer, Commander Richard W. Meade, signed a treaty with the Samoan chieftains that gave the United States possession of the harbor of Pago Pago as a possible naval base and coaling station. The United States was still far from being interested in overseas expansion, however; the Senate rejected the proposed treaty. Nevertheless, Secretary of State Hamilton Fish dispatched a special commissioner to Samoa with instructions stating that it was "not unlikely that perhaps in the not distant future" the United States might want a naval station there.

The new commissioner, A. B. Steinberger, turned out to be a colorful and irresponsible adventurer who soon became deeply involved in the rivalries of the resident American, English, and German traders. He took it upon himself to spread abroad reports that the United States might establish a Samoan protectorate and, when rebuked for these activities, had himself appointed the "premier" of Samoa, through intrigue with the native king. Although Steinberger finally had the grace to resign his post as American commissioner, he had succeeded in stirring up a hornet's nest of local strife and awakened the alarm of both the British and the Germans by his talk of an American protectorate.

Even after Steinberger was officially out of the picture, other

American residents in the islands indicated their approval of a protectorate. They were fearful that either Germany or Great Britain might set one up if the United States failed to do so, and they prevailed upon a native Samoan chief to journey to Washington and propose either American annexation or American guardianship. His offer was debated by the members of President Hayes's cabinet and was ultimately turned down, but the Samoan chieftain did not return empty-handed. A treaty was signed in January 1878, and later approved by the Senate, whereby the United States obtained the right to establish a naval station at Pago Pago, and in return agreed to offer its good services in the event of any dispute between the Samoan government and any foreign power.

In the meantime the foreigners in the islands found themselves even more at odds in their incessant bickering over commercial privileges, and the resident consuls—American, British, and German—grew highly belligerent in defense of what they considered national rights. Their home offices were not greatly concerned over such disputes—Samoa was very far away—but the local situation became highly confused. The consuls' backing of different native claimants to the Samoan throne, unauthorized proclamations of protectorates, plotting and counterplotting at the local seat of government, set the stage for an *opéra bouffe* of international rivalry that gradually took on serious proportions.

The American consul at this time, one Berthold Greenebaum, was quite as active as his German counterpart in these island intrigues. Doubling as the agent for a firm making patent overalls, he perhaps envisaged a great market for his company's products throughout the South Seas. Whether or not this was his bright dream, no one could have been more zealous in seeking to block every move made by the German consul to advance German interests. When the latter attacked the authority of the recognized king, set a rival on the throne, and proclaimed a German protectorate, Greenebaum countered by affirming his continued support for the first king, challenging the actions of the German consul, and running up his own country's flag as sign and symbol of an American protectorate.[1]

It was these untoward events in Samoa, seemingly coming to something of a climax in 1886, that first aroused the concern of the Cleveland administration. For, as conflicting reports of what was actually happening in the distant South Sea islands reached the capitals of the nations involved, diplomatic wires began to hum. Secretary Bayard promptly and vigorously protested any German effort to establish a protectorate, and then found it necessary to disavow the actions of the overzealous American consul in raising the American flag. In very much the same manner, the German foreign office took the position that the activities of its representative did not have official backing, and Germany had no intention of trying to establish a Samoan protectorate.

Cleveland was convinced that something had to be done to clarify the situation. "The moral interests of the United States with respect to the islands of the Pacific, necessarily dependent in greater or less degree on our own American system of commonwealths," Bayard informed the consul at Apia upon reporting the President's views, "would counsel us to look with concern on any movement by which the independence of those Pacific nationalities might be extinguished by their passage under the domination of a foreign sovereign." In line with such rather vague principles, the United States thereupon suggested that after suitable investigations the three powers—the United States, Germany, and Great Britain—

[1] The term "king" is used advisedly. On his first visit to the chieftain he was to support, the American consul had a disconcerting experience. A guide led him to a large hut, reads a contemporary account, "and paralyzed Greenebaum by announcing that it was the royal palace. . . . Just as Greenebaum removed his hat and bowed his head to enter the low doorway, a big hog made a sudden rush from the interior, dashed between Greenebaum's legs and threw the disgusted consul into a heap of kitchen refuse by the side of the door."

hold a conference in Washington in an effort to arrive at a common Samoan policy.

This conference met in the summer of 1887, and Secretary Bayard proposed a tripartite agreement which would at once recognize Samoan independence and provide some measure of international control over island affairs by three-power representation on the native government's executive council. But the conferees could not agree. The discussions dragged on endlessly, and the conference seemed to be completely futile. Cecil Spring-Rice, present as a member of the British delegation, left a vivid description of the dreary proceedings.

"The Secretary clears his throat and makes a speech in senatorial style—very eloquent and rather long," he wrote. ". . . Then the German says (in English) he will read a written statement. Of course wholly irrelevant to Bayard's speech. Then West [the British minister, Sackville-West] reads a written statement. Then Bayard asks questions but is too deaf to hear the answers, and resumes his speech where he left it off. . . . Then we all get hungry and yawn. Then the sitting is adjourned and we telegraph home. This has been going on for some days."

As the summer brought hotter and hotter weather, and tempers shortened, the conference at last adjourned permanently, having accomplished nothing whatsoever.

In the meantime, while the diplomats were spinning out their endless words, things had begun to go from bad to worse in Samoa itself. New claimants to the native throne appeared, and rivalry among the unabashed consuls in supporting their candidates grew even more frenzied. The Germans drove one king off the throne and installed another with the support of marines landed from a gunboat in the harbor at Apia; the British and American consuls refused to recognize him; a native revolt broke out and a third chieftain took over control.

Finally, in January 1889, the forces from the German gunboat were again sent ashore to combat the revolt against the

chieftain still receiving German support in opposition to the
backing given his rival by both the British and American
consuls. Someone blundered. The German forces were caught
in an ambush and some twenty of them killed by natives.
This was virtual war—between Samoa and Germany. The
American consul frantically reported that the Germans were
"shelling and burning indiscriminately, regardless of American
property. Protests unheeded. Natives exasperated. Foreigners'
lives and property in greatest danger. Germans respect no
neutral territory."

President Cleveland, now nearing the close of his term of
office, grew even more disturbed over these developments than
he had been two years earlier and suspicious of what Bismarck,
the German Chancellor, might really have in mind. Still without any idea of asserting exclusive American authority, Cleveland ordered three warships to Samoa to safeguard national
interests; and in his communications with the German government he insisted that "the autonomy and independence of
Samoa should be scrupulously observed." In a final message
to Congress on January 21, in which he termed the Samoan
imbroglio a very "delicate" situation, the President reviewed
the steps he had taken and somewhat ominously left any
further action to the "wider discretion conferred by the Constitution upon the legislative branch of the Government."

There was, for a time, excited talk in the newspapers of
compelling Germany to respect the American position by a
show of force. "If ordinary protests shall not be heeded," cried
one newspaper, "then we must give him [Bismarck] a lesson
with shotted guns." Congress appropriated $500,000 for the
protection of American lives and property as Senator Reagan
of Texas, expressing the views of many other congressmen,
insisted that the President "assert our rights in such a way that
there can be no mistake about his meaning and what his
powers are."

For all the noisy clamor of the firebrands—an article in the
New York *Herald* warned of the "extreme probability that the

German fleet may threaten to shell New York"—the press generally began to adopt a more temperate tone as the possible consequences of a clash in Samoa were better understood. The *New York Times* stated that the "talk about war . . . is nonsense." Other papers agreed that nothing could be more ridiculous than for the United States to take up arms "on account of some black people thousands and thousands of miles away in the Pacific." The *Nation* sarcastically decried "running this wild goose chase respecting a group of islands in the South Pacific Ocean more distant from our shores than Berlin itself. . . . The more the matter is looked into," its editorial continued, "the more plainly does it seem, on our part, an outbreak of sheer Jingoism and meddlesomeness in other peoples' affairs."

Conditions in Samoa might nevertheless have led to real trouble had not Germany promptly acceded to the strong protests that Cleveland had sent to Berlin. Bismarck made it clear that he considered the whole affair a local fracas and did not want further controversy with the United States. Stating emphatically that Germany had no intention of placing the independence of Samoa in jeopardy or of challenging the rights of the other powers in the islands, he proposed the resumption in Berlin of the negotiations that had broken down two years earlier in Washington. Cleveland was glad to accept this suggestion. He left to the incoming Harrison administration a free hand to try to settle the vexatious issue of Samoa's future status as best it could.

The drama in the islands themselves was not yet played out. In these early March days, seven foreign warships—three American, three German, and one British—tossed uneasily in the harbor at Apia. There were repeated rumors that they had clashed—that an American vessel had fired on one of the German ships, that an American gunboat had been sunk by a torpedo. On one occasion, excited crowds gathered about the newspaper offices in San Francisco on the report of incipient German-American hostilities. This was not the news that finally arrived from Samoa—it was that of a disaster even more dramatic, if far less dangerous to world peace.

On the night of March 15, as the local situation grew ever more tense in spite of the conciliatory moves made by diplomats, Samoa was suddenly struck by a storm of hurricane force. All the next day it swept over the islands, building up a tremendous, raging sea in the usually calm waters of Apia's harbor. On the morning of the seventeenth, only one of the foreign warships was still afloat. Two of the American vessels were partially sunk and the third beached; the three German ships were either sunk or broken on the reefs, and only the British vessel had succeeded in riding out the storm and escaping to sea after narrowly avoiding collision with one of the American gunboats. Some forty-four American sailors had been swept off their ships and into the sea during this frantic battle against the elements. The beach of Apia was heaped high with the debris of the wrecked ships.

"In what seemed the very article of war," said Robert Louis Stevenson in *A Footnote to History,* written in Samoa shortly afterward, "the sword-arm of each of the two angry powers was broken; their formidable ships reduced to junk; their disciplined hundreds to a horde of castaways. . . . Both paused aghast; both had time to recognize that not the whole Samoan archipelago was worth the loss in men and costly ships already suffered."

When word of the catastrophe reached the United States, even the most rabid warmongers completely subsided. "Men and nations," wrote the New York *World,* "must bow before the decrees of nature."

As Cleveland's term of office expired, there was still—in spite of these developments in Samoa or those affecting Anglo-American relations—little to suggest any departure from the principles of foreign policy the President had so cogently set forth in his inaugural address. The fisheries dispute had been at least temporarily settled through the *modus vivendi;* and

while the Samoan problem was still unresolved, it no longer had
very serious implications.

In his final message to Congress in December 1888, Cleveland had dwelt very little on foreign policy. He made no
general statement other than to express his conviction that
there were no questions in dispute that could not be settled
by "frank diplomatic treatment." He regretted there had been
no final settlement of the fisheries issue and drew attention
to the continuing controversy over Samoa. He referred briefly
to the question of Chinese immigration, the revision of foreign
treaties with Japan, the reception of a diplomatic mission from
Korea, and a new treaty with Hawaii. He spoke also of minor
affairs affecting relations with the countries of South America.
Europe would appear to have been nonexistent.

His successor in the White House was able, on this record, to
reaffirm in his inaugural address that "we have happily maintained a policy of avoiding all interference with European
affairs." President Harrison's statement, indeed, again emphasized the provinciality of the national outlook while mildly
warning against it. Even though "our interests are so exclusively American," Harrison said, ". . . . our entire inat-
tention to any events that may transpire elsewhere can never
be taken for granted."

This was still the period which Mr. Dooley, the irrepressible
bartending philosopher created by Peter Finley Dunne, would
later look back upon so nostalgically as "th' good old days befur
we became . . . . a wurruld power." Those were the times,
he told his friend Mr. Hennessy, when "our fav'rite sport was
playin' solytare . . . . We didn't care f'r th' big game. . . ."

CHAPTER IV

BACKGROUND OF ADVENTURE

IF THE FIRST CLEVELAND ADMINISTRATION CAME TO A CLOSE
without materially breaking the pattern of the past in foreign
affairs, the next decade was to usher in the future. Politicians,
publicists, and editorial writers began to stress as never before
that with the world growing constantly smaller—Europe less
than a week from American shores—the United States could
no longer afford to be so indifferent to what happened abroad
and could not hope to escape international entanglements. The
subtle forces of a new era were creating a popular demand for
a more positive foreign policy. The way was being prepared
for imperialism and world power. As early as 1890, Alfred
Thayer Mahan, observing the current scene with both historical
perspective and imaginative foresight, stated succinctly what
more and more people would come to believe. "Whether they
will or no," Mahan wrote, "Americans must now begin to look
outward."

The very year in which Cleveland had emphasized isolationism so heavily in his inaugural address, two well-known publicists set forth views that were greatly to bolster new conceptions
of the manifest destiny of the United States. John Fiske,
historian and philosopher, wrote that the superiority of the
Anglo-Saxon people, and the natural growth of their power,
could leave no doubt that, having already spread over two
hemispheres, this favored race would continue to maintain its
sovereignty of the sea and its commercial supremacy. And
Josiah Strong, noted evangelical leader and social reformer,

expressed in a popular little book entitled *Our Country* a comparable view which further postulated the transfer of the seat of Anglo-Saxon power to the United States, and from this new base moving "down upon Mexico, down upon Central and South America, out upon the islands of the sea, over upon Africa and beyond."

In their reflection of the impact of the theory of evolution upon racial concepts, the views expressed by Fiske and Strong were extremely important. The idea of the Anglo-Saxon's innate superiority, his impressive lead in the struggle for racial survival, and his inevitable future triumphs, had become generally accepted in America by the 1890s. Had not Darwin himself stated that the wonderful progress made by the United States and the energetic character of the American people were the result of natural selection? Had not Herbert Spencer declared that Americans could reasonably look forward to the time when they would have produced a civilization grander than anything the world had known to that time?

Strong quoted these statements in *Our Country*, and he unquestioningly accepted them. He told the many thousands of persons he reached with his books and other writings that the world was entering upon the final competition of races. After speaking of the Anglo-Saxon spreading out from North America over all the earth, he concluded with the rhetorical question, "and can anyone doubt that the result of this competition will be the 'survival of the fittest'?"

The pre-eminence of the Anglo-Saxons—and especially the Americans—he widely credited to their possession of two great ideals: pure spiritual Christianity and civil liberty. It must be admitted that Strong had one reservation in his otherwise enthusiastic acceptance of the triumphs awaiting the race. It had somehow to avoid being "devitalized by alcohol and tobacco." If this hazard were surmounted, however, he had no doubts of the steadily expanding moral and political influence of his own country. The introduction to his book stated this thesis with concise brevity: "As goes America, so goes the world."

There was of course nothing new in the idea of an American world mission. The role of the United States had often been historically viewed as that of leading all mankind to peace and liberty. A good many years earlier, John Adams had expressed this view in terms that might have given pause even to Fiske or Strong. "Our pure, virtuous, public-spirited, federative republic," he had written Thomas Jefferson in 1813, "will last forever, govern the globe, and introduce the perfection of man." The application of evolutionary doctrine in charting the future of America was no more than a further endorsement of a very old idea. What had once been considered inherent in the national destiny and foreordained by Providence was now sanctioned by social Darwinism.

Strong himself was not yet thinking, in 1885, of political power or overseas expansion. His concern was the spiritual redemption of the world, and he saw his countrymen in the van of a great movement which would extend Christianity and democratic principles through precept and teaching. This was the age when the slogan of the missionary movement was "the evangelization of the world in our generation." Nevertheless, the emphasis that Strong placed on the role of the American people in this divine scheme supported at every point the parallel concept of the extension overseas of national power. Here was the foundation for what would later be called "the imperialism of righteousness." It provided whatever justification was necessary for promoting American commercial and political interests in the far corners of the earth.

Strong himself was to accept the lesson so naturally drawn from the identification of moral purpose with evolutionary doctrine. There could be no avoiding what was at once destiny and duty. He emphatically endorsed overseas expansion. It was time for Americans, he stated in a later book, published in 1900, "to recognize the place in the world which God has given us and to accept the responsibilities which it devolves upon us in behalf of Christian civilization."

The superiority of the Anglo-Saxon race and the consequent obligation to extend the blessings of American civilization to other peoples—or what was sometimes called the law of conquest and empire for the "dominant evolved race"—were stressed in countless books and articles of this period. One of the most effective spokesmen of such views, however, was found not among American philosophers, political scientists, or publicists, but in the person of a young English poet.

Rudyard Kipling, as already noted, visited the country in 1889 and again in the 1890s. Like so many English observers, he was somewhat taken aback by the brash self-confidence of Americans, and their belligerent attitude toward his own country rather appalled him. Describing a banquet in San Francisco during his tour in 1889, he wrote:

"It was my first introduction to the American Eagle screaming for all its worth . . . I sat bewildered on a coruscating Niagara of—blatherskite. It was stupendous. . . . Then, according to rule, they . . . hurled defiance at 'our natural enemy . . . with her chain of fortresses across the world.' Thereafter they glorified their nation afresh . . . in case any detail should have been overlooked."

For all his ridicule, however, Kipling sensed in the raucous patriotism of such affairs, and even more in the nascent imperialistic spirit of the country, an attitude of mind with which he was in hearty sympathy. No one could have been more chauvinistic than Kipling himself, and he believed so completely in Anglo-Saxon superiority and the consequent need for close Anglo-Saxon cooperation that he welcomed every stirring of American ambition. Having long felt that Great Britain had world obligations almost beyond her, he was eager to have American participation in a task that the two great English-speaking nations might share. As the United States looked outward at the close of the century, he issued a stirring call to the American people "to take up the White Man's burden," and became overnight the prophet of the new imperialism devolving upon the superior race:

> "Take up the White Man's burden—
> Send forth the best ye breed—
> Go bind your sons to exile
> To serve your captives' need;
> To wait, in heavy harness,
> On fluttered folk and wild—
> Your new-caught, sullen peoples,
> Half-devil and half-child."

Two Americans who hardly needed to be convinced by this poetic summons to overseas expansion—it might be noted in passing—warmly welcomed Kipling's aid in arousing public opinion. "Rather poor poetry, but good sense from the expansionist standpoint," Theodore Roosevelt wrote Henry Cabot Lodge. "I like it," Lodge replied. "I think it is better poetry than you say, apart from the sense of the views." As illustrative of the dichotomy in so much thinking on this issue, William Allen White once wrote of being "bound to my idols —Whitman, the great democrat, and Kipling, the imperialist."

The idea of Anglo-Saxon racial responsibilities, however, was to reach its apogee in the fulsome rhapsodies of Albert J. Beveridge. This brilliant young man was to take his place in the Senate just as the imperialism for which Kipling was such an inspired advocate came into full flower; and no one, throughout the length and breadth of the land, embraced it more enthusiastically. He was to advance many arguments in favor of the cause, but the role of the United States in carrying out its obligations as the torchbearer of civilization was always strongly emphasized.

Beveridge believed that the American republic was part of a race movement—of the most masterful race in history—and that nothing could stop this movement's further progress. But the nation also had a stern duty to carry forward the tasks to which it was appointed. "God has not been preparing the English-speaking and Teutonic peoples for a thousand years for nothing but vain and idle self-contemplation and self-admiration," Beveridge would declare in 1900. "No! He has made us the master organizers of the world to establish system where chaos reigns. . . . And of all our race He has marked the American people as His chosen nation to finally lead in the regeneration of the world." It was all very simple in his mind: the Americans were "trustee, under God, of the civilization of the world."

The general idea that, in fulfilling both its destiny and its duty, the United States should now look outward, also received significant support from changing conditions within the country. Just at this time—the actual date was 1890—the Census Bureau made its famous report that the frontier as it had existed throughout American history had finally "disappeared." There were still vast stretches of free land to be homesteaded, but the unsettled area in the western plains had been so broken into by isolated bodies of settlement, to quote the report, "that there can hardly be said to be a frontier line." In comparison with the circumstances of nearly three centuries, continental America had become a closed domain.

The American people did not read this report and at once become convinced that they should advance overseas and seek out colonial possessions. Quite naturally, few of them saw it, or would have recognized the report's significance if they had. However, the disappearance of the frontier was gradually brought home with the dwindling of free land and final completion of western settlement. It had a subtle psychological influence which helped to condition the public to the idea of expansion overseas. What was more natural than for a nation which had become great through the steady extension of its boundaries to look still further westward after the tide of settlement reached the shores of the Pacific?

As America stretched out toward the ancient East and the "equation of the horizon" was solved, the novelist Frank Norris summed up the future: "March we must. Conquer we must."

Nor was it only the end of the frontier that pressed home the realization that there were territorial limits to the boundless expansion symbolized by the American West. The pioneers who had staked out their farms in the vast area of the Great Plains and so hopefully plowed its tough, matted soil to plant their corn and wheat found their great expectations were not always fulfilled. In the early 1890s, drought and insect plagues, poor harvests and low prices were casting a heavy pall over the Myth of the Garden—that enticing dream of a great agricultural utopia. No longer did the West seem to represent the opportunities that an aggressive, demanding people had come to consider their due right.

The discouragement and even despair of many of the Midwestern pioneer settlers were somberly recorded in such contemporary stories as those of Hamlin Garland. In harshly realistic tones he depicted the unceasing toil, the drudgery, the deadening monotony of the lives of the men and women of the Middle Border. In telling incident, he described their embittered sense of frustration when their crops failed and all their hopes were disappointed. Discontent was spreading through the prairie states; it was soon to find violent expression in the rising tide of Populism and a nationwide farm revolt.

In these circumstances it was natural that many people should look out beyond the frontier—even if that frontier were now the Pacific shore—for opportunities that no longer seemed to exist in continental America. The old custom of moving on toward the setting sun was not easily broken. If there was no more room for further westward expansion in the traditional pattern of the past, the idea of extending the nation's boundaries overseas and acquiring new possessions awoke a natural response.

Toward the close of the 1890s, and on the eve of war with

Spain, the close interrelationship between the disappearance of a frontier once symbolic with opportunity and this new urge for overseas expansion was forcefully stated in the pages of the *Overland Monthly*. The subjugation of a continent had been a sufficient job to keep the American people busy for a century, its editor said, but now that this great task had been completed, they were looking "for fresh worlds to conquer." Stressing the innate colonizing instinct of the Anglo-Saxon in terms reminiscent of those used by Fiske and Strong, he declared that, whether conservative stay-at-homes liked it or not, this compelling force "is now pushing us out and on to Alaska, to the isles of the sea—and beyond."

More specific economic pressures also began to exercise their influence in favor of an energetic foreign policy and ultimate overseas expansion during these years. The rapid increase of industrial production, as mines, mills, and factories multiplied and grew, accounted for a greater volume of goods than the domestic market seemed able to absorb. Foreign trade and commerce took on a new importance. The cry was raised that the United States was turning out such a surplus of manufactures that new foreign markets were a vital necessity. Outlets beyond our borders had to be found, wrote one economist, "in order to prevent business depression, idleness, and suffering at home. . . . The United States are compelled by the instinct of self-preservation, to enter, however reluctantly, upon the field of international politics." Statements from the Department of Commerce also stressed this same problem, and the consequent necessity of national conversion from a people absorbed in the development of a virgin continent to a nation prepared to become a great commercial power. "We are Anglo-Saxons," one spokesman of such views asserted, "and must obey our blood and occupy new markets and, if necessary, new lands."

All this clearly meant an aggressive search for trade, the building up of a sadly depleted merchant marine, and a national policy that would safeguard and promote foreign commerce. And such a program was immediately linked up with the agitation already underway for a more powerful navy. The proponents of naval expansion, whatever their underlying motives, eagerly seized upon these economic arguments to emphasize the importance of building a fleet and obtaining the bases that would rank the American navy among those of the great powers.

The great industrial interests of the country did not originally urge such policies. In the early 1890s they remained absorbed in domestic problems. At first hard hit by depression, they did not raise their sights to an expanded trade, a strong navy, and possible overseas possessions. When the country then began to recover, they were afraid that foreign adventure might interrupt the hopeful progress being made toward the return of domestic prosperity. Before the Spanish-American War, it was the big-navy advocates, zealous for the assertion of national power in its own right, who were the most vocal advocates of commercial expansion and overseas colonies as a means toward the ultimate goal of America's world leadership.

The question had begun to be asked as early as the beginning of the 1880s: Could the United States hope to exercise any influence whatsoever in international affairs, or maintain its trade and commerce, while allowing its navy to sink to a position not only inferior to that of the fleets of other major powers, but to the fleets of Turkey, China, and Chile? In 1880, Representative Whitthorne of Tennessee, anticipating the famous thesis of sea power set forth by Alfred Thayer Mahan, had marshaled all the historical arguments in favor of naval supremacy.

"It is singular to note," Whitthorne told Congress, "what is the seeming lesson in the history of those nations which have attained the highest rank of dominion, power, and civilization: that they have flourished most in wealth and prosperity when they had powerful navies and commercial marine. I need not ask you, in order to establish this, to review in detail the history of Phoenicia, Carthage, Rome, Venice, Naples, Spain, Portugal, France, and England. The mere mention of these names in this connection will make manifest the proposition I assert."

The "new navy" first began to get underway as an expression of growing American ambitions when, during the Arthur administration, three steel ships were built to supplement the wooden, sail-rigged vessels then making up the fleet. Further progress was recorded under Cleveland. Congress made appropriations for five protected cruisers and the battleships *Texas* and *Maine*, the nucleus of the famous White Squadron; and an able Secretary of the Navy, William C. Whitney, pushed ahead energetically with a program for the complete modernization of his department.

Cleveland was fully aware of what he termed "the irresistible tide of commercial expansion," and it was on such grounds that he was prepared to support the building of both merchant ships and additional naval vessels. In keeping with his basic isolationist attitude, however, he thought entirely in terms of a navy for continental defense. He had no idea of trying to build up a striking force that would be in a position to protect American trade in all parts of the world and challenge the navies of other powers. Indeed, it was not until 1890—after he had left office—that a report of the Naval Policy Board first proposed an American fleet that would be strong enough to safeguard the highways of commerce and enable the United States to exercise overseas power. And even in that year, popular misgivings over such a policy caused the big-navy advocates ambiguously to label the new vessels for which they were seeking appropriations "seagoing coastline battleships."

The navy continued to grow steadily after this initial expansion. It attracted increasing support which at once reflected the desire for a more positive foreign policy and still further intensified such a desire. Moreover, the expansion of the navy soon began to create a demand for the bases and

coaling stations that would enable it to operate [...], and [...]
also gave fresh vigor to earlier proposals f[or] b[...]
isthmian canal that would link the Atlantic a[nd] [...]

The foremost big-navy advocate was Alfr[ed] Tha[yer]
and it was he, more than anyone else, w[ho] lin[ked]
power with commercial expansion. This s[...]y, reser[...]
naval officer—a tall thin man with a [...]sharply [...]
beard—had had a long period of rou[tine] sea [...]
—"drifting on the line's simple res[...]ectability a[...]
one very well could"—until he wa[s] called [...]
College in 1885. His lectures [...]here were [...]
published under the title of *Th[e Influence* [...]
History, and his fame was esta[b]lished. Engl[...]
hailed a book that explained [...] her own wo[...]
made it required reading f[or] German n[...]
promptly translated into [J]apanese.

Not without honor i[n] his own c[...]
directly the political [and] naval p[...]
administrations in W[a]shington, [...]
decisive influence o[...] sea power [...]
in the inherent g[...]atness [...]
carefully formul[...]ed program [...]
secure its rightful p[...]ce. [...]
United States should deve[lop] its trade [...]
marine, establish a navy that c[ould] protect [...]
wherever it might be threatene[d], [a]nd acqui[...]
bases that would enable the fleet to ope[...]te effectively [...]
its home waters. The isolation that had bee[n] practiced [...]
earlier period of national growth was no longer [...]
was convinced, if the United States were not to fa[...] hope[...]
lessly behind in the march of nations. Not only had the Ame[...] skillfully [...]
can people to *look* outward; they had to *act* in such a way as [...]
to expand their power and influence beyond the borders that Alfre[d] Thayer Ma[...]
had heretofore marked the national horizon.

Mahan was immensely persuasive. His magazine articles [...] If the laws o[...] evolu[...]
especially had a powerful impact upon public thinking. Per- tional boundaries no[...]

Valley, Great Britain was constantly seeking to obtain new concessions in central China. Germany, a new, but for that reason an all the more zealous, entry in the imperial sweep-stakes, was ready to make even more dictatorial demands upon the crumbling dynasty that controlled the fortunes of the once great Chinese Empire. And even more menacing was the in-sidious penetration in Manchuria of the agents of the Russian Czar. In 1894 China fought a disastrous war with Japan. The European powers nobly called upon the victorious Japanese to give up their conquests (except Formosa), but imperial Russia was soon taking over the very holdings which Japan had been compelled to surrender—Port Arthur, Darien, and control of the Manchurian railways.

"The various powers," lamented the last of the great Manchu rulers, the despotic old Empress Dowager Tzu Hsi, "cast upon us looks of tigerlike voracity, hustling each other in their en-deavours to seize upon our innermost territories."

If the United States was never concerned with Africa and had no part in these aggressive moves in China, it had interests extending far out into the Pacific. There were Hawaii and Samoa. Any suggestion that the forces of European expansion might precipitate a struggle for domination of the western ocean was viewed with anxiety. As Secretary Bayard stated in 1885, the United States did not seek control in this part of the world for itself, but it could not accept any doctrine whereby other nations "might roam at will over the Pacific seas and absorb jurisdiction of the islands." National policy under Cleveland went no farther than the reiterated declara-tion that the United States would demand respect for the independence of any such island nations with which it had treaty relations. It was hardly surprising, however, that, con-fronted with European imperialism, public opinion should in-sist upon a more determined stand in upholding and ad-vancing American interests abroad.

While there were those who continued to cry out that, come what might, the United States itself should never em-

brace imperialism, there was a contagion in the air that had
disturbing implications in terms of traditional American policy.

The full reaction to these expansive forces was not of course
to take place until the end of the decade. Even in the early
1890s, however, a new chauvinism—it universally went by
the name of "jingoism"—seemed to be sweeping the country.
This martial spirit both reflected the deeper forces that were
making for a changed attitude toward America's world role
and added a new explosive ingredient to them.

Jingoism had been clearly manifest during the fisheries
dispute with Canada and Great Britain. The Detroit News,
indeed, had helped to popularize the term at this time by
paraphrasing the verses which had been originally responsible
for its modern connotation. The News had written:

> "We do not want to fight,
> But, by jingo, if we do
> We'll scoop in all the fishing grounds
> And the whole Dominion, too."

This heady spirit soon found expression in a further series
of unusual incidents. The Samoan episode and brief excitement over relations with Germany has already been noted.
Another dispute with Great Britain over sealing rights in the
Bering Sea would again find the more bellicose newspapers
demanding rigid insistence upon American rights even at the
risk of war. There was a flare-up of excitement in relations
with Italy over the so-called Maffia affair, growing out of the
lynching of some Italians in New Orleans, which for a brief
moment led to further irresponsible talk of war. A more
serious controversy with Chile—to which we shall return—
caused even so astute an observer as Cecil Spring-Rice to write
very soberly from Washington in 1891 that "we are on the
verge of war here." And finally there was the clash with Great
Britain over Venezuelan boundaries three years later, again
under circumstances to be later discussed, which created a

very real danger of war. Many Americans seemed to be spoiling for a fight in their new-found restlessness and in their bellicose determination to uphold national honor.

That hostilities could possibly result from such minor incidents as those which led to the successive periods of tension in relations with Germany and Italy, Chile and Great Britain, would be unimaginable today. But in the 1890s war was popularly considered a very limited action, to be fought by professional armies and navies, and unlikely to involve any countries other than the original parties to the quarrel or seriously to affect even the belligerents. The jingoes did not think in terms of dangerous national conflict, but rather of picturesque naval battles and exciting cavalry charges—flags, bands, and glory.

"War now not only occurs more rarely," wrote Mahan, "but has rather the character of an occasional excess, from which recovery is easy."

It was a point of view romantically held by an English visitor to American shores (of whom Theodore Roosevelt, incidentally, took a very dim view) in the person of the young Winston Churchill. Many years later, in 1930, looking back with the perspective of more than thirty years on his experiences as a foreign observer in revolutionary Cuba, Churchill recalled an age long past: "The minds of this generation, exhausted, brutalized, mutilated, and bored by war," he wrote, "may not understand the delicious yet tremulous sensations with which a young British Officer bred in the long peace approached for the first time an actual theatre of operations . . ."

The jingoes' attitude often seemed completely childish. Secretary Bayard once complained bitterly of those who proposed "to deal with the vast issues of war or peace between great states in the spirit of prize fighters or scuffling bootblacks." It was somewhat in this frame of mind that the martial-minded Roosevelt so often talked of war and what it might mean in restoring the morale of a nation too lax in defending its honor and prestige. He was always impatient with what he believed to be the popular apathy throughout the country when it came

to standing up for American rights and taking a leading position among the nations of the world. Together with his
fellow jingoes, he wanted to see the United States demonstrate,
if necessary by force of arms, that it had become a great power
not on any account to be trifled with by any other country.

There were a number of serious discussions of this extreme
chauvinism. A contributor to the *North American Review*
declared that the American people appeared to be "inflated
with a national vanity" that made them supersensitive in their
relations with other countries. Another contemporary observer
wrote in an article for the *Arena* that unless the signs were
entirely misleading, the United States was initiating a foreign
policy "which will soon reflect our worst national characteristics." The *Nation,* singled out by James Bryce as "the best
weekly not only in America but in the world," carried on an
unrelenting campaign against the "professional frothings of
the incurable jingoes."

"The number of men and officials in this country who are
now mad to fight somebody is appalling," wrote E. L. Godkin
in a trenchant editorial in 1894. "Navy officers dream of war
and talk and lecture about it incessantly. The Senate debates
are filled with predictions of impending war and with talk
of preparing for it at once. . . . Most truculent and bloodthirsty of all, the jingo editors keep up a din day after day
about the way we could cripple one country's fleet and destroy
another's commerce, and fill the heads of boys and silly men
with the idea that war is the normal state of a civilized country."

Jingoism was a part of the background of the whole imperialistic movement. Certainly it contributed greatly to the
climate of public opinion that made for war with Spain in
1898, and then for overseas expansion in both the Pacific and
the Caribbean. Long before the sensational newspaper campaign playing up Spanish atrocities in the Cuban war and
then crying for retaliation after the sinking of the *Maine,*
the American people had become conditioned to the idea that

the United States should be ready to fight whenever the national honor was affronted. It was an attitude aptly expressed by Senator Cushman K. Davis of Minnesota. "The United States has ceased to be the China of the Western Continent," he declared grandiloquently. "We are alive, thank God, and must not be insulted by any power in this world, great or small."

So it was that the changing tide of events and of public opinion in the early 1890s set the stage for America's imperial years. The concept of racial superiority merged with the historic sense of national mission to bid America take up its task of world regeneration. A new restlessness, born of the closing of the frontier, coincided with the stirrings of worldwide imperialistic competition and economic rivalry to emphasize a growing popular conviction that the nation's future could no longer be constricted by continental bounds. And a sense of mounting power found expression in an assertion of national honor and national rights that was a direct reflection of these basic factors in the country's evolution.

Some writers have maintained that the wholly decisive factor in the imperialism of 1898 was the pressure of capitalistic development calling for new foreign markets. "It was Messrs. Rockefeller, Pierpont Morgan, and their associates," J. A. Hobson has stated, "who needed Imperialism and who fastened it upon the shoulders of the great Republic of the West." But the evidence for any such simplified interpretation of events is simply not available. The early proponents of imperialism did not reflect such influences. They were indeed basically unsympathetic to the pushing industrial and financial interests of the day. They sought national power and national influence primarily for America's greater glory, rather than for her greater profit. It remains highly significant that commercial spokesmen did not at first support expansion. There can be no question that economic factors were to play an increasingly important role in the final stages of imperialist advance, but they were

originally very much subordinate to the other interrelated forces
—political and psychological—coming to a head in the 1890s.

James Bryce, giving a friendly warning to the United States
on what he considered the futility of overseas expansion, once
suggested that a powerful, but unrealized, motive in the
minds of many Americans was no more than the idea "that it
is a fine thing for a great country to have territories, and to
see marked as her own, on the map of the world, dominions
beyond her natural borders." There was obviously something
more to imperialism than such national self-assertiveness. Yet
Bryce's comment seems highly significant as one looks back
upon the exuberant enthusiasm with which the American
people responded to the more subtle causes serving to break
down their traditional isolation.

CHAPTER V

THE FIRST STIRRINGS OF IMPERIALISM

IT WAS AGAINST THE BACKGROUND OF SUCH EMERGENT FORCES
making for a new foreign policy that the Republicans returned
to office after the defeat of Cleveland in 1888. Although domestic issues naturally bulked larger in the campaign, one of
their parting shots at the outgoing administration was that
its operation of the State Department had been "surpassing
in imbecility and pusillanimity anything that has been known
in the annals of American diplomacy." It was generally expected that the Republicans, so insistent upon a firm stand
against Great Britain in the fisheries dispute and highly suspicious of Germany in Samoa, would give new force and vigor
to national policy all along the line.

Such expectations were not confined to this country. Bismarck already envisaged the United States as a nation certain to play a large role in world affairs and in a position to take issue with the European nations' ambitions for colonial expansion. In 1887 his son, Count Bismarck, had warned Lord Salisbury, the British Foreign Minister, that the United States wished to bring both Hawaii and Samoa under its exclusive control and was interpreting the Monroe Doctrine as though "the Pacific Ocean were . . . an American lake." Hoping to conclude an Anglo-German entente, the Iron Chancellor instructed the German ambassador in London, on the very eve of President Harrison's inauguration, to point out to the British Foreign Office that if America knew that England and Germany were working together, she would "not be inclined to give expression by war to the chauvinistic tendencies of her future government."

One reason for the widespread belief in more active American participation in world politics was Harrison's appointment of James G. Blaine as his Secretary of State. The latter's intense nationalism—it led to his being called "Jingo Jim"—had been demonstrated during his former brief tenure in the State Department under President Garfield, and it was generally taken for granted that he would dominate the new administration. This was not actually to be the case, however. Although the dashing Blaine, the Plumed Knight of so many political battles, personally overshadowed the new incumbent of the White House, it was to be a Harrison rather than a Blaine administration.

The personalities of the two men could hardly have offered a more striking contrast. The President was not a very impressive figure. He was highly conscientious, had a great sense of the dignity of the position he occupied, and in all his contacts was austere, cold, and aloof. One contemporary described Harrison as a "rather circumspect, erudite, self-willed, dainty little aristocrat"; another said that he was "as glacial as a Siberian stripped of his furs." Blaine, on the other hand, was the most popular man in public life. His generous, outgoing spirit and easy affability, his engaging friendliness and great personal charm, had won him a place in the hearts of his countrymen that no contemporary could rival. Yet the White House ever remained beyond his eager grasp. His somewhat elastic conscience raised such doubts as to his fitness for the high office of the presidency that, while the American people continued to love him, they withheld the great prize which was always the object of his political ambition.

It was not, however, the youthful politician of the flashing smile and incredible charm who served in Harrison's cabinet. Blaine had greatly aged in 1889. With his tall, spare figure, snow-white hair, and still brilliant eyes, he remained a man of great personal distinction, especially in comparison with the dumpy little President, but the fire of an earlier day had been dampened by the frustration of his ambitions. Blaine remained a staunch champion of American rights and an avowed expansionist. Nevertheless he was not as zealous for high adventure in foreign affairs as he had once been, and there were several occasions when he exercised a moderating influence on his chief. As time went on, moreover, increasing ill health limited his activities in the State Department and finally led him to resign.

Whatever the respective roles of Blaine and Harrison in the conduct of foreign affairs during these years, popular expectations of "a spirited policy" were generally realized. There was a distinct break with the ancient traditions so sternly upheld by Cleveland. Repeated efforts were made to secure bases in the Caribbean—Samana Bay in the Dominican Republic, a coaling station in Haiti, the entire Danish West Indies. Support was renewed for a Nicaraguan canal under exclusive American control. A three-power protectorate was set up over Samoa and a treaty of annexation signed with Hawaii. Among these projects, only the Samoan protectorate was successfully carried through during the Harrison administration; but here were concrete signs of an entirely new ap-

proach to foreign affairs and significant harbingers of imperialism.

A policy that during the next presidential campaign was
characterized by the Democrats as one of "irritation and
bluster with the alternative of humiliation or war," and by
the Republicans as one seeking the "achievement of the
manifest destiny of the Republic in its broadest sense," marked
the first youthful signs of America's coming of diplomatic age.
Expansionism was in the air. Some little time after Harrison's defeat in 1892, a correspondent of the Washington *Star*
wrote that there was good reason for believing that, had he
been returned to office, "an aggressive foreign policy would
have been the most marked feature of his administration." This
correspondent continued: "The end of another four years would
have found this country in possession of strong points of advantage, from a naval point of view, in the South Atlantic
and the Pacific. . . ."

On February 10, 1889, Mrs. James G. Blaine wrote to her
son, "Your Father is now looking up Samoa on the map."
Little wonder that the new Secretary of State was searching
out the location of this distant island—as many other Americans must also have been doing—for this was a first and
immediate issue with which he would have to deal. If the
outgoing Cleveland administration had ridden safely through
the flurry that had given rise to excited talk of a clash with
Germany over Samoa's status, it had left to the Harrison
administration a final settlement of this troublesome question.
It was Blaine's task to outline the policy that the American
delegates would follow at the conference which Bismarck
had suggested should be held at Berlin.

If his more enthusiastic followers expected him to live up
to his old nickname of "Jingo Jim," they were disappointed.
For Blaine was not prepared to defy Germany or move
toward American annexation of Samoa. On the contrary, he
accepted in good faith Bismarck's disclaimer of any German

ambition to take over the islands. There is no evidence that he considered the Samoan question in itself of any great importance, or thought of it other than as a situation from which the United States could not in good conscience try to escape. Nevertheless the policy that he now proposed, somewhat along the lines Bayard had suggested two years earlier, marked a first distinct departure from the nation's traditional isolationism. It involved a measure of international control over Samoa in which the United States committed itself to joint action in cooperation with the two other powers concerned in Samoan affairs.

In his instructions to the American delegates at the Berlin Conference, Blaine strongly reaffirmed the interest of the United States in Samoa's autonomy. This country's developing trade and the prospect of opening up an isthmian canal, he stated, had so changed the American position in the Pacific that any alteration in the island's status would be highly unfortunate. This country could not fail to regard such a move "as inconsistent with that international consideration and dignity to which the United States, by continental position and expanding interest, must always be entitled." Notice was clearly served on Germany, that is, of the Secretary of State's firm determination to uphold American rights.

Bismarck continued in his conciliatory mood. He had no idea of challenging the United States. Indeed, Germany and Great Britain, under the stress of more important issues involving their imperialistic rivalry in other parts of the world, were very anxious to work out a mutually satisfactory settlement of the troublesome but still very minor problem of Samoa. There was one occasion toward the close of the negotiations when newspaper reports suggested that Bismarck had sought to impose his will on the conference and that Blaine had forced him to back down. The story ran that the American delegates, unduly impressed by the Iron Chancellor's storm and bluster, cabled home fearfully that further concessions were perhaps in order, and that the Secretary of State there-

upon bluntly replied that "the extent of the Chancellor's irritability is not the measure of American rights."

There was no truth whatsoever in this report. Bismarck did
not actually attend the conference, the attitude of Germany
was always moderate, and at no time was there any dangerous
clash of interests. The Blaine message which gave rise to the
story of his defying Bismarck was actually a rebuke to members
of the American delegation for allowing any "irritability" on
the part of either their English or German associates to prevent their taking full time to complete some minor details of
an agreement already generally accepted.

The negotiations, following the lines laid down by Blaine,
resulted in the signature of the so-called Berlin General Act
and established what was in effect a three-power protectorate
over the Samoan Islands. The system whereby such control was
to be administered was highly complicated; it ultimately broke
down completely. At the time, however, it appeared to promise
an end to the controversy and dissension, the threat of more
serious clashes, which had for so long bedeviled the "Samoan
problem." And the Berlin General Act, accepted by President
Harrison as an "honorable, just, and equal settlement," was
duly approved by the Senate.

This agreement had a significance which some contemporaries realized, and which was later to be emphasized even
more strongly. There could be no denying its violation of that
age-old tradition which had heretofore blocked American participation in any international engagement with political implications. Although most of the comment of the time stressed
what was regarded as a diplomatic triumph in forestalling
German naval expansion in the Pacific, at least one paper
expressed the view that the agreement should have been incorporated in individual treaties rather than in a joint undertaking for preserving Samoan autonomy. "In that way," it was
said, "we should have maintained that policy of independence
from complications with European governments which has
been our consistent policy from the foundation of the Union."

It would be an exaggeration to characterize the Berlin General Act as an entangling alliance. Nevertheless it was an engagement without precedent in our national history, an assumption of responsibilities that showed a new concern with affairs outside our continental borders, and an entering wedge for overseas expansion and imperialism.

Although circumstances had forced Blaine to consider Samoa as the first item of business when he took over the State Department, he was more interested in other aspects of foreign policy. His primary concern was relations with Latin America, where he hoped to carry through plans for a closer accord which he had originally launched during his earlier days as Secretary of State under Garfield. Also he was personally convinced of the desirability of building an isthmian canal and obtaining the naval bases necessary for its defense. If his expansionist ambitions did not reach as far as the South Pacific, he still believed that the United States should extend its sphere of influence in the Western Hemisphere and over such outlying islands as fell within reasonable bounds.

In this policy he had the support of Harrison. Writing in 1891, the President declared that while he was "not much of an expansionist," he felt that in some directions, as to naval stations and points of influence, "we must look forward to a departure from the too conservative opinions which have been held heretofore."

Underlying both Blaine's interest in a canal and his desire to bring about a greater degree of cooperation among the Latin American republics was a strong feeling of the importance of promoting foreign trade and of the desirability of reversing the unfavorable balance that had long existed in the commerce of the United States with its southern neighbors. It was an unusual coincidence that Congress had proposed an international conference on American affairs, fruitlessly urged by Blaine eight years earlier, at the very time that he was once again Secretary of State. Historical accident enabled him to issue the official invitations for this so long delayed meeting and to preside over the first cooperative effort to meet the various problems of communications, trade, and peace affecting the Western Hemisphere.

When the Latin American delegates first gathered in Washington in October 1889, Blaine extended to them an invitation to make a tour of the cities of the East and Middle West. Before they returned to the capital, they had traveled six thousand miles on the special train placed at their disposal; had everywhere been met by welcoming committees and brass bands; had been taken on tours of factories, industrial plants, department stores, and other local sights; and had been, in general, royally entertained. The newspapers had a heyday describing the reactions of the bewildered participants in this tremendous junket. While the view was widely expressed that the principle result of the tour was probably the complete exhaustion of all those who were on it, the press generally agreed that the Latin American delegates must have learned something of this country, and that the people of the United States were awakened to a greater interest in Latin American affairs than ever before.

When the delegates at last returned to Washington, they carefully took up the successive issues presented to them and deliberated for five long months. However, the agreements for which Blaine was so anxious proved impossible of realization. His plans for a customs union that would facilitate trade and commerce were rejected; a proposed arbitration treaty failed to win majority support. For all his eloquence —and the Secretary of State left the chair to plead in person for his treaty—mutual suspicions and general distrust of the United States blocked any effective action. Blaine's hopes for a "new Magna Carta" which would substitute arbitration for war in the relations of the New World were frustrated. Except for the establishment of an International Bureau of American

Republics, later to become the Pan-American Union, the results of the Washington conference were generally inconclusive.

Blaine was ahead of the times in his interest in Latin American cooperation. Yet, despite its failure, the conference marked the beginning of a movement that was ultimately to carry his ideas into effect. For what Blaine tried to do in 1889 was to be achieved, in large measure, through the Pan-American conferences of later days and the conclusion of the reciprocity agreements and mutual security pacts of the mid-twentieth century.

Two years after this conference there occurred an incident which reflected the underlying distrust between the United States and the Latin American republics and gave occasion for angry recriminations and a further outburst of American jingoism. This was the excited controversy with Chile in 1891 that led to widespread fears—in some quarters, happy expectations —of actual war.

The trouble grew out of a complicated background of revolution, gunrunning, American seizure of a Chilean vessel on the high seas, and diplomatic blundering. Its immediate cause was a riot in Valparaiso. A party of sailors on shore leave from the American ship *Baltimore* became involved, on October 16, 1891, in a saloon brawl that rapidly took on heroic proportions. As the disorder spread, angry mobs fell upon American sailors throughout the city of Valparaiso and beat them up unmercifully. One man was shot dead, another died of knife wounds, others were severely injured. Then, to add insult to injury, the police, who had complacently stood aside throughout the riot, carted the hapless Americans off to prison.

Captain Schley of the *Baltimore* bitterly complained about the Chilean authorities' failure to protect his men and declared that they had been sober, quiet, and peaceful. The latter contention would appear somewhat doubtful. It was, indeed, flatly contradicted by another naval officer, Captain "Fighting Bob"

Evans of the gunboat *Yorktown,* which arrived at Valparaiso shortly after the riot. Evans admitted that the sailors were "probably drunk, properly drunk. They went ashore, many of them, for the purpose of getting drunk." His theory was that under such circumstances they were all the more entitled to the police protection they did not get. Whatever the potency or effects of the drinks served in the local saloons, however, the fact remained that American sailors had lost their lives— "foully murdered," their officers said—and on the receipt of reports from Valparaiso, the State Department sent a stern official protest to the Chilean government.

When no immediate apology was forthcoming, tempers flared in both official and popular circles in the United States. With jingoistic editors throughout the country demanding action, President Harrison brought the issue before Congress in his annual message in December. After outlining the facts as they had been reported in Washington, he stated that if there were any further delay on the part of the Chilean government in answering the American protest he would bring the matter up again "for such action as may be necessary." This led to a counterblast from Chile's foreign minister. He stated that the information on which President Harrison had based his interpretation of the incident was "erroneous or deliberately incorrect"; assailed the American minister in Santiago for pursuing what he said was an unfriendly policy; and declared that the rights and dignity of Chile would be upheld "notwithstanding the intrigues which proceed from so low a source and the threats which come from so high a source."

Here were the makings of a fine quarrel and an open invitation to warmongers to make the American eagle scream. They did not hesitate to do so. In the immediate flurry of excitement and talk of war, the Chicago *Tribune* led the way. Even before the Chilean foreign minister's statement, it had called upon the Administration "to get its warships on the coast as speedily as possible and enforce its demands . . . . if necessary the nitrate beds should be seized and held." It now declared belligerently that, if Chile continued in its insolent attitude, "there must be no fear of factious or partisan opposition to the declaration of war. The whole nation would demand it."

Other newspapers, without outlining just what steps should be taken, called for a vigorous defense of national honor. Great Britain, Germany, and Italy had all been taught their lesson, Frank Leslie's *Illustrated Newspaper* declared, "and now Chile is learning that it cannot insult with impunity the representatives of our Government." The New York *Sun* stated that if proper reparation were denied the United States, "we must teach men who will thenceforth deserve to be called snarling whelps of the Pacific that we cannot be snapped at with impunity."

There was a sharp response to such inflammatory editorials in many other newspapers. The New York *Tribune* commented soberly that "a nation really great does not permit itself to lose its temper—but waits." The Charleston *News and Courier* reflected very much the same attitude. "The talk about 'maintenance of National dignity and self-respect' on the part of the United States in this quarrel with Chile," it commented, "is all stuff and jingoism. It is like John L. Sullivan shaking his fist at a little street gamin. . . . There is no dignity to be maintained or reputation to be gained in a war with Chile."

Still, popular excitement mounted, with Washington full of rumors of further anti-American demonstrations in Chile including a rumor that the *Baltimore* had been blown up. Preparations were made by both the army and navy for possible hostilities, and orders given for new military equipment. With the support of most of his cabinet, President Harrison was believed to be determined upon decisive action whatever the consequences. Only Blaine—the "Jingo Jim" of an earlier day—stood out for a more moderate policy in the interests of the Pan-Americanism that he had sought to promote at the Washington conference two years earlier.

"Blaine's influence is for peace," wrote Cecil Spring-Rice. "It is curious, with his reputation, what an anti-jingo he is. He has done everything he can against war. I hope it may still be avoided, but the President is bent on it."

In this jingoist mood the United States sent to Chile, on January 21, 1892, a stiff note that was in effect an ultimatum. Unless Chile promptly apologized for her failure to afford adequate protection for the sailors from the *Baltimore* and for the offensive note of her foreign minister, there would be no alternative to breaking off diplomatic relations. Although signed by Blaine, this note was in reality written by Harrison. The President had rejected a more conciliatory text prepared by his Secretary of State and substituted his own sharper wording. Nor was the bellicose Harrison willing to await Chile's reply before further stirring the embers of controversy. Four days after the note had been dispatched, he sent a long special message to Congress in which he again reviewed the entire situation, said he had not yet heard from Chile, and concluded that he felt he should not delay any longer in once again bringing these matters to the attention of Congress.

Fortunately Chile now recognized that any further provocation of an aroused United States might invite war. Her answer to the final American *démarche* was a complete apology for the slurs that had been made upon the President and the American minister, and a promise that an indemnity would be paid for the loss of lives in the Valparaiso rioting. Even the most rabid jingoes, both within and without the government, could not but be satisfied with Chile's retreat. Secretary Blaine was able to make a friendly response in behalf of the United States ("It may seem to you too cordial," he wrote Harrison almost apologetically, "but I believe it to be in the highest sense expedient"); and another ephemeral war scare passed into history.

"The triumph for peace is great," the Philadelphia *Press* exulted. "The proof of patriotism has been as broad as the land and overflowing as the sea. There is not an American who does not thrill with a sense of national power exerted for international right."

Other interpretations of the incident struck a different note.

It was Spring-Rice's view that both the President and the Secretary of the Navy were anxious for war—"one to get re-elected, the other to see his new ships fight." And John Hay, writing to Henry Adams, suggested that the crisis had been averted only because Blaine, standing out against the political-minded President, "had got the strings in his hand." Moreover, the jingoist press, with complete irresponsibility as to the possible consequences of war, helped to blow the incident up out of all proportion. Yet there remained a fundamental truth in the comment of the Philadelphia *Press*. The stand taken by the United States was a significant expression of a new spirit in the realm of foreign affairs and of a national determination to sustain the honor and dignity of the United States.

Almost exactly a year after the Chilean war scare, events in the Pacific foreshadowed even more clearly what was to be the new role of the United States in upholding and expanding the national interest overseas. This was the movement, that appeared to come to a climax under exciting circumstances in January 1893, for the annexation of Hawaii. Blaine, who had so long favored annexation, was no longer Secretary of State. He had resigned on the eve of the presidential campaign the year before and was a very sick man. It was as he lay on his deathbed that an Hawaiian commission hurried to the United States to conclude the annexation treaty that he had envisaged as a first step in his expansive policy for the promotion of American interests in the Pacific.

The key figure in the Hawaiian situation was Queen Liliuokalani, last of the line of native monarchs that had ruled the Hawaiian Islands ever since they first swung within the orbit of American interest. This unusual woman, whom the American public was in coming months to consider variously as a bloodthirsty tyrant and as the deeply injured victim of cruel circumstance, greatly influenced the course of American expansion. The United States would almost surely have annexed Hawaii some day, whether or not there was a Liliuokalani on the throne. But her policies precipitated the crisis in January 1893, and then so confused the situation in Hawaii that its logical outcome was postponed for another five years.

The propaganda of her enemies and of the proponents of Hawaiian annexation was to picture Liliuokalani as thoroughly depraved, vicious, and corrupt—an untutored savage exercising ruthless power. Imperious and self-willed she may have been, reactionary according to all American standards, but unbiased reports constantly stressed her innate dignity, her superior culture, and her high sense of morals. In 1887 she had visited London for Queen Victoria's jubilee ("quite stylish, and dressed according to the best Parisian mode," wrote a contemporary), and she was also briefly in Washington that same year. On both these visits to foreign capitals she made a very favorable impression. After the dispute over her role in Hawaiian affairs had died down, Senator Hoar was to apologize for his use of the phrase "barbarous queen" in describing her, and courteously acknowledge that she was "an excellent Christian woman."

Liliuokalani was indeed gifted in many ways. She was well educated, spoke perfect English, and had a special interest in poetry and music. She wrote verse and among her musical compositions was the famous "Aloha Oe," still sung in Hawaii. In later years, when the islands were safely within the American fold, the onetime queen lived on quietly in retirement, with her books and music, flowers and canaries. She was loved and respected by Hawaiians of all ranks.

The story of Hawaii, however, does not begin with this intriguing monarch, and some background must be given to set the stage for the abrupt blotting out of her kingdom in 1893. It was a full century earlier, in fact, that the first contacts had been made between Americans and Hawaiians. The old China traders, making what were then known as the Sandwich Islands a port of call between the Northwest Coast and Canton, and the New England whalemen wintering at Honolulu in the course of their long voyages to the North Pacific, forged the first links between the United States and Hawaii. Missionaries and merchants then followed their trail around Cape Horn and further encouraged American interest in the islands.

Long before the feverish debates of the 1890s, the Hawaiian Islands were called the "key to the Pacific." From the days of Webster and Marcy, their ultimate annexation—and until that day came, rigid insistence that no other nation should occupy them—was the declared policy of all expansionist statesmen. While efforts to bring about annexation had failed, both in the mid-1850s and after the close of the Civil War, the project was never entirely forgotten.

The possibility that Great Britain might rush in where the United States appeared so reluctant to tread had originally fired Blaine's imperialistic ambition. He expressly stated, in reviewing Pacific developments during his first term of office in the State Department in 1881, that should the islands be unable to maintain their own neutrality, "this government would unhesitatingly meet the situation by seeking an avowedly American solution for the grave issues presented."

Cleveland's opposition to annexation during his first term, and the no less firm position taken by Secretary Bayard, had never led them to the point of minimizing Hawaii's importance to the United States. It was in 1887 that the cession of a naval station at Pearl Harbor was incorporated in a renewed reciprocal trade treaty. Granted that this move was the result of Senate amendment to the treaty, originally opposed by Bayard, the fact remains that Hawaii was at this time brought more than ever within the orbit of American interest. Also, the Cleveland administration summarily rejected a proposal by Great Britain for a joint protectorate over the islands on the ground that the United States could not tolerate the admission of any foreign interest in Hawaii.

Soon thereafter, matters came to a head through domestic developments in the islands. When Liliuokalani ascended the throne in 1891, factional strife and corruption generally characterized local politics. Her predecessor, King Kalakaua, had signally demonstrated that the line of the old native dynasty was running out. "He was inclined to drunkenness," read one report, "and was morose, did not act nicely." The Americans in the islands, controlling business and commerce, exercising a generally dominating influence over local affairs, had long favored annexation to the United States. They now became convinced that it was the one and only answer to Hawaiian problems.

This conviction was further strengthened, moreover, by the effects of the McKinley tariff of 1890. This measure had placed sugar on the free list and thereby destroyed the preferential position Hawaiian planters had previously enjoyed in the American market through the provisions of the existing reciprocity treaty. Trade and commerce were very adversely affected. Only through annexation could the old market be restored. It appeared to have become an economic as well as political necessity.

Queen Liliuokalani, however, had no idea of promoting annexation or in any other way encouraging the American party. When the reciprocity treaty was renewed, she had tersely noted in her diary: "Today a day of importance in H. history. King signed a lease of Pearl Harbor to U. States . . . It should not have been done." She was stubbornly determined to revive the power of native rule, break away from all foreign influence, and assert her own authority. "Hawaii for the Hawaiians" was her goal. In its pursuit the Queen allied herself with the most reactionary of the native leaders, and let herself be advised by a small group of adventurers who played upon her vanity and pride for their own usually corrupt purposes.

In their growing conviction that annexation was the only way both to block Liliuokalani's despotic designs and to recover the market for Hawaiian sugar, the American residents had a strong ally in the United States minister to Hawaii. John L. Stevens had been hand-picked by Secretary Blaine because of his annexationist sympathies, and his stay on the islands persuaded him that the time had come for what his chief called "an avowedly American solution" of the entire Hawaiian problem. Stevens' reports to the State Department repeatedly declared that annexation was the only way to prevent Great Britain from fishing in these troubled waters, and he significantly asked for instructions as to his course in the event a revolution should break out. His dispatch of November 20, 1892, concluded: "The golden hour is near at hand."

The excuse for action, so impatiently awaited by the annexationists, presented itself when Liliuokalani, incensed at the opposition of the legislature to her program, arbitrarily moved to proclaim a new constitution which would have abolished the assembly and restored the old prerogatives of the crown. Her ministers grew fearful of the consequences of such a move, however, and secretly informed the leaders of the American party of what was underway. The Queen hesitated to act under these circumstances and postponed any further moves until she felt more sure of herself. In spite of this temporary retreat, however, it was clear that a crisis was at hand. The American residents, feeling that they were "living on a volcano," consequently took matters into their own hands. On January 16, 1893, they set up a Committee of Public Safety, called a mass meeting of all Hawaiian citizens, and demanded the abdication of the Queen.

The plot now thickens as a result of the role played by the American minister. Stevens was away from the islands when the first rumors of trouble began to circulate; but, promptly returning, he immediately got in touch with the leaders of the revolt. A clear understanding was reached. In response to a request from the Committee of Public Safety for the protection of United States forces, Stevens ordered a landing party from the USS *Boston*, fortunately for the American party, in port at this critical juncture, to take over the task of preserving law and order. The Committee thereupon issued a proclamation abrogating the monarchy and establishing a provisional government to take over full control of Hawaiian affairs until union with the United States should be successfully concluded.

The Provisional Government then asked for *de facto* recognition by the American minister. Even though on the previous day the leaders of the revolt had admitted that "we are unable to protect ourselves without aid," Stevens immediately acceded to this request. Nor was the precipitate American minister content with recognizing a regime that could still produce no evidence of either popular support or of its ability to take over the government. He granted it official protection and ran up the Stars and Stripes over the administration buildings.

Liliuokalani was helpless. She had no alternative other than to surrender her authority. In doing so, however, she registered an embittered protest. She had yielded, "to the superior force of the United States of America, whose minister plenipotentiary, his excellency John L. Stevens, has caused United States troops to be landed at Honolulu and declared that he would support the said Provisional Government."

Events had moved rapidly. The Queen had summoned the assembly which she had originally intended to inform of the new constitution on January 14; two days later the Committee of Public Safety had demanded her abdication and called for American aid; within another twenty-four hours Stevens had recognized the Provisional Government. Nor did the pace of these hectic developments slacken. The new regime at once appointed a commission to negotiate an annexation treaty. It reached Washington in the first week of February, and four days later full agreement had been reached with representatives of the State Department. An annexation treaty was signed on February 14—just thirty-two days after the revolt against Queen Liliuokalani's rule had been launched.

The Harrison administration, not surprisingly in view of its general policies, was ready to accept annexation of Hawaii without a second thought. John W. Foster, who had replaced Blaine as Secretary of State, was very much of an imperialist. An able and industrious international lawyer, rather than a statesman, his was in a sense an interim appointment, but his influence was aggressively exerted in favor of taking over the islands. "It is, in my opinion," he wrote, "the plain duty of the

United States to annex them to its territory." There were, however, only a few more weeks before Harrison's term of office
would expire and Cleveland, re-elected to the presidency during the previous autumn, would once again be in the White
House. If the outgoing administration were to annex Hawaii,
the Senate would have to act immediately and Secretary Foster
would have little time to prepare his case for the treaty's ratification.

The American people proved to be somewhat more hesitant
than the Republican leaders about taking such a hasty step.
The idea of overseas expansion, in spite of increasing popular
interest, was still too much of a novelty to be taken so easily in
the nation's stride. And even those who believed that sooner
or later Hawaii would necessarily become an American possession could not help being disturbed by the way things had been
rushed by the enthusiastic Stevens and were now being further
hurried by Foster. A spirited debate in the press, colored as
always by intense partisanship, revealed highly conflicting
views as to whether the treaty should be approved and the
United States embark on a new colonial policy.

The expansionist arguments, generally advanced by Republican papers supporting the outgoing Harrison administration,
stressed the commercial and strategic importance of Hawaii in
the light of expanding American interests in the Pacific, and the
danger that if the United States did not take advantage of this
opportunity to annex the islands, some other nation surely
would. The Washington *Post* particularly, in both its news
columns and in its editorials, played up purported moves, first
on the part of Great Britain, and then by Japan, to take over
Hawaii should the crisis not be promptly resolved by American
action. Where the flag had once been raised, other papers declared in what was to become a recurrent theme, it should
never be lowered. "The American people are not fools," said
the New York *Sun*. "Congress will annex Hawaii; and one number in the program of manifest destiny will have been performed." Any possible question of the attitude of the Hawaiian

people themselves was easily brushed aside by the jingoistic Baltimore *American*. "The interests at stake are too serious," it declared, "to admit of mawkish sentiment about the rights of a queen who does not know how to govern, or a people who do not want to govern, but prefer to be governed by the United States."

Such papers as the *New York Times* and the New York *World*, however, expressed strong doubts of the advisability of annexation and, even when begging that basic question, severely criticized what they declared to be the indecent haste with which the whole business had been carried through. Their principal point was that settlement of the issue should at least be postponed until the Cleveland administration was installed and the public had been allowed time to consider annexation's full implications. The question could wait a couple of weeks, said the *Times*, "without injury to anybody except the schemers who have precipitated it."

Many Republican papers felt that the criticism of their partisan rivals was entirely due to a desire to have the new administration get the credit for a move for which its predecessor was responsible. The Democrats would see matters differently, they maintained, once they were in office. In suggesting this shift in attitude, an editorial in the Philadelphia *Inquirer* reflected the underlying ideas on both sides of the question.

"All we would get, it is said, are a few active volcanoes, several thousand savages, about a thousand lepers, and a parcel of adventurers, speculators and sugar kings," the *Inquirer* commented. ". . . If we get nothing else we get the key to the Pacific, and this is something that our Democratic brethren will begin to see after noon on Saturday."

Whatever the merits of the dispute, the Senate was not to be hurried unduly. No action was taken in the brief period before Cleveland's inauguration. The country then waited expectantly to see what the new President might do. Was he prepared to fall in line with what appeared to be the growing annexationist sentiment throughout the country, or would he still stand for that traditionalism in foreign policy that he had asserted so emphatically during his first term of office?

CHAPTER VI

MR. CLEVELAND RETURNS

MANY MORE SERIOUS PROBLEMS THAN THE ANNEXATION OF Hawaii confronted Cleveland in March 1893. One newspaper, the Detroit *Evening News,* commented that it was of comparatively little consequence "what he does about the tariff or the currency, if, in the situation now presented by Hawaii . . . . he proves himself a true American—an American like Jefferson —equal to the greatness of his country's possibilities." This was of course far from the case. The problems of tariff and currency had become of immediate and vital urgency. The country was facing a sharp and dangerous business decline, panic was over the horizon, and soon a nationwide depression would settle ominously over the land.

The opening years of the new Cleveland administration, indeed, have been called one of the most perilous periods in the nation's history, apart from those years when the country was actually challenged by war. They were not only depression years. They were a time of smoldering popular discontent, of embittered labor strife, and of what was widely interpreted— especially in the conservative East—as threatened social revolt. Populism was sweeping through the agrarian states of the South and Midwest as fanatical orators—"Pitchfork Ben" Tillman, "Bloody Bridles" Waite, "Sockless Jerry" Simpson, and Mary Elizabeth Lease—called upon the farmers, in the latter's famous phrase, "to raise less corn and more Hell."

Infuriated railroad workers walked out in the great Pullman strike of 1894, tying up all traffic, and, in defiance of federal troops, angrily attacked railroad property. Here was "rebellion," cried conservatives; and among other newspapers the *New York Times* denounced the gentle Eugene V. Debs, the strikers' leader, as "a lawbreaker at large, an enemy of the human race." During this same tumultuous spring General Coxey led an army of the dispossessed, hundreds of ragged unemployed workers, in a march on Washington, protesting the failure of the government to satisfy their demands. Although this invasion ended with the members of Coxey's army arrested for trespassing on the Capitol grounds, the faint-at-heart trembled.

These were developments, actual or threatened, that far overshadowed foreign policy as Cleveland again took up the reins of office. Still, Hawaii was an issue that had to be settled. The new administration had to take a stand at once on what was to be done with the annexation treaty pending in the Senate.

The Secretary of State charged with the immediate responsibility for dealing with this question, Walter Q. Quesham, advised Cleveland to withdraw the treaty until a full investigation could be made of just what had taken place in Hawaii. The President, without hesitation, accepted this proposal. On March 9, he informed the Senate in a curt message that he wished the treaty to be returned "for the purpose of re-examination."

In a private letter to Carl Schurz about this time, Cleveland said that he did not regard "annexation in all circumstances and at any time unwise," but was convinced that the country should very carefully "stop and look and think." Gresham's views were more positive. "I am opposed to annexation," he stated flatly, "especially of territory not a part of our continent." Although Cleveland was to swing ever more strongly against expansion and would never approve the annexation of Hawaii, it was his Secretary of State who most resolutely took this stand in March 1893.

Gresham was a onetime Republican, a bitter foe of Harrison

who had defeated him for the presidential nomination in 1888; and contemporaries sometimes attributed his opposition to the Hawaiian annexation treaty to a desire to undo the work of a political rival. There is little to sustain this interpretation of his attitude. Gresham was a man of strong idealistic principles; he was also generous and humane. His wife has implied that his personal sympathy for Queen Liliuokalani importantly affected his policy on Hawaii. "A woman in trouble!" she wrote. "My husband would certainly side with her against the power, greed, and lust of man." Whatever there may have been of the sentimental in his make-up, however, there is no question of a stronger basis for his position. "A free government," was his emphatic answer to all annexationists, "cannot pursue an imperialistic policy."

The Cleveland administration's second step in regard to Hawaii was to dispatch a special commissioner to the islands. James H. Blount, former chairman of the House Committee on Foreign Affairs, undertook this assignment with complete authority to conduct such investigations as he saw fit and take whatever measures he deemed necessary to protect the interests of American citizens. Upon his arrival in Honolulu, Blount promptly ordered the lowering of the American flag, so impetuously raised by Stevens as a symbol of an American protectorate, and insisted that the American sailors and marines who had been sent ashore for the ostensible purpose of maintaining order return at once to their ship. It was quite clear that American policy had changed. While there might still be some conjecture as to the nature of the report Blount would make after his interviews with both American and Hawaiian leaders, annexation had suffered a sharp rebuff.

The press in the United States was widely divided as news of these developments reached home. The Republican papers were generally bitter; the Democratic papers usually approving. It was maintained on the one hand that such a propitious moment for annexation would never occur again; and, on the other, that the annexation movement was a plot with which the

United States could not in good faith associate itself. Cleveland came under heavy fire for repudiating his predecessor's policy and allowing the American flag to be hauled down. The Chicago *Tribune*, expressing the widespread Republican sentiment that the United States had every right to intervene in Hawaii, soberly warned that if the islands should, through negligence or hesitancy, be allowed to fall into the hands of any foreign power, "the American people will never forgive the guilty party." Other papers were no less condemnatory of this apparent repudiation of the whole program of Hawaiian annexation. "The dream of an American Republic at the crossroads of the Pacific," the *Commercial Advertiser* commented bitterly, "has been shattered by Grover Cleveland, the Buffalo Lilliputian."

Rallying to the President's support, the Democratic press applauded the courage and statesmanship that led Cleveland to reject a policy that was a denial of the basic tenets of democracy. Many newspapers stated that there could be no reconciliation between colonialism and republicanism; others declared that the wise teachings of Washington would be effectively set at naught if the United States embarked on the road to imperial conquest.

The periodical discussion of the issue brought forth an effective article by Alfred Thayer Mahan, insisting upon the necessity of annexation; and a sharp rebuttal by Carl Schurz, who declared that possession of the islands would weaken, rather than strengthen, the United States. Both men took a broader view of possible overseas expansion than immediate policy toward Hawaii. Mahan called for annexation of the islands, not as a mere sporadic effort, but as "a first fruit and a token" that the nation was at last aroused to the necessity of carrying its life "beyond the borders which heretofore have sufficed for its activities." Schurz countered by stating that the adoption of any such course under the sign of "manifest destiny" would mean the total abandonment of the traditions of national policy, deterioration in the character of the American people, and "a future of turbulence, demoralization, and final decay."

While the press at home argued about what should be done, Blount was quietly pursuing his investigations in Hawaii. The pro-annexationist forces did everything possible to win his support. They endeavored to prove that the revolution had popular backing and, without too great subtlety, tried to win him over to their side by personal favors. "He is a genial, pleasant man," one of the Hawaiian commissioners in Washington had advised the annexationist leaders, "one who would appreciate attention"; another suggested that "it is the after dinner talk over the cigar, when one feels comfortable and well filled, that effective work is done." Blount, however, remained immune to such blandishments, carrying out his difficult task with what was generally accepted as admirable objectivity.

His report was to prove devastating to the annexationist cause. On the basis of the evidence he had so laboriously assembled, he came to two major conclusions. There had been collusion between the revolutionary leaders and the American minister, and the whole movement was without popular support. "The undoubted sentiment of the people," Blount wrote in startling summary, "is for the Queen, against the Provisional Government, and against annexation."

This analysis was accepted by the Cleveland administration as basically sound, but it left open the very delicate question of what, under such circumstances, the United States should do next. Secretary Gresham was prepared to make a definite recommendation. "Should not a great wrong done to a feeble but independent State by an abuse of the authority of the United States be undone by restoring the legitimate government?" he asked. "Anything short of that will not, I respectfully submit, satisfy the demands of justice." Other members of the cabinet, most notably Attorney General Olney, did not believe that it would be quite so easy to unravel the Hawaiian tangle. Less romantic than Gresham, who, again according to his wife, did not think that "the weakness and frailties of a woman, even if they existed, should be made the basis for dethroning her," Olney was unwilling to ignore altogether the interests of the

American party. He pointed out that the United States had a certain responsibility for a government which had come into existence with the aid of the American minister and American armed forces. If influence were to be exerted for the restoration of the Queen, he urged, it should only be done on the basis of a clear understanding that Liliuokalani would extend a complete amnesty to all those who had taken part in the revolution.

Cleveland decided to follow Olney's advice. Albert S. Willis, who had been named minister to Hawaii and accredited to the Provisional Government operating under the presidency of Sanford B. Dole, the son of a former missionary, was charged with carrying out the new policy. Gresham's instructions called upon Willis to express to the Queen the President's regret for the "flagrant wrong" done her; secure an undertaking on her part that she would grant an amnesty; and, having obtained such assurances, inform the Provisional Government that it was expected promptly to relinquish to the Queen her constitutional powers.

While the American authorities in Washington apparently thought that this plan would work out rather easily, Willis was to find the situation in Hawaii a good deal more complicated than the State Department realized. He met Liliuokalani on November 13 and asked her whether, if she were restored to her throne, she would grant a full amnesty to all those concerned with the revolution. The Queen hesitated a moment, according to his later report, and then slowly and calmly gave her answer.

"There are certain laws of my government by which I shall abide," she said with regal dignity. "My decision would be, as the law directs, that such persons should be beheaded and their property confiscated to the Government."

The startled American minister was taken aback. Here was an impasse he had hardly foreseen. At a loss how to proceed in the face of this emphatic refusal to consider an amnesty, Willis at once informed Washington: "Views of the first party so extreme as to require further instructions." As nonplused as his envoy, Gresham replied that he should continue to insist on the amnesty. If the Queen remained obdurate, he stated, the President would have no alternative other than to cease "interposition in her behalf."

Liliuokalani remained obdurate. Imperious and self-willed, she saw no occasion to condone the injustice done her. Only after several weeks of persuasion by her more practical-minded advisors did she at last back down and agree to the amnesty. Willis then turned to the Provisional Government and submitted the proposal that the Queen should be restored to power. Dole withheld his answer at this first meeting; but three days later, in a firm and dignified reply, he declared that the Provisional Government "respectfully and unhesitatingly declines to entertain the proposition . . . . that it should surrender its authority to the ex-Queen." Having finally succeeded in carrying out the first phase of his instructions, Willis was now peremptorily rebuffed in seeking to complete the second phase.

Cleveland was already despairing of finding any way to reconcile the conflicting positions of the Queen and the Provisional Government and prepared to admit the collapse of his own program for dealing with Hawaii. On December 18—actually the very day of Liliuokalani's capitulation, but five days before Dole's statement—he had sent a message to Congress that in effect surrendered executive responsibility and deposited the entire issue in the lap of the legislative branch of government. The President emphatically stated his own conviction that the Provisional Government had come into power only as a result of the intervention of armed United States forces in the domestic situation, and that despite the failure of his own policy, "our duty does not, in my opinion, end with refusing to consummate this questionable transaction." He did not, however, give Congress any slight hint of what he thought could now be done.

The attention of the public had been diverted to other matters during the dreary depression months of 1893, but interest flared up once again as the news of these further developments became known. And once again newspaper reaction conformed pretty generally to political alignments. The idea of seeking to restore the Queen was assailed by Republican papers as "stupid and outrageous," "a source of universal ridicule," and "an act of national self-stultification." There was perhaps no more bitter attack on Cleveland's policy than that of the *Congregationalist*, which reflected the outraged view in some religious circles of trafficking with an unprincipled "barbarian." The President was using national power and prestige, the *Congregationalist* asserted, "to impose on decent people the authority they had overthrown of a vicious, immoral, irresponsible woman, surrounded by knavish advisors, to the destruction of the guarantees of protection of life, liberty, and possessions."

The Democratic press often found it difficult to uphold the idea of the United States intervening in behalf of royalty. Since when, asked one newspaper, had it become the policy of a democratic nation to place monarchs on the thrones of neighboring countries? The *New York Times*, however, expressed a more general Democratic view in praising Cleveland's policy. "Nothing could more strengthen the Administration in the mind of fair-minded and right-thinking men," the *Times* declared on announcement of the original plan to restore the Queen, "than the act of justice to Hawaii which is announced in the letter of Secretary Gresham."

It was significant that in this public debate relatively little was said about the possible annexation of Hawaii. The press generally assumed that, at least for the time being, the project was dead. The disclosures of the Blount report had too clearly demonstrated that, whatever the advantages or disadvantages of acquiring the islands, this was hardly the occasion on which the United States could act with a clear conscience. This general attitude was also reflected in political debate in Congress. There were some few expansionists who continued to urge Hawaiian annexation whatever the circumstances, but more generally Congress simply wanted to let the matter drop.

The final decision in which both the Senate and House concurred was that the Hawaiian people had an inherent right to establish and maintain their own form of government, and that the United States should not interfere in their domestic politics. Congress nevertheless made it very clear that, in this new hands-off policy, the United States was in no sense giving up its historic interest in the islands. Intervention in Hawaiian affairs by any other government, the congressional resolution stated explicitly, "will be regarded as an act unfriendly to the United States."

Here the situation was left—temporarily. The Provisional Government under President Dole proceeded to establish the Republic of Hawaii, and the unfortunate Queen Liliuokalani finally accepted as incontrovertible fact the permanent loss of her throne. Annexation had also been defeated for the time being, and Cleveland was rid of a troublesome problem. But the idea was by no means abandoned—either in Hawaii or among American expansionists. It was certain to come up again. The mounting imperialist sentiment throughout the country suggested that as soon as the Republicans were returned to power they would almost surely submit a new annexation treaty for national consideration.

The Cleveland administration's action in blocking Hawaiian annexation was not an isolated incident in its stand against overseas expansion. The President remained firmly opposed to any move along such lines. Setting his face grimly against every proposal for an extension of American territory beyond continental bounds, he even opposed a bill that would have provided cable communications with Hawaii because he did not want "to boom the annexationist craze."

He had no desire, for example, for continued entanglement in the confused situation still prevailing in Samoa. Referring in his annual message to Congress in 1893 to developments in those far-off islands, where the system of control set up at the Berlin Conference appeared to be breaking down, he expressed the greatest skepticism as to what the United States had gained through the tripartite treaty. Dissensions had not been stilled, nor had rivalry among the competing native claimants for the throne. A joint military effort on the part of the three powers participating in the Samoan protectorate failed to bring to an end the prevailing disorder. "This incident and the events leading up to it," Cleveland flatly stated, "signally illustrate the impolicy of entangling alliances with foreign powers."

He would have liked to bring the whole arrangement to an end and was fully supported in this position by his Secretary of State. In a report in 1894, Gresham elaborated on what he considered the complete failure of the General Act of Berlin to remedy the evils it was designed to correct. "We may well inquire," he wrote, "what we have gained by our departure from our established policy beyond the expenses, the responsibilities, and the entanglements that have so far been its only fruits . . ." Nothing was done at the time, but neither Cleveland nor Gresham changed their view that the Samoan involvement was a great mistake.

Cleveland also remained strongly opposed to the idea that the United States should attempt to set up exclusive control over the projected isthmian canal. He was sympathetic to the proposal that a canal should be built and believed that it should be "accomplished under distinctively American auspices," but by this he did not mean that the United States should acquire or control the territory through which a canal might pass. The project should be undertaken, if at all, he reiterated, in the interests of the international community; and the canal should always, in war as in peace, be open to the ships of all the world.

Summarizing his views on the whole question of obtaining new territories—whether in the Caribbean or in the Pacific—Cleveland expressly stated his conviction that any such program would not only be contrary to historic national policy, but a perversion of America's basic goals. "The mission of our nation," he stated, "is to build up and make a greater country out of what we have, instead of annexing islands." His final message to Congress in 1896 found him reaffirming the sentiments he had set forth in his first inaugural address eleven years earlier. "Its own ample and diversified domains," he said in discussing the country's future, "satisfy all possible longings for territory, preclude all dreams of conquest, and prevent any casting of covetous eyes upon neighboring regions, however attractive."

If Cleveland's policies were thus sternly directed against territorial expansion, it is nevertheless true that he gave a new impetus to the burgeoning imperialist spirit of the times by his actions in another quarter. When confronted with the situation arising out of the boundary dispute between Great Britain and Venezuela in 1894, which he interpreted as involving a threat to the Monroe Doctrine, Cleveland took so firm a stand that the imperialist and jingo elements in the country hailed him as a nationalist hero. Critics of his attitude toward Hawaii and Samoa abruptly reversed themselves. Senator Lodge was "bubbling over with delight," and wrote exultingly: "I am no longer lonely—Jingoes are plenty enough now."

In later years Cleveland could never understand how, in spite of his opposition to expansion, one of his close friends could call him "the father of imperialism." Yet his belligerent defense of the Monroe Doctrine in the Venezuela dispute not only served to heighten the American people's sense of national power, but emphatically increased their desire for the exercise of such power. His policy gave an impetus to the latent forces of imperialism that far overshadowed the temporary check administered by the withdrawal of the Hawaiian annexation treaty.

The boundary dispute between Great Britain and Venezuela had been simmering for half a century before Cleveland felt compelled to take a hand in it. A tentative line drawn up in 1840 by Sir Robert Schomburgk to mark the territories of Venezuela and British Guiana had never been accepted by Venezuela, and in the course of years additional British settlements to the west of this line had encroached still farther on what Venezuela considered her territory. At stake were both control of the mouth of the Orinoco River and the possession of newly discovered gold fields. Venezuela's claims were admittedly extravagant, yet British statesmen haughtily turned a deaf ear to every Venezuelan request that the entire issue be submitted to arbitration. England was willing to consider negotiations in respect to the title to the new settlements that had been made west of the Schomburgk line, but the Foreign Office insisted that the boundary proposed in 1840 could not be questioned.

Relations between the two countries were finally broken off in 1887; and although on several occasions the United States attempted to exercise its good offices in healing the breach, the crisis deepened. In his annual message in 1894 the President, reiterating his belief that it was of the utmost importance "to remove from this hemisphere all causes of differences with powers beyond the sea," said that he would renew these earlier efforts to induce Great Britain and Venezuela to submit their controversy to arbitration.

As England continued to maintain her intransigent attitude, the American public became aroused over the issue and anti-British feeling once again flared up dangerously. Taking advantage of such sentiment, an astute Venezuelan agent, William L. Scruggs, published a pamphlet provocatively entitled *British Aggressions in Venezuela, or the Monroe Doctrine on Trial*. It had a sensational effect, and the newspapers began to insist that the United States interest itself in the dispute more directly. In February 1895, Congress adopted a resolution calling upon England to accept arbitration; and in response to public pressures, Secretary of State Gresham undertook to prepare still another note to Great Britain.

Before this note was sent, Gresham died and was replaced in the State Department by Attorney General Olney. He was a man of an entirely different stripe from the rather easy-going Gresham. While he knew little of foreign affairs, he was an able lawyer with pronounced views and the utmost frankness in stating them. "Rather rugged," Henry White wrote, "and unlike his predecessor, of ability and force." Olney was impatient and demanding, harsh and imperious. He was not a man to brook opposition on any course on which he had decided. Tall and powerfully built, with a bulldog face and figure, his manner reflected the ruthlessness with which he had dealt with the Pullman strike, and was now prepared to deal with what he considered Great Britain's challenge to the Monroe Doctrine.

Secretary Olney promptly drew up a new note—July 20, 1895—to replace the one written by Gresham. It was designed to shock Great Britain into an awareness that the United States considered the Venezuela dispute a matter of grave concern. Some of its phrases, Olney was later to write, were "undoubtedly of the bumptious order." He continued: "The excuse for them was that in English eyes the United States was then so completely a negligible quantity that it was believed only words the equivalent of blows would be really effective."

Olney bluntly stated that the controversy between Great Britain and Venezuela was one in which the United States, under the terms of the Monroe Doctrine, felt that both its honor and its interests were involved. Any move on the part of a European power forcibly to deprive an American state of the right and power of self-government would be deemed an act unfriendly to the United States. There could be no interference by Europe in the affairs of the Western Hemisphere. This country was prepared to defend its rights. "Today," Olney said belligerently, "the United States is practically sovereign on this continent, and its fiat is law upon the subjects to which it confines its interposition . . . its infinite resources combined with its isolated position render it master of the situation and practically invulnerable as against any or all other powers."

Great Britain's refusal to arbitrate the entire boundary dispute could not be defended, Olney further stated, "and it seems therefore quite impossible that this position of Great Britain should be assented to by the United States, or that, if such position be adhered to with the result of enlarging the bounds of

British Guiana, it should not be regarded as amounting, in substance, to an invasion and conquest of Venezuelan territory. . . ."

The Secretary of State was concerned over whether Cleveland would approve so forceful a statement of the American position, but he had no need for misgivings. Cleveland's conservative attitude on foreign policy, as we have seen, embraced rather than excluded the firm defense of American interests; and he believed thoroughly in upholding a broad interpretation of the Monroe Doctrine. On reading the note he assured the anxious Olney, "It is the best thing of the kind I have ever read."

For five months there was no reply from Great Britain. The British Prime Minister and Foreign Secretary, Lord Salisbury, was affronted by the peremptory tone of Olney's dispatch; and he failed to realize the gravity with which the Cleveland administration regarded the affair. When he finally replied, it was to deny dogmatically the applicability of the Monroe Doctrine to the Venezuela controversy—"the disputed frontier of Venezuela has nothing to do with any of the questions dealt with by President Monroe"—and blandly to reiterate the British position that there could be no arbitration affecting the original Schomburgk line. Salisbury had underestimated his man, but the fault was not entirely his. The American ambassador in London, the affable and conciliatory Thomas Bayard, whose pro-British sympathies were demonstrated in the old fisheries negotiations, was not in sympathy with Olney's stand and minimized American concern with the issue.

In failing to impress upon the British Prime Minister that it was a serious situation, Bayard most certainly did not help matters. Olney was to complain bitterly. The United States government, he wrote in reviewing the situation, "had been handicapped by having in England a diplomatic agent who has not sympathized with its policy." And he went on to characterize Bayard as a man "who through sentiment, self-conceit, physical infirmity, and otherwise, has been practically disabled from rendering the service rightfully expected of him." Even John Hay, a pronounced Anglophile, wrote disparagingly of Bayard's "slobbering over the British."

When Salisbury's belated reply was received, in any event, President Cleveland, hastily summoned back from a duck-shooting expedition, was reported to be "mad clear through." This was a rebuff that could not be tolerated. Moreover the public—which had not been informed of the exchange of notes, although some hint of them had leaked out—was becoming highly critical of what appeared to be the administration's dilatory policy. Many newspapers followed the lead given them in a contemporary magazine article by Lodge. "The supremacy of the Monroe Doctrine," the ever-belligerent senator wrote, "should be established and at once—peaceably if we can, forcibly if we must." Although the Springfield *Republican*, with its usual moderation, deprecated any talk of possible conflict "over a matter so trivial," the Washington *Post* reflected a much more general view in asserting that the United States should be ready to defend its interests, whatever Great Britain might choose to do.

Cleveland needed no prodding from the press. He strengthened a message to Congress that Olney had already drawn up and—without consultation with his cabinet, which he bluntly informed, "I am about to send this message"—laid things squarely on the line.

The President insisted, in this message of December 17, 1895, upon the correctness of Olney's interpretation of the Monroe Doctrine and on the necessity for vigorous enforcement of American interests. He asked Congress to appropriate the funds necessary for an investigation of the boundary between British Guiana and Venezuela. And finally he stated his conviction that when the investigation was made, the United States should be prepared to resist as willful aggression any move by Great Britain to assert her authority over territory that the United States might determine belonged of right to Venezuela.

Cleveland declared that he was fully alive to the responsibility incurred in making his recommendations and to the consequences that might follow. If there were no other way of impressing upon Great Britain that the United States would not tolerate any violation of the Monroe Doctrine, he was quite clearly ready for war.

The message evoked the greatest enthusiasm. Congress unanimously voted the appropriations for the investigating committee, and throughout the country newspaper editorials excitedly hailed this ringing assertion of American rights. The editors of the *Literary Digest* reported that "the overwhelming majority of the newspapers applaud the message as American, vigorous, and eminently just."

The Washington *Post,* true to its own convictions, devoted its entire front page to the message with the over-all headline: "Clear and Patriotic—The Law of Monroe Must Stand." It reported congratulatory messages pouring in at the White House and a burst of patriotic feeling throughout the capital as "old veterans of the late war talked exultingly of what they were prepared again to undertake at the call of their country." The New York *Sun* declared that the American people would deal harshly with any representative or senator who might seek to cripple the hand of the Executive in vindicating the national honor, and the Cincinnati *Enquirer* said the message was an exhibition of backbone that every American would applaud. Perhaps the Atlanta *Journal* expressed what, for the moment at least, was the most general reaction. "In supporting the President in this position," it stated, "the people of this country will stand as one man. Party lines will vanish like smoke and sectional divisions will be forgotten. The honor of the country is at stake. We have a President who means to defend it and we are all with him."

The latent jingoism of the day was immensely stimulated. A nation grievously disturbed by its domestic problems happily let its attention be diverted to a foreign issue on which the United States could take a vigorous and forthright stand. Here was something to applaud and cheer. The deeper significance of the position Cleveland had taken was temporarily ignored in the immediate exulting over an America confronting the world with so bold an assertion of her rights.

There was a note of hysteria in much of the comment. "Let the fight come if it must," wrote Theodore Roosevelt. "I don't care whether our seacoast cities are bombarded or not; we would take Canada." Senator Stewart of Nevada declared that war would "rid the country of English bank rule." Commenting on the flood of bellicose newspaper stories and editorials upholding Cleveland's message, the pacific *Nation* said that "rational sober-minded people" were driven to silence for fear of being charged with "un-Americanism."

Yet more sober counsels were soon to prevail as the implications of what the New York *World* called the "jingo bugaboo" were more fully realized. This newspaper, indeed, took the lead in trying to marshal the peace sentiment both in this country and in England.

"There is no menace in the boundary line," an editorial of December 21 declared, "it is not our frontier, it is none of our business. To make it such without cause, and to raise the spectre of war over a false sentiment and a false conception, is something more than a grave blunder. If persisted in, it will be a colossal crime."

As the immediate chauvinistic outburst gradually subsided, the forces on either side of the Atlantic making for peace gathered headway. The British people showed remarkable forbearance. Responsible leaders in and out of the government declared an Anglo-American war unthinkable, and some 354 members of Parliament supported a resolution endorsing arbitration of any dispute that might arise with the United States. In response to such friendly overtures, the more conservative and peace-minded groups in this country reaffirmed their opposition to a policy that could conceivably lead to hostilities and expressed a firm friendship for England. All but the most rabid jingoes began to realize that war between the two great English-speaking peoples would be an unmitigated tragedy.

The next move, nevertheless, remained up to Great Britain.

Consequently there was immediate relief when Lord Salisbury, in contrast with his answer to Secretary Olney's original note, gave every indication of being willing to pursue a conciliatory policy. His decision to seek a settlement of the dispute through negotiation, and ultimate acceptance (although still with some reservations in respect to the Schomburgk line) of the principle of arbitration, was due not only to friendship for America but to certain European developments. When the German Kaiser, on January 3, 1896, sent a telegram congratulating the Boers for their successful defense against the Jameson raid on their territory, the British government was sharply reminded of the importance of allies in the face of mounting Anglo-German rivalry. It became all the more important, from its point of view, to strengthen the ties between England and the United States as fresh difficulties developed in maintaining the uneasy balance of power in Europe.

Negotiations went on for many weary months before the Venezuela issue was finally settled, but the public lost all interest in the matter as the war talk died down. A treaty which provided for the submission of the dispute to arbitration was finally signed by Great Britain and Venezuela in February 1897, but an award was not made until more than two years later. It generally followed the Schomburgk line, but Venezuela was given a little additional territory and control of the mouth of the Orinoco.

The Venezuela episode, for all its anti-climactic conclusion, was of utmost importance in the development of American foreign policy. Cleveland's position on the Monroe Doctrine may have been untenable according to international law, and his virtual ultimatum to Great Britain unjustified on many counts. Yet he had made not only England, but the rest of the world, realize that the United States was prepared to defend its self-declared interests in the Western Hemisphere and would go to any length in upholding the principles of the Monroe Doctrine. America was asserting the rights and privileges of a great power. There remained a certain irony in the fact that the

President, who in so many ways represented the older traditions of American policy through his stern opposition to overseas expansion and foreign entanglements, had taken the lead
in asserting an entirely new role for the United States on the
world stage. Yet this was just what Cleveland had actually
done.

Various factors affected Cleveland's policy. He was under
heavy political pressure because of Republican attacks on his
general approach to foreign affairs. He was criticized not only
for what was considered his unpatriotic attitude toward Hawaiian annexation, but for failure on other counts to uphold
the national interest. His defense of the gold standard had
been tied in by the proponents of free silver with a general subserviency to Great Britain. The prevailing popular sentiment
would not condone any such attitude.

Moreover, the jingoistic spirit that in part inspired such criticism, and on which only the year before the penetrating editor
of the *Nation* had commented so caustically, was in itself becoming a force that could not be wholly ignored, as an expression of a popular desire to escape through foreign adventure
from the grave and seemingly insoluble problems confronted
on the home front. As Charles Francis Adams noted at the time,
the only remedy for this excited talk of war would be the return
of national prosperity. "I have always observed," he said, "that
when people are employed and prosperous, they cease to be
jingoes." But in the hard times of the early 1890s, prosperity
did not seem to be even around the corner.

Caught up by the impact of untoward events at home, the
President may well have felt driven to divert popular attention
from the dangerous implications of industrial unrest and deepening agrarian discontent by taking a patriotic stand that would
not only rally support for his administration, but quiet the
clamor of restless farmers and sullen industrial workers. At
least one congressman—Representative Paschall of Texas—
specifically advised him, in rather inelegant terms, that a strong

position on Venezuela would "knock the pus out of the anarchistic, socialistic, and populistic boil."

Yet Cleveland's forthright defense of the Monroe Doctrine on the Venezuela issue was in no sense out of character. It did not necessarily represent submission to political pressures. For he had repeatedly shown that in spite of his opposition to overseas expansion and foreign entanglements, he was resolute—sometimes aggressively resolute—in defending the national interest wherever he believed it to be threatened. While he opposed the acquisition of either Samoa or Hawaii, no one could have been more determined to prevent the establishment of a paramount foreign influence over either of these Pacific islands. If he did not want to see the United States become involved in the affairs of Europe or Asia, he was always adamantly opposed to the intervention by any other nation in the affairs of the Western Hemisphere. The policy that he had enjoined upon his countrymen in his first inaugural address ten years earlier was one not merely rejecting any share in foreign broils, but "repelling their intrusion here." In his defense of the Monroe Doctrine in 1895, Cleveland felt himself on entirely justifiable grounds. Far from wishing to stir up trouble with England, he expressed his bitter disappointment, in a letter to Ambassador Bayard, that the British Government had not understood his position "in the midst of all this administration has had to do in attempts to stem the tide of 'jingoism.'"

Cleveland considered himself bound to sustain national honor and national rights. His fundamental ideas were perhaps most clearly set forth in the conclusion of his famous message to Congress calling Great Britain to account. "There is no calamity which a nation can invite," he declared, "which equals that which follows upon supine submission to wrong and injustice, and the consequent loss of national self-respect and honor, beneath which are shielded and defended a people's safety and greatness." Possibly he was himself unconsciously affected by the jingoistic spirit of the times, but he acted as he did in 1895 out of conviction rather than political-mindedness.

If the most obvious result of his policy was to heighten nationalist feeling and build up the American people's sense of their own power, it also had another and unexpected consequence. The risk that such an arbitrary stand might conceivably embroil the United States in war with Great Britain drove home among American leaders—and the American people— a realization that, in assuming a larger part in world affairs, this country could hardly afford a break with that nation with which the ties of race, language, and natural sympathy afforded so natural a basis for international friendship. However paradoxical it may seem, the flare-up of the old hostility toward Great Britain in 1895 actually paved the way for a new Anglo-American entente. It swept the slate clean; it aroused both nations to the realities of the world situation. There were never again to be such violent outbursts of anti-British sentiment as had generally characterized the early 1890s.

"There is a patriotism of race as well as of country," Secretary Olney himself declared in 1898, "and the Anglo-American is as little likely to be indifferent to the one as to the other." For all the "family quarrels" that had occurred in the past and would surely take place again, he continued, it was not permissible to doubt that the two nations "would be found standing together against any alien foe by whom either was menaced by destruction or irreparable calamity."

This prophetic utterance was to be realized in the two great wars that lay over the horizon of the twentieth century. However, the more immediate effect of the Cleveland administration's bold assertion of nationalism was to give the United States a new standing in the eyes of other nations and to place a further emphasis upon that vigorous foreign policy which the generation of the 1890s so stridently demanded.

"It indicates, as I believe and hope," observed the thoughtful Captain Mahan, "the awakening of our countrymen to the fact that we must come out of our isolation . . . and take our share in the turmoil of the world." In more flamboyant terms, Henry Watterson, the fiery editor of the Louisville *Courier-Journal* who had previously written that Olney's original message "called down the despots of Europe," declared that henceforth the United States was "destined to exercise a controlling influence upon the actions of mankind and to affect the future of the world as the world was never affected, even by the Roman Empire itself."

CHAPTER VII

BEHIND THE SCENES

LATE IN SEPTEMBER 1895, THE SUGGESTION WAS MADE TO President Cleveland that he appoint to the State Department a young man named William Phillips. The President was not impressed. "I learn that he is a good deal of a club man," he wrote, "and what is a settler with me, that his close associates are John Hay, Henry Adams, Henry Cabot Lodge, and such."

Whatever the implications of this comment as respecting the mores of Washington society, it was hardly surprising that the anti-imperialist Cleveland should veer away from naming any member of this group for a position involving the formulation of foreign policy. For the men he mentioned formed the nucleus of an intimate circle—the "and such" would certainly have included Theodore Roosevelt—which was already helping to build up the momentum that would precipitate imperialist expansion in 1898. And if Henry Adams remained always in the background—"stableman to statesman," as he himself characterized his role—the others in the group were to play a dynamic part in directing national policy during the McKinley administration.

An oddly assorted lot in some ways, they were drawn together by the closest ties of social position, wealth, and intellectual sympathies. Henry Adams—"queer to the last degree," as Cecil Spring-Rice described him on first being introduced into a circle of which he was to become an increasingly intimate member—never overcame the burdensome heritage of family tradition. Shy and sensitive, a man of ideas rather than action, he could not find his place in life. Temperamentally unable to assume the political role his forebears had played in the making of the nation, he fell back upon a critical attitude toward national affairs which reflected an unhappy blend of frustration and cynicism. With an Adams relegated to the wings, it was only natural that he should pessimistically see the world rapidly going to the devil. Yet there was a great deal of shrewd foresight in his caustic comments on the passing scene. No one ever questioned Henry Adams's intellect or imagination. He understood the forces that were soon to bring about such momentous changes in the global balance of power far better than most of his contemporaries.

At the time of the Venezuela crisis, he recognized that, with America united and Europe divided, Great Britain had no choice in the face of Cleveland's stalwart defense of the Monroe Doctrine other than "to crawl down or fight." He was hardly surprised when Lord Salisbury accepted American policy. Adams also foresaw in the expanding United States of these days the formation of a new world culture, and he believed that it would only be offset by "the Russian center forming across Asia."

He was greatly influenced by his brother Brooks Adams, who was no less concerned over the cloudy future. The latter had become convinced—and would convince Henry Adams—that power was primarily based on economic factors. "Brooks Adams had taught him," as Henry wrote in *The Education of Henry Adams*, "that the relation between civilizations was that of trade." The United States could only save itself in the growing competition among nations, according to such theories, by moving out across the Pacific and winning control of the trade and commerce of the Orient. And here again the great protagonist was Russia. America could not afford to stand aside, both Adamses believed, as a new century approached in which imperialist conflict would determine the world's future.

Brooks Adams only occasionally visited Washington. There was a period in 1897, however, when he was there (he had married the sister of Mrs. Henry Cabot Lodge) and was described by Roosevelt, who lunched with him daily, as "simply revelling in gloom." This could hardly be expected to appeal to the always effervescent "Teddy"; and the latter was, indeed, highly skeptical of his luncheon companion. He strongly criticized Brooks Adams's treatise on *The Law of Civilization and Decay* and wrote Spring-Rice that he would have handled it even more brutally in his review article if he had not been persuaded that its author's mind was "a little unhinged." He was prepared to condone what he termed the extraordinary intellectual and literary dishonesty of the book only on this account, but hastily warned Spring-Rice, "for Heaven's sake don't quote this, as I am very fond of all the family."

A good many years later, when Roosevelt became President, his attitude toward Brooks Adams was quite different. He was greatly impressed by Adams's ideas on the role the United States should play in international affairs; took over a number of his ideas on far eastern policy, especially in relation to China and Russia; and frequently borrowed phrases from his writings.

It was Henry Adams, however, who was the key figure in the group that aroused Cleveland's distrust in the mid-1890s. His major interest was always foreign affairs; and as he later wrote in *The Education of Henry Adams,* he "felt most keenly the nightmare of Cuban, Hawaiian, Nicaraguan chaos." With his usual somewhat oblique approach, he believed that it was essential for the United States to take over the Caribbean islands; and when the question then arose of possible acquisition of the Philippines, he became greatly concerned over the balance of Pacific power. He accepted expansion and finally wrote that "he could see that the family work of a hundred and fifty years fell at once into the grand perspective of true empire-building."

The only occasion on which Henry Adams appears to have taken a direct part in the developments that led to imperialism occurred in December 1896. After sounding out Hay, to whom he had written some months earlier: "that we must recognize the independence of Cuba next winter is, I think, as nearly inevitable as any future policy can be," Adams drew up a resolution to effect such recognition; and it was submitted to Congress by Senator J. Donald Cameron of Pennsylvania. This was a curious maneuver. For Cameron was a close friend of Lodge and Roosevelt as well as of Adams, very much one of the group ("the relation was daily," Adams wrote); and the contemporary correspondence suggests that their idea was to force upon the Cleveland administration a war which the incoming Republicans could then carry through to a victorious conclusion. "I certainly wish the matter could be settled this winter," was Roosevelt's blunt comment.

The Cameron resolution was unanimously approved by the Foreign Relations Committee ("Stroke for Cuba—Congress Asked to Take Action That May Result in War," headlined the Washington *Post*) in spite of a two-hour plea by Secretary Olney that it should be rejected. Nevertheless the continuing opposition of the Administration—Olney stated that even if the resolution were passed it would be completely disregarded —resulted in its never being called up for debate. Adams's one direct intervention in expansionist politics had proved rather futile.

The closest friend of Henry Adams in these Washington days was John Hay. The two men had adjacent and connecting houses at the corner of Sixteenth and H streets, and their association was constant whenever they found themselves in the capital. They saw each other almost every hour of the day and often took walks together.

Suave and polished where Adams was self-conscious and brittle, a man of great charm, and a wonderful conversationalist, Hay was in the early 1890s almost as much outside politics as his retiring friend. His service as Lincoln's secretary had been the great experience of Hay's life; but he was also poet, biographer, diplomat, and amateur politician. Although he was a Republican, his ambitions for an important diplomatic career had been constantly thwarted by his support of the wrong man when his own party was in power; and during the Cleveland administration there was, of course, even less opportunity for him to find something to do. That he intended to get back into the political swim was suggested in a letter to Henry Adams in May 1894: "I think I must take office again," he wrote, "when youalls get out." He was to work vigorously for McKinley's nomination and election; and as his reward he was to be, first, ambassador to Great Britain, and then Secretary of State.

Like so many other Republicans who were to stand in the vanguard of imperialism, Hay welcomed the strong stand taken by Cleveland on the Venezuelan issue, even though he perhaps wished it had been the Republican party that was getting political credit for this bold assertion of American rights. It so happened he was in England in the summer of 1896, and he took occasion to write Secretary Olney of his conversations with a number of British leaders. He reported that he had warned them not to expect any change of policy should McKinley be elected—"that the public sentiment of the United States was virtually unanimous in support of the administration's action in this question; that no steps backward would be taken by McKinley. . . ."

Although not a jingo in the more extreme sense, Hay became an expansionist and believed, as he wrote McKinley early in 1898, that "the greatest destiny the world ever knew is ours." His biographer has written that in the turgid days

on the eve of war with Spain he had nothing to say: "It may
be doubted whether he had opinions on the subject; he was
thinking." Nevertheless Hay was soon writing a correspondent
that, while he detested war and had hoped he might never
live to see another one, the contest with Spain was "as
necessary as it is righteous. I have not for two years seen
any other issue." He favored the annexation of Hawaii, accepted the necessity for taking over the Philippines, and
promoted the acquisition of Samoa "in the interest of our
Pacific work."

Hay was to have some qualms about his conversion to the
imperialist cause from an earlier attitude of strong opposition
to overseas expansion. Once he had written:

> "Far be it from our principles of state
> On distant reefs and islands to display
> Our power and motives."

He had been won over—a man of adaptability rather than
strong principle—by the persistent infusion of the ideas of the
company he kept and by political pressures. He was himself
to explain his changed attitude on broader grounds. "No man,
no party," he wrote, "can fight with any chance of success
against a cosmic tendency; no cleverness, no popularity, avails
against the spirit of the age."

If Henry Adams was always on the sidelines, and John Hay
in the early 1890s still an impatient observer of events in
which he had no active part, Lodge was already the practical
politician among the familiar visitors to the two adjacent
houses at the corner of Sixteenth and H streets. And perhaps
no one in Washington—unless it was Roosevelt—was more
enthusiastically, aggressively imperialistic. His insistence upon
the protection of American rights in Samoa, his emphatic endorsement of the need to annex Hawaii, and his demand for
vigorous support of the Monroe Doctrine demonstrated this
beyond question.

Lodge had already won a reputation in Washington for chilly aloofness. Tall and thin, with a short, close-cropped beard, very dapper in appearance, he had what a contemporary described as "an air of well-bred hauteur." While his self-assured manner and clipped Harvard accent did not endear him to his fellow senators, he was widely recognized as a very able parliamentarian, an effective speaker, and an industrious, hardworking member of Congress. With such friends as he met in the circle revolving about Adams and Hay, he could be gracious and charming.

Adams's relations with Lodge, as the former wrote in *The Education of Henry Adams,* had been those of an elder brother or uncle since "Cabot Lodge had left his examination papers on Assistant Professor Adams' desk, and crossed the street to Christ Church in Cambridge to get married." There were frequent travels abroad together—"where Mrs. Lodge summoned," wrote Adams, "one followed with gratitude"; and it was of Washington life in 1893 that he also commented on how, among the few houses which he could enter without being asked and quit without being noticed, "one was John Hay's; another was Cabot Lodge's." The ties between these houses, to which Adams also added that of Senator Cameron, became a powerful social and political force. "Whatever one's preference in politics might be," he said, "one's house was bound to the Republican interest when sandwiched between Senator Cameron, John Hay, and Cabot Lodge, with Theodore Roosevelt equally at home in them all, and Cecil Spring-Rice to unite them by impartial variety."

Lodge's partisanship was perhaps to mark his career more than any other single factor in his make-up. Aristocratic and conservative by nature, he accepted the Republican party as generally representative of the things in which he believed; and, right or wrong, he stood by the party. His early imperialism, however, seemed to be an obsession and led him, almost in spite of himself, to praise Cleveland in 1896. In season and out, he spoke and wrote of the desirability of driving Europe entirely out of the Western Hemisphere (and this included taking over Canada), of the need for overseas bases, and of the vital importance of building up American naval strength.

One of his greatest efforts along these lines was a speech in the Senate on March 2, 1895. The immediate subject was Hawaii, but Lodge ranged over the entire world in emphasizing the importance of the "sea-power that is essential to the greatness of every great people" and the value to the United States of what he called "the necessary outworks" to reinforce its continental position. He brought out on the Senate floor a great map of the world with red Maltese crosses marking the naval bases of Great Britain. The lesson was clear and heavily underscored the danger of letting Hawaii drift into the hands of any foreign power.

"I was in desperate earnest," Lodge wrote his mother after this speech. ". . . As I spoke the Senators came in from the cloakrooms, members of the House appeared, the messengers and doorkeepers came in. . . . When I sat down everybody crowded around to shake my hand."

The substance of this speech was incorporated in an article for the *Forum* that Lodge entitled "Our Blundering Foreign Policy." In his fervid plea for building an isthmian canal and annexing not only Hawaii and Samoa, but also Canada, he declared that such expansionist policies were the only ones that American statesmen could follow "if they would prove themselves worthy inheritors of the principles of Washington and Adams."

After the Venezuelan incident, Lodge felt that the general cause for which he spoke was certain to make headway; and he was even more confident when McKinley came into the presidency in 1897. He was prepared to exert all his influence —for a time seeing the new President almost daily—to promote territorial expansion. He realized that recognition of the Cuban rebels might well lead to war, but this did not deter him from strenuously urging such a move. Lodge indeed felt that hostilities were not an unmitigated evil. A nation far too prone to think in terms of material gain would greatly profit, he suggested on several occasions, from an infusion of the martial spirit that would rally the people to uphold national honor and national glory.

In this phase of his thinking, Lodge reflected the views of the entire group with which he was so closely associated. None of them had any real sympathy, in spite of their support for the Republicans, for the business interests which that party so generally represented. They were conservatives, but in a traditional sense, and far removed in spirit from the contemporary supporters of the new industrial society. And they were all of them highly scornful of the pacifism of the "aristocratic upper crust" and of the timidity in commercial circles toward the adoption of a strong foreign policy. There were many things worse than war, Lodge repeatedly said, and the nation should always be ready for it. "It was painful," he wrote at the time of the Venezuela crisis, "to read the telegrams and letters from frightened stockbrokers and bankers."

Whatever may be said of Lodge's chauvinism was, of course, doubly true in the case of Roosevelt. When he came to Washington as a civil service commissioner under President Harrison, he had naturally gravitated to the exclusive circle dominated by Adams, Hay, and Lodge; and he was to become increasingly intimate with Lodge—"the staunchest friend I have ever known." The two men's views on the country's future could not have coincided more closely. Roosevelt was not only an impetuous jingo, but proudly boastful of it and deeply scornful of anyone who did not accept his point of view.

"These solemn prattlers," he wrote of the anti-imperialist, antijingo faction, "strive after an ideal in which they shall happily unite the imagination of a green grocer with the heart of a Bengalese baboo."

Roosevelt was a brash young man in these days—just thirty-seven in 1895—and already noted for his enthusiasm and cocky spirit. Adams enjoyed his company but maintained a

somewhat skeptical attitude toward him; Hay regarded him
with both amusement and awe. Contemporary descriptions
already emphasized those characteristics that were later to
become even better known—"his teeth are big and white, his
eyes are small and piercing, his voice rasping." He was a
tremendous talker. Rudyard Kipling came to know him in these
days (Roosevelt found the Englishman "a pleasant little man,
bright, nervous, voluble, rather underbred") and used to enjoy
hearing him hold forth at the Cosmos Club. "I curled up on
the seat opposite," Kipling wrote, "and listened and wondered
until the universe seemed to be spinning around and Theodore
was the spinner."

This happy facility for talking, of course, Roosevelt never
lost. Some years later, when Roosevelt was President, Hay
wrote amusingly to Adams of how their young friend was
conducting himself: "He began talking at the oysters, and the
pousse-café found him still at it. When he was one of us, we
could sit on him—but who, except you, can sit on a Kaiser?"

Roosevelt's martial fervor was an instinctive expression of his
own character and also a mark of his emphatic reaction to
what he believed with Lodge to be the "animal sloth and ease"
of contemporary American society. He wanted to see the
United States become a great power; he believed thoroughly
in its imperial destiny; he was ready to welcome war as a
means to revive the national spirit. And he always wanted to
practice what he preached: "If there is a muss I shall try to
have a hand in it myself." There is a wonderful picture of
Roosevelt in a letter from Hay to Adams at the time of the
Chilean affair. "He goes about hissing through his clenched
teeth that we are dishonest," Hay wrote. "For two nickels he
would declare war himself . . . and wage it sole."

Roosevelt's views led to a lively controversy with Charles
W. Eliot, president of Harvard, who attacked both him and
Lodge as "degenerated sons of Harvard" for their jingoistic,
chip-on-shoulder attitude. Roosevelt, as might be expected,
was incensed, and wrote Lodge of "the futile sentimentalists

of the international arbitration type" who would deny the great fighting qualities of the race. In an effort to save Harvard from degeneracy, and convinced as a result of the clamor of the peace faction that the country really needed war, he published a letter in the *Harvard Crimson* urging the students to uphold the stand taken by Cleveland during the Venezuela crisis.

Roosevelt was greatly influenced, as was Lodge, by the teaching of Alfred Thayer Mahan. He enthusiastically reviewed Mahan's first book on *The Influence of Sea Power on History*, and their subsequent correspondence clearly reveals how much the younger imperialist owed to the great advocate of sea power. Again and again Roosevelt acknowledged this debt—"you are head and shoulders above all of us"; and when he became Assistant Secretary of the Navy, he emphatically told Mahan that "all I can do toward pressing your ideas into effect will be done."

One of the most interesting Roosevelt letters of this period, revealing the close ties linking Roosevelt, Lodge, and Mahan and their common agreement on national policy, was written to Mahan on May 3, 1897. After expounding his views on the Navy, a Nicaraguan canal, purchase of the Danish West Indies and Hawaii ("hoist our flag over the island, leaving all details for after action"), Roosevelt wrote:

"I need not say that this letter must be strictly private. I speak to you with the greatest freedom, for I sympathize with your views, and I have precisely the same idea of patriotism, and of belief in and love for our country. But to no one else excepting Lodge do I talk like this."

Among other associates of the imperialist-minded clique was Henry White. This able and experienced diplomat, whose affability and charm, appealing modesty, and sympathetic attitude led him to be characterized by all who knew him as "a great gentleman," had a natural entree into the most ex-

clusive of Washington's social circles. While the greater part
of his life was spent in a series of diplomatic posts overseas,
which he filled with marked distinction, he too was in Washington in 1895. His diary shows how very often, at suppers,
dinners, and other evening parties, he saw Adams and Hay,
Lodge and Roosevelt. They were almost invariably among the
guests he listed as on hand at these functions. When Mc-
Kinley came into office, Roosevelt and White each worked
for the other's interests; and on one occasion we find Roosevelt
writing affectionately: "Now, old man, don't you bother about
me."

White was never an important formulator of foreign policy,
but few of his contemporaries had broader contacts among
foreign diplomats or was more useful in explaining American
foreign policy in European capitals. Roosevelt would later
characterize him as "the most useful man in the diplomatic
service." He had no official assignment during the Cleveland
administration, but Olney nevertheless called upon his services
when White was visiting in England in 1896. His acquaintanceship among the elite was so wide that within ten days he was
able to talk with almost every British leader, generally during week ends at one or another of the great English country
houses, and he proved a far more effective defender of American policy than Ambassador Bayard.

White fully approved the stand on Venezuela taken by
Cleveland as the employment of his services suggested. "As
to the Monroe Doctrine," he wrote one correspondent, "I do
not find the modern interpretation of it extravagant, considering the great power of the United States. It is evidently not
a piece of international law, but what matter so long as the
United States has the power to maintain it as a policy." Yet
he rarely expressed himself in his private correspondence, let
alone public statements, on the issues of imperialism. President
McKinley gave him the choice of minister to Spain or first
secretary in London. He chose London.

Another diplomat in this same circle, but quite a different

sort of man, was William W. Rockhill, future architect of the Open Door policy and already recognized as an authority on eastern Asia, as a result of a tour of duty in China and extensive travels in Tibet and Mongolia. There was little of White's charm and affability about this rather enigmatic individual—a tall man with a drooping red mustache and "an almost washed-out fairness"—whose scholarly interests made him a good deal of a recluse. But while he had little liking for social life—one diary comment on the functions he had to attend was the expressive "stupider, stupider, stupider!!!!"—he apparently cast off his customary austerity among close friends and won both their affection and respect. For a time Adams, Hay, and Rockhill maintained a sort of seminar on world relations; and at one time, in Hay's absence, Adams wrote that he was "quite alone . . . . except for Rockhill, in the atmosphere of foreign affairs."

Rockhill became Assistant Secretary of State under Cleveland—"Three cheers," Roosevelt wrote enthusiastically—and accepted without reservation Cleveland's policy on Venezuela. He was never won over to the advisability of recognizing Cuba's independence, however, and remained very skeptical of the plank urging such action placed in the Republican platform in 1896 by his friend Cabot Lodge—"I do not think he has distinguished himself by so doing."

When McKinley was elected, Rockhill's friends hoped for —and zealously promoted—his appointment as minister to China, but he was sent instead to Greece. In time, however, Hay brought him back to Washington, nominally in a post dealing with Latin America but more importantly to serve as an advisor on far eastern affairs. Rockhill had a keen appreciation of the expanding role the United States was playing in the Pacific, recognized the need to safeguard and promote American interests in Asia, and was always deeply sympathetic toward China's aspirations for freedom from foreign interference in her internal affairs. The problem of Asia, he consistently maintained, was the most important international issue with which the world was faced, and he was always afraid that in resolving the tangle Russia would come out ahead.

Even though White and Rockhill, who stand out as virtually the first career diplomats in the foreign service of the United States, may not have been fervid imperialists, they were notable exponents of the theory that the United States should play a larger and more responsible role in international affairs. And their close association with such men as Adams, Hay, Lodge, and Roosevelt serves further to stress the significance of the part played by this rather exclusive group in pointing the way to America's rise to world power.

Other Washington figures on the periphery of the group, or occasionally swinging within its orbit, included a number of the most aggressive contemporary imperialists. There was Whitelaw Reid, militant editor of the New York *Tribune* and aspirant for the London embassy, who led a constant campaign for overseas expansion. Spring-Rice speaks of breakfasting with him in the company of Lodge and Roosevelt. On another and later occasion Roosevelt referred to him "as always, delightful . . . excellent about the Philippines." Albert Shaw, editor of the *Review of Reviews,* and Walter Hines Page, at this time editor of the *Atlantic* and subsequently editor of *World's Work,* welcomed the articles of Roosevelt and Lodge and in other ways promoted and encouraged the expansionist cause. Page was to comment happily, after visiting Washington early in 1898, "We see already the beginnings of an 'Imperial' party."

One more journalist who often dined with these people on his occasional visits to Washington was Henry Watterson. He enjoyed the talk—"Lodge, cool and wary as a politician should be; Hay, helter-skelter, the real man of the world crossed on western stock . . . . Adams something of a littérateur, a statesman and cynic."

Still additional names might be cited as both being closely associated with the Adams-Hay-Lodge-Roosevelt circle and vigorous exponents of expansion. There were, for example,

Senators John T. Morgan of Alabama, Cushman Davis of Minnesota, and Redfield Proctor of Vermont. "A jingo!" Roosevelt wrote of Proctor, "and it is rather a relief to see a man who can't be touched by the timid people of wealth." And a Roosevelt letter further suggesting how men of like minds were brought together these days is a note introducing Josiah Strong to Captain Mahan.

Somewhat later there would be added to the group the brilliant young man from Indiana. "Senator Beveridge was out here yesterday," Roosevelt wrote Lodge in the fall of 1899. ". . . . His views on public matters are almost exactly yours and mine. I want you to meet him."

The association of the principals among these statesmen, diplomats, and publicists was closest during the mid-1890s. It was to be abruptly interrupted after the change of administration in 1897.

"Suddenly Mr. McKinley entered the White House and laid his hand heavily on this special group," wrote Henry Adams. "In a moment the whole nest so slowly constructed was torn to pieces and scattered over the world. Adams found himself alone. John Hay took his orders for London. Rockhill departed to Athens. Cecil Spring-Rice had been buried in Persia. Cameron refused to remain in public life either at home or abroad . . . Only the Lodges and Roosevelts remained, but even they were at once absorbed in the interests of power."

If this was regret and loneliness for Adams, it was opportunity for his friends. They were now to play a dominant role in the making of foreign policy. If the larger part was to be that of Roosevelt—first exercising no little influence as Assistant Secretary of the Navy in preparing the way for war with Spain; and then as President, implementing the larger world role of the United States in the opening years of the twentieth century—the others had a part only less important. The diplomacy of John Hay would be held responsible for the great development of American interests in Asia through the promulgation of the Open Door policy, and Lodge was a guiding spirit in winning approval on the part of his fellow senators for the acquisition of Hawaii and the Philippines. Rockhill was not only the real author of the Open Door notes, but the principal negotiator in settlement of the Boxer Rebellion troubles in China. White, moving from one important diplomatic post to another, would represent American interests at the Algeciras conference.

Here was the fulfillment of much that must have been discussed when the group gathered for "the usual pleasant evenings and parties" in the Washington of pre-McKinley days; during the morning horseback rides of Roosevelt and Lodge; on the walks when Adams picked up Hay for their customary afternoon stroll; and, as the written record shows, in the correspondence among them all—Adams, Hay, Lodge, Roosevelt, White, Rockhill, Mahan. . . .

The interwoven threads linking these men suggest a fascinating pattern of political influence. They did not operate as a unit. Here is neither intrigue nor conspiracy. Their combined influence, indeed, cannot possibly be accurately evaluated. But the exchange of ideas, action, and counteraction most certainly helped to win over the McKinley administration, and Republican political circles generally, to imperialism.

"No man or group of men," Mahan was later to write, "can pretend to have guided and governed our people in the adoption of a new policy, the acceptance of which has been rather instinctive—I would prefer to say inspired—than reasoned." Perhaps this was true. The tide of imperialism was rising as a result of underlying forces—social, political, economic—that were beyond the control of individuals or any group of men. Still, the direction in which these forces were to move depended on direction and leadership. The way had to be prepared for overseas expansion. "Reflection and discussion, voice and pen," Mahan himself also said, "had broken up the fallow ground left untilled by the generations which succeeded the fathers of the republic."

This preparation for empire was the role played in the development of foreign policy by the Adamses, the Hays, the Roosevelts, the Lodges, and the Mahans, who directly or indirectly sought to impress upon the American people the need to look beyond national boundaries and to be ready to assume a new role of world leadership.

CHAPTER VIII

THE RISING TIDE

WHEN CLEVELAND LEFT OFFICE IN 1889, HE HAD BEQUEATHED to Harrison the troublesome problem of Samoa; four years later Harrison in turn handed over to the returning Cleveland the unresolved issue of the annexation of Hawaii. As Cleveland reached the end of his second term in March 1897, he followed this familiar pattern in the realm of foreign policy. He left to his successor, William McKinley, still another and far more critical problem involving American policy toward the rebellion that had broken out in Cuba against Spanish rule. This issue was, of course, far to overshadow Samoa and Hawaii—or even the Venezuelan incident—for it provided the impetus that started the United States on the road to empire and served once and for all to shatter the traditional isolation of the nineteenth century.

In finally taking up arms to secure Cuba's independence in the Spanish-American War, the United States embarked upon a course that led to establishment of American domination of the Caribbean, the extension of national interests and territory to the shores of Asia, and inevitable entanglement in the web of world politics. So basic a change in policy appears sudden and abrupt, however, only when it is divorced from the background of the 1890s. Richard Olney, whose stand on the Venezuela issue had so directly contributed to the growth of imperialist sentiment, was one contemporary who fully realized this.

"Though historians will probably assign the abandonment of the isolation policy of the United States to the time when this country and Spain went to war over Cuba, and though the abandonment may have been precipitated by that contest," Olney wrote in 1900, "the change was inevitable, had been long preparing, and could not have been long delayed."

McKinley had been elected on a platform whose foreign planks called for control of the Hawaiian Islands, construction of a Nicaraguan canal, purchase of the Danish West Indies, and an expression of sympathy for the Cuban rebels. These issues had been completely ignored, however, in an exciting, vituperative campaign that largely centered about William Jennings Bryan's demand for free silver. The Republican victory owed nothing to the party's stand on foreign questions. It was the triumph of the conservative forces of the industrial East over the agrarian radicalism of the South and West. Vachel Lindsay would later sing:

> "Election night at midnight:
> Boy Bryan's defeat.
> Defeat of western silver.
> Defeat of the wheat.
> Victory of letterfiles
> And plutocrats in miles
> With dollar signs upon their coats,
> Diamond watchchains on their vests
> And spats on their feet."

As the new President McKinley stood firmly for a laissez-faire economy, establishment of the gold standard, and a protective tariff. He reflected the views of the business interests that directed the domestic policies of the Republican party and which had so far shown no sympathy whatsoever, in spite of the platform's foreign policy planks, in any overseas extension of national territory. Something over a month before the inaugural ceremonies, the Washington *Post* asserted authoritatively: "President-elect McKinley does not favor the annexation of either Hawaii or Cuba." About this same time, McKinley himself assured Carl Schurz that there was to be "no jingo nonsense under my administration." It appeared to be abundantly clear that he did not want any foreign adventure that might interrupt the recovery, already under way, from the depression of the mid-nineties.

In conformity with this attitude, McKinley said nothing about foreign policy in his inaugural address which could have been challenged by even so staunch an anti-imperialist as Grover Cleveland. Reaffirming the traditional policy of nonentanglement bequeathed by Washington, he stoutly declared: "We want no wars of conquest; we must avoid the temptation of territorial aggression."

There was nothing, indeed, in McKinley's background to suggest any interest in the country's playing a broader role in world affairs. He was an Ohio politician who had been taken under the wing of Mark Hanna, that stern and unabashed champion of the *status quo*, and was presented to the Republican convention as a foremost advocate of high tariffs and the gold standard—"Bill McKinley, author of the McKinley Bill, advance agent of prosperity." Easy-going, affable, and pliant, he won the warm affection of those close to him; and while he had none of the magnetism of a Blaine, he was to become highly popular as President. It was said that if men would not die for him, they were very happy to vote for him. He symbolized the best conservative traditions of his party.

McKinley very much looked the part of a president. An unusually handsome man, with a fine massive head, he made an impressive public appearance at all official functions. In-

variably dressed in the conventional political uniform of that
day, a well-pressed and stately Prince Albert with gleaming
white vest and striped trousers, he was dignity incarnate. As
a symbol of rectitude and high moral standards, he took himself very seriously. For example, no one could have more liked
to smoke, but to safeguard the nation's youth McKinley always
tried to avoid being photographed with his otherwise customary cigar.

The President completely lacked, however, the qualities
that make for effective, dynamic national leadership. He was
cautious as well as conservative. Although a man of deep
religious convictions and moral earnestness, he was at all
times ready to follow popular opinion rather than attempt to
lead it. He did not have Cleveland's unswerving devotion to
principle nor his dogged determination in following through
on any course he had adopted. McKinley accepted what the
people wanted and then invariably convinced himself that
Providence had decreed the policies that he was following.
Perhaps his outstanding characteristic was this sensitivity to
the changing tides of popular opinion and consequent willingness to be swept along by them rather than to try to check
them.

If the new President was totally inexperienced in foreign
affairs, he could not look for any help from his Secretary of
State. Political exigencies—supposedly the ambition of Mark
Hanna for the Senate and the consequent need to create a
place for him—had been largely responsible for the appointment of the aged Senator Sherman of Ohio to this key post.
Sherman was to prove completely incapable of carrying on
his arduous duties as a result of the progressive enfeeblement
of his powers and loss of memory. Assistant Secretary William
R. Day soon replaced him. The latter was thoroughly com-
petent—McKinley believed he had "a genius for common
sense"—but he could hardly be compared in stature with such
men as Blaine and Olney, or his successor, John Hay.

Foreign policy was not made during these epochal days

at the turn of the century by those constitutionally charged with its direction. There was a strange irony in the fact that such momentous changes in the whole approach of the United States to world affairs should take place while a McKinley was in the White House. Although the President was to have some part in helping to direct the imperialistic forces of the day into the channels they ultimately took, he was not in any real way responsible for the nation's venturing along such new and untried paths. The changes ushered in with the Spanish-American War came about as a result of the impact upon the country of those underlying forces that had been gradually building up the spirit of imperialism. They were most directly instigated by those ambitious expansionists who, throughout the 1890s, were appealing so successfully to the restless stir for power in a people newly awakened to the inviting possibilities of America's future world role.

Before the developing crisis in Cuban affairs led to that irresistible popular demand for intervention which overwhelmed McKinley in 1898, a first concrete sign of mounting imperialist sentiment was a renewed drive for the annexation of Hawaii. Many Republican leaders, however lukewarm McKinley's own original attitude, considered this to be highly important unfinished business. Former Secretary of State Foster was pressing for annexation. A number of prominent senators followed his lead, and the Hawaiian minister in Washington soon took up with the President the possibility of negotiating a second annexation treaty.

Theodore Roosevelt, the new Assistant Secretary of the Navy, and Senator Lodge also lost no opportunity in urging action to secure Hawaii before the opportunity was lost; and they were soon able to report to their common mentor on such matters, Captain Mahan, highly encouraging progress. "All I can do toward pressing our ideas into effect will be done," Roosevelt wrote Mahan on May 17, 1897; and some three weeks later he expressed his confidence that the President had been persuaded that Hawaiian annexation was necessary. And such confidence was justified. In spite of his professed opposition to overseas expansion and all earlier statements, McKinley now authorized further negotiations with the Hawaiian Republic and on June 16 submitted to the Senate a new annexation treaty with his strong endorsement.

There had been, in the spring of 1897, further developments in Hawaii that may have influenced McKinley more than the urgings of such expansionists as Lodge and Roosevelt. Japanese immigration in the islands was greatly increasing, a number of sharp disputes had arisen between the Japanese and Hawaiian governments, and there was a growing fear that Japan might have designs that would endanger American interests in this part of the Pacific. Moreover, such fears seemed to be confirmed when, on announcement of the negotiations looking toward a new treaty, Japan protested that American annexation of the islands would jeopardize the rights of Japanese subjects in the islands and declared that maintenance of the *status quo* was essential to the peace of the Pacific. The arrival of a Japanese warship at Honolulu underscored this emphatic protest and threatened to create what might have become a difficult situation. On July 10, the State Department consequently moved to sustain American interests. The United States minister was instructed that in the event of any attempted interference by Japan in Hawaiian affairs he was to "confer with local authorities and Admiral, land suitable force, and announce provisional assumption of protectorate pending consummation of the annexation treaty."

This potential crisis was resolved by Japan's withdrawal of her protest in the face of the strong stand taken by the United States, but the interest that Tokyo was taking in Hawaii aroused American expansionists to a new flurry of excitement. They saw Japan annexing the islands unless this country acted promptly. McKinley was himself alarmed and told Senator Hoar that Japan undoubtedly had her eye on

Hawaii and if something were not done "there will be before long another revolution, and Japan will get control." It seemed imperative to the imperialist-minded that the Senate at once approve the new treaty submitted by the President and confront Japan and the other Pacific powers with an accomplished fact.

Once again, however, the Senate was not to be hurried. In spite of strong support for annexation, political alignments within Congress made it extremely unlikely that the treaty would command the two-thirds majority necessary for approval. While the Republicans could be generally counted upon to sustain what had now become administration policy, the Democrats adhered to the position Cleveland had adopted and refused to fall in line. Consequently, no action was taken during the current session of Congress, and further consideration of the treaty was put off until the spring of 1898. The administration then decided to resort to the precedent provided in the case of Texas and seek annexation by congressional resolution, with its requirement of only a simple majority. In March such a resolution was favorably reported in both the Senate and the House.

By this time more exciting developments than the possible annexation of Hawaii were taking place in the realm of foreign affairs. Intervention in Cuba was very much in the forefront of popular interest; and, in response to the clamorous war spirit aroused by the sinking of the *Maine* in the harbor of Havana, the United States was about to go to war with Spain. To that story we shall, of course, return. It is sufficient to note at this point that the final chapter in Hawaiian annexation was to be written against a highly charged emotional background of patriotic fervor and martial adventure.

Moreover, as the Spanish-American War opened up the possibilities of other additions to American territory, it became clear that much more than the future of Hawaii was at stake in the impassioned debates in Congress on possible overseas expansion. The real issue underlying nearly everything said was whether the United States should hold firmly to the traditions of the past, rejecting all idea of colonies, or whether it should embrace a new policy and a new destiny. Captain Mahan had already suggested the underlying significance of Hawaiian annexation from this point of view in declaring that it should be considered only a first step in carrying the nation's life beyond its continental borders.

Although partisanship continued to dominate the congressional debates to a very large extent, there were both advocates and opponents of annexation who tried to come to grips with the issue on broader grounds. The former asserted that possession of Hawaii was necessary to assure American domination of the Pacific, and only such domination could adequately guarantee national security, protect American trade and commerce, and enable the United States to take its rightful place among the nations of the world. The anti-annexationists countered with the charge that whatever the possible benefits of controlling Hawaii, this first step toward empire would plunge the United States into the rivalries that plagued the European powers and also lead to the disintegration of the republic as it had traditionally existed. It is interesting to note that all the arguments—strategic, commercial, and moral —that were to come up in the later debates on the Philippines were first expounded in the discussion over Hawaii.

One man who sought to promote Hawaiian annexation and yet disassociate himself from more ambitious schemes of overseas expansion was Senator George Frisbie Hoar. He had been won over to the advisability of taking this mid-Pacific island base because of the threat that Japan might do so if the United States stood aside any longer, but he remained obdurately opposed to imperialism as a general policy.

"If this be the first step in the acquisition of dominion over barbarous archipelagoes in distant seas; if we are to enter into competition with the great powers of Europe in the plundering of China," Hoar declared in one forthright speech, ". . . . then let us resist this thing in the beginning, and let us resist it to the death. . . . But, Mr. President, I am satisfied, after hearing and weighing arguments and much meditation on this thing, that the fear of imperialism is needless alarm."

It soon became apparent, whatever was said in debate, that the mounting expansionist spirit engendered by war would really decide the issue. The Congress and the American people were now ready to take the step from which they had so long hung back. When the proponents of annexation were able to advance the final argument, however specious it might actually be, that Hawaiian annexation had become necessary as a war measure to safeguard American interests in the Pacific— that it was a matter of high strategy—there could no longer be very much effective resistance. The House voted for annexation in mid-June; some three weeks later the Senate followed suit. When, on July 7, President McKinley signed this joint resolution for the nation's first acquisition of overseas territory, he proudly announced that in view of the close ties so long prevailing between Hawaii and the United States, "annexation is not change; it is consummation."

The President was in a sense correct so far as the immediate question was concerned. Yet the annexation of Hawaii had a far deeper meaning and a broader significance. "The Rubicon has at last been crossed," the Boston *Transcript* editorialized. "The country enters upon a policy that is entirely new. It has thrown down its former standards, cast aside its old traditions." Certainly Captain Mahan was right in declaring that Hawaiian annexation would be a step toward further overseas expansion; and Senator Hoar was wrong in implying that it was not such a move and that the fear of imperialism was needless alarm. However logical American control of Hawaii might be, the acquisition of the islands clearly broke the pattern of the past.

"Hawaii is ours," growled former President Cleveland. "As

I look back upon the first steps in this miserable business and as I contemplate the means used to complete the outrage, I am ashamed of the whole affair."

In the meantime, the war with Spain was already rushing to its victorious conclusion. It is necessary, however, to turn back to discover how the United States became involved in these hostilities, before relating further events during the crowded summer of 1898.

The Cuban rebels, following a not unfamiliar pattern, had risen up against their rulers in 1895, and before many months had passed were wreaking havoc throughout the island. The economic depression that had hit Cuba a year earlier, with American adoption of high tariffs on sugar, was in part responsible for the outbreak, but it also reflected the long simmering discontent of the Cuban people with Spanish control, and a natural assertion of the right to freedom. American sympathies were at once engaged on the side of the rebels. The United States had long had an interest in Cuba; there was an instinctive reaction in favor of a colonial people so close to American shores struggling for liberty, and sensational reports of the brutal attempts of the Spanish military to crush the revolt by herding the Cuban people into reconcentration camps heightened the feeling that the United States could not ignore what was happening. In response to growing popular pressure, Congress overwhelmingly passed a concurrent resolution in the spring of 1896 favoring recognition of Cuban belligerency.

Such a move would have been direct intervention in the internal affairs of a friendly country and tantamount to a challenge of war with Spain. President Cleveland, true to his antijingo and anti-imperialist principles, refused to consider recognition. He was determined to meet the problem of Cuban rebellion without any conflict with Spain. Paying no attention to the action of Congress, he continued to seek some solution of the issue through diplomatic negotiations. On one occasion he is reported to have said that even if Congress should declare war, there would be no hostilities, for "I will not mobilize the army."

His attitude at once drew down upon his head, with the usual partisan undertones, the maledictions of both the imperialist-minded and of those jingoistic elements that had for so long been spoiling for a fight—with almost any nation —to test the mounting power of the United States. Nevertheless Cleveland held his ground, and in the summer of 1896 popular attention was largely diverted from Cuba to the excitements of the presidential election. But the issue could not be ignored. As warfare continued in the island and the yellow press played up the atrocities that marked the campaign of "Butcher" Weyler, the Spanish commander, in seeking to suppress the revolt, the American public was again aroused. Before leaving office Cleveland sternly warned the Spanish government that United States intervention would become inevitable if the struggle degenerated into "senseless slaughter."

With the advent of the new McKinley administration, the popular demand for some form of intervention in Cuba was stepped up by two related, though in some measure contradictory, impulses animating the American people. There was still the conviction among the imperialist-minded that the revolt in Cuba offered an unique opportunity for the United States to drive Spain out of the Western Hemisphere, and also a more widespread feeling that, entirely apart from its own interests, the United States was morally bound to uphold the cause of liberty by aiding the people of Cuba in their struggle against Spanish tyranny. Self-interest and idealism were linked in a common cause. Imperialists and anti-imperialists were drawn together in favor of a positive action, even at the risk of war with Spain. Those elements in the country that refused to be carried away either by ambition for national aggrandizement or by sympathy for the Cuban people, who wished at all costs to avoid war, found themselves more and more in the minority.

Once again Roosevelt stands out as a symbol of the forces most vigorously urging intervention. As early as May 3, 1897, he was writing Captain Mahan that Spain should be driven out of Cuba and that if he had his way, "that would be done tomorrow." Some six months later, he wrote William Wirt Kimball that he regarded possible war with Spain from two viewpoints:

"First, the advisability on the ground of both humanity and self-interest of interfering on behalf of the Cubans, and of taking one more step toward the complete freedom of America from European domination; second, the benefit done our people by giving them something to think of which isn't material gain. . . ."

One further point Roosevelt sometimes made: war would be a good test for the Navy, and an engagement between the American and Spanish ironclads would provide "a very pretty fight." During these months, moreover, Roosevelt was doing everything possible to impress his views upon McKinley and to win his approval for a disposition of naval forces that would enable the United States to strike promptly and effectively should war come. "The President has been most kind," he wrote Lodge after one of these sessions at the White House. "I dined with him Friday evening, and yesterday he sent over and took me out to drive again." Nor was it only in private conversations that the impetuous young Assistant Secretary of the Navy pled his cause. On March 30, 1898, he wrote William Sheffield Cowles that he had "advised the President in the presence of his cabinet, as well as Judge Day and Senator Hanna, as strongly as I know how, to settle this matter instantly by armed intervention."

It would appear, however, that Roosevelt may have overplayed his hand. Just five days after reporting the meeting with the Cabinet, he told another friend that he had preached the doctrine of armed intervention in such plain language that the President "will no longer see me."

Senator Lodge's attitude was more circumspect. His private correspondence clearly shows that he felt as strongly about matters as did Roosevelt, but he was too political-minded to risk falling out of presidential favor. He also realized the dangers to the party should there be a rift between the executive and Congress over Cuban policy. Recognizing the President's strong opposition to any move that might lead to war, he was consequently ready to cooperate with him in trying to find a peaceful resolution of the problem that would still enable the United States to aid the Cuban rebels and pursue the more general expansionist goals in which Lodge so firmly believed.

The partisans of intervention continued to find their most faithful allies in the press. Following the lead of the New York *World* and the New York *Journal,* which were engaged in a frenetic circulation battle, newspapers throughout the country played up the situation in Cuba for all it was worth —and often a good deal more; provocatively they headlined every incident that could be made to have a sensational appeal, and zealously fanned the flames of popular excitement. They spiritedly vied with one another in asserting that intervention—whether in the form of recognition of Cuban independence or more direct action—was the only way in which the United States could be true to its principles of safeguarding and promoting liberty wherever it was endangered.

So widespread was popular sympathy for the Cubans under this barrage of propaganda that the Democrats were soon outdoing the Republicans in trying to demonstrate that their party was the more zealous supporter of Cuban freedom. Nor did the Populists, for all their continued concern with domestic issues, lag behind their political rivals in insisting that the Administration should recognize the rebels. They appeared ready to bolster a cause which had so disastrously gone down to defeat in 1896 by linking the challenge of Free Cuba to their old cry of Free Silver.

If President McKinley hesitated further, the Chicago *Times*

Herald declared in an editorial in March 1898, "who dares doubt that 'war for Cuban liberty' will be the crown of thorns the free-silver Democrats and Populists will adopt at the elections this fall? And who can doubt that by that sign, held aloft and proclaimed by such magnetic orators as William J. Bryan, they will sweep the country like a cyclone. . . . Cold imagination cannot picture the possibilities for national dishonor that lie in the triumph of the Democracy through such a campaign of passion and convulsion."

Politics clearly demanded support for the cause of liberty. " 'Our Charley,' " William Allen White was to write of Charles Curtis, Kansas representative who was destined to be Vice President under Herbert Hoover, "knew nothing about the deep currents of imperialism that were sweeping the world in the nineteenth century. He was out after votes to hold his job, and 'free Cuba' was a vote-getter."

In spite of all such agitation, however, the conservative business interests in the country steadfastly resisted any idea of intervention. They remained fearful of its possible effects on the national economy, and they still saw no advantage in the possibilities of overseas expansion that war with Spain might open up. Commercial and banking journals almost without exception declared that war would endanger the newly established currency stabilization, interrupt commerce, and injure all business. Support for this position by the moneyed class created what often seemed to be a sharp division of opinion along social lines. One contemporary letter writer stated that he had not met a single man in "the aristocratic upper crust" who felt that there was any justified cause for hostilities with Spain, but when one went "below that crust . . . . the wish for war is almost universal."

As on previous occasions, the jingoist clique was incensed at this attitude on the part of "the utterly selfish money interests" which failed to recognize that here was a great opportunity to make the power of the United States known and felt. Such a position was castigated as cowardly: those responsible for making policy should have more faith "in the popular instinct." There is the well-known story of an angry Roosevelt shaking his fist in Mark Hanna's face and saying, "We will have this war for the freedom of Cuba in spite of the timidity of the commercial interests."

Throughout 1897 McKinley was nevertheless conscientiously trying, in the face of all such excitement, to make good his promise that there would be no jingo nonsense about his administration. He patiently sought to induce Spain to come to terms with the rebels and bring about the pacification of war-ridden Cuba. With the succession to power of a more liberal Spanish ministry in October, there seemed very real hope that in spite of the popular demand in this country for immediate intervention, a peaceful solution of the conflict could be found. The Spanish Government recalled General Weyler, substantially modified the reconcentration policy, and prepared to grant the Cubans a considerable measure of autonomy. "No War with Spain—All Indications Point to Peace," headlined the Washington *Post* on November 6. And in his message to Congress a month later, the President reviewed the situation hopefully, expressing his own opposition to recognition of Cuban belligerency, or any other overt act that might precipitate hostilities. While he warned Spain, as had Cleveland before him, that should the fighting continue, the United States could not indefinitely stand aside and "action will be determined in the light of indisputable right and duty," the whole tone of the message was moderate and pacific.

Under these circumstances public concern again appeared to be subsiding. The press showed a greater interest in other foreign matters—the threatened partition of China by the European powers, the drama of France's notorious Dreyfus case—and largely ignored Cuba. Yet this was only the lull before the storm. Soon imperialists and jingoes were stepping up their pressure for intervention, as the promised Cuban reforms failed to materialize and the yellow press discovered

new stories of Spanish atrocities. Then, in the opening months
of 1898, a series of untoward events provided the final impetus
that was to hurry the nation along the final stage of the road
to war. In vain did the more conservative and peace-minded
elements within the country, including not only the President
but most of his cabinet, seek to allay this new upsurge of
martial excitement.

The first incident was the publication of a personal letter of
the Spanish minister in Washington, Dupuy de Lôme, in which
this indiscreet diplomat took it upon himself to describe
President McKinley as "weak and a bidder for the admiration
of the crowd, besides being a would-be politician who tries
to leave a door open behind himself while keeping on good
terms with the jingoes of his party." The second was the sinking of the battleship *Maine,* which had been sent to Havana
to safeguard American lives and property, with the tragic loss
of more than 250 officers and men. And the third was a dramatic report by Senator Proctor of Vermont on the consequences of Spanish policy. Even conservatives, the *Wall Street
Journal* said, found themselves converted to the need for
intervention when they read Proctor's appalling description
of the conditions in which several hundred thousand Cuban
people were living in the concentration camps: "Torn from
their homes, with foul earth, foul air, foul water and foul
food or none, what wonder that one half have died and that
one quarter of the living are so diseased that they can not be
saved?"

A public already strongly prejudiced saw all its worst fears
of Spanish treachery and Spanish inhumanity confirmed by
these developments. A number of newspapers, recognizing
the gravity of the situation, tried to encourage a rational stand
even in the face of admitted provocation. The Washington
Post stated that the De Lôme letter should not be allowed
to affect American policy, and after the Spanish government
had accepted the offending envoy's hasty resignation, declared

that "the incident is closed." Moreover, the *Post* called for
reserved judgment on the sinking of the *Maine* until a commission of inquiry could report on the cause of the explosion.
Among other papers the Philadelphia *Press* also spoke of the
American people's "continued duty to sobriety and reserve of
judgment," while the Kansas City *Star* declared that "a great
nation can afford to take time to be perfectly just." In contrast
to such moderate statements, however, the jingo press let out
all the stops in their shrill call for immediate measures to
uphold national honor, revenge the sinking of the *Maine,* and
rescue the Cuban people from their unhappy lot.

"Now let us have action, immediate and decisive," shouted
the New York *Journal.* "The flag of Cuba Libre ought to
float over Morro Castle within a week." Quoting a statement
by Hanna that there would be no war, it extravagantly assailed those conservatives who considered the suffering of the
Cubans and the loss of American lives in the sinking of the
Maine of less importance than "a fall of two points in the price
of stocks." If the President failed to take prompt and decisive
action to uphold national honor, the Denver *News* insisted in
an equally extreme editorial, he deserved the most profound
contempt of all the American people. The New Orleans *Times-
Democrat* declared that McKinley might not have the backbone to act, but "war in this country is declared by Congress."

In the editorials of several newspapers there was a further
significant note which recalled the popular reaction to Cleveland's stand on the Venezuela dispute. The possibility of war
was welcomed as a means of allaying the popular discontent
that had flared up in the Populist revolt and the embittered
class warfare of the presidential campaign of 1896. There had
been earlier warnings that existing party divisions would encourage a renewed war spirit. "This state of flux, of instability,
is the despair of the politician," Theodore S. Woolsey wrote in
1897. "What a godsend to him, therefore, would be such a
foreign embroilment as would replace or at least overshadow
in the party platform and in the popular mind these difficult

internal problems." And so it was that the Richmond *Times* now stated that war "would undoubtedly have a wholesome effect in knitting the bonds of the Union closer together, and in allaying sectional and class strife," while the Chicago *Times Herald* declared that " 'war for Cuba' looms before us as the only rallying standard of the legions of our own national discontent."

Consciously or unconsciously, the desire to slough off internal problems and unite the country certainly affected the situation in March 1898. Without waiting for any report on the sinking of the *Maine,* Congress immediately appropriated $50,000,000 as an emergency fund for national defense, the army and navy departments hastened war preparations, and orders went out for new ships, submarines, gun mountings, and other military equipment. As ever more sensational headlines reported these developments, the war fever spread from coast to coast. When the official board of inquiry finally reported at the end of March that the *Maine* had been blown up by a submarine mine, even though it made no attempt to fix responsibility for the explosion, all doubts of its being Spain's treacherous doing were swept away in the mounting wave of hysteria. The cry of the day was:

> Remember the *Maine!*
> To hell with Spain!

Roosevelt excitedly wrote Brooks Adams that "the blood of the Cubans . . . who have perished by the hundred thousands in hideous misery . . . and the blood of the murdered men of the *Maine* . . . calls for the full measure of atonement which can only come by driving the Spaniard from the New World." Lodge declared that "this gigantic murder, the last spasm of a corrupt and dying society . . . cries aloud for justice."

In the face of the mounting clamor, with political rallies throughout the country calling for action, and growing signs that a restive Congress might take matters into its own hands, President McKinley still sought to avert the mounting crisis.

There is no question that he wanted above everything else to avoid war, but he was under terrific pressure. Although the spokesmen of the business elements within his party continued to uphold his search for a peaceful solution, other political advisors warned him emphatically that unless he conformed to the war spirit, both his administration and the party would be repudiated at the polls. Always a man who, both by temperament and philosophy, believed in keeping his ear close to the ground, McKinley was cruelly torn by his desire for peace and his desire to satisfy his constituents.

Throughout this period the negotiations that were being conducted with the Spanish government actually showed further encouraging progress. Assistant Secretary of State Day instructed the American minister in Madrid, Stewart L. Woodford, to make it clear that "we do not want the island" and that the President's only interest was the restoration of peace. He asked him to explore the possibilities of securing a temporary armistice as a basis for negotiations, in which the United States would be glad to offer its friendly offices. In response to such overtures, the Spanish government let it be known at the end of March that it had withdrawn its reconcentration order and was prepared to consider plans for pacification of the island. Although this reply still did not specifically promise an armistice, Minister Woodford cabled on April 3—just a week after the report of the official inquiry on the *Maine*—that he was convinced that the Spanish government, although forced by political circumstances to move slowly, was sincerely anxious for peace. "If you can still give me time and reasonable liberty of action," he stated, "I will get you the peace you desire so much and for which you have labored so hard."

The next few days appeared to bear out his expectations. Against a background of complicated diplomatic maneuvers— in which the Pope intervened in Spain and the European powers made an appeal to the United States for peace—the government in Madrid seemed about to give way completely. On April 10 the Queen ordered the military commander in

Cuba "to grant immediately a suspension of hostilities for such length of time as he may think prudent to prepare and facilitate the peace earnestly desired by all."

After all the American demands had apparently been met, Woodford happily cabled President McKinley that he was even more satisfied that the Spanish government "is going, and is loyally ready to go, as fast and as far as it can." He was confident that a settlement could be reached that would provide either for Cuban autonomy on terms acceptable to the rebels, for Spanish recognition of the island's independence, or for the cession of Cuba to the United States. "With your power of action sufficiently free," he concluded this significant message, "you will win the fight on your own lines. . . ."

The President, however, had become persuaded that his power of action was no longer free. Congress was running ahead of even an inflamed public opinion. The jingoes in both House and Senate were calling for intervention with a reckless irresponsibility that seemed ready to ignore any concessions that Spain might make, even her complete acceptance of the terms that the United States had stipulated for peace. Newspaper after newspaper noted that there was war talk everywhere. The *World* conducted a poll of every congressional district from which it enthusiastically concluded that the national sentiment was "No more delay." In later years McKinley was to say that if he had been let alone, he was certain that he could have secured Spanish withdrawal from Cuba without a war. In April 1898 he was not let alone.

Those who saw him in these final days of the crisis were agreed that he was almost breaking under the strain. "He has been robbed of sleep, overworked," Secretary of the Navy Long wrote in his diary on April 4, "and I fancy that I can see that his mind does not work as clearly and as self-reliantly as it otherwise would." Twelve days later the presidential secretary, George B. Cortelyou, made a comparable entry in his diary: "The President does not look well at all. . . . His haggard face and anxious inquiry for any news . . . tell of the sense of tremendous responsibility."

It was under these circumstances that McKinley surrendered to the war party. Almost his entire cabinet still favored peace; Mark Hanna and other leading Republican senators of his party were "ferociously against war"; and Speaker Reed of the House also opposed any form of intervention. But the President did not feel that he could stand out any longer. A stronger man might have been able to hold Congress and the country in check, but McKinley was not made of such stern stuff. The popular current was too strong for him. He decided to lead the war movement rather than resist it at the risk of shattering his party. His deep and sincere sympathy for the Cubans, and a natural skepticism as to whether Spain would actually carry out her new pledges, undoubtedly helped him to rationalize his surrender to the popular hysteria of the day. "I did all that in honor could be done to avert the war," McKinley would say in 1901, "but without avail."

On April 11, 1898—two days after the virtual capitulation of Spain to his demands—the President sent a message to Congress asking for authority to use the Army and Navy to bring an end to hostilities in Cuba. The message had been under preparation for some days (its actual transmission held up to allow the Americans in Cuba to leave the island), and word of the armistice Spain was prepared to grant the rebels was received in Washington after McKinley's message had been approved. So it was that following the passage in which he asked authority to intervene and stated that "the issue is now with Congress," McKinley added, almost parenthetically, that since preparation of the message he had learned of new Spanish concessions, and very briefly outlined what they were.

Some newspapers which had confidently expected a forthright request for an immediate declaration of war were disappointed in what they termed the President's equivocation. Yet this was an unwarranted interpretation of the stand he had taken. Authority to intervene was a declaration of hostilities.

McKinley knew this very well. And perhaps it was now too late for any other outcome to the crisis. All warnings that idealism should be tempered by a sense of reality and that the consequences of a resort to arms should be further considered fell on deaf ears. The yellow press and other jingoistic spokesmen had played so successfully upon the emotions of the American people that open conflict had become as nearly inevitable by early April as it well could be.

In response to McKinley's request, congressional leaders promptly introduced a joint resolution that declared the people of Cuba to be free and independent, called for the complete withdrawal of Spain from the island, directed the President to use the Armed Forces of the nation to secure these ends, and disclaimed any intention on the part of the United States to annex Cuba.

The latter provision, the so-called Teller Amendment, reflected the force of those humanitarian and idealistic sentiments that animated the great body of the American people. Whatever the part played by advocates of Cuban annexation and by irresponsible jingoes in creating the popular demand for intervention, the general public thought in terms of aiding the Cuban people, sustaining the cause of liberty, and upholding national honor. While the imperialist spirit that had been building up through the 1890s provided the background for the Spanish-American War and was to flare up once again with the dramatic victories that crowned American arms, it did not entirely account for intervention in Cuba. The immediate cause for war was an idealistic impulse rather than any thought of territorial aggrandizement or economic benefit. A possible peaceful solution of the situation was sacrificed—needlessly sacrificed—for want of resolute presidential leadership, but the motives of the American people in taking up arms were not ignoble.

"We intervene not for conquest, not for aggrandizement, not because of the Monroe Doctrine," Spooner of Wisconsin told an excited Senate; "we intervene for humanity's sake . . . . to aid a people who have suffered every form of tyranny and who have made a desperate struggle to be free." His words were echoed by Senator Cullom of Illinois, slow to take such a stand and now commanding rapt attention as he rose to his feet in the final day of debate. "If the people of this country shall do nothing more in this century than drive the Spaniards from this hemisphere," Cullom declared, "we as a people shall earn the praises of every lover of freedom and humanity the world over." And Senator Chilton of Texas also emphasized—however chauvinistic his speech's undertones—what he believed to be the special obligations of the United States. "I believe that in the economy of Providence," he said, "responsibility always goes with power . . ."

Although war was in all probability not necessary to secure freedom for Cuba, it was in the name of liberty that Congress adopted and the President signed the joint resolution calling for intervention by armed force. Not unnaturally Spain at once broke off diplomatic relations. McKinley thereupon ordered a blockade of the Cuban coast, together with offensive operations against the Philippines, and on April 25 the Congress recognized a state of war which it said had been in existence for four days.

CHAPTER IX

"A SPLENDID LITTLE WAR"

TEN WEEKS AFTER PRESIDENT MCKINLEY SIGNED THE CONGRESsional resolution recognizing war with Spain the fighting was over. An eager and delighted public had read with mounting enthusiasm of Dewey's spectacular victory at Manila Bay, of the heroic charges of the American troops at San Juan, and of the destruction of Admiral Cervera's fleet off Santiago. While a few more weeks were to pass before the protocol embodying the terms of Spanish surrender was officially signed, victory was already secure. It had been, in Hay's memorable phrase, "a splendid little war."

The American people were carried off their feet by the martial fervor that swept the land in 1898. Everywhere volunteers rushed lightheartedly to the colors, and when these raw recruits then marched off to war, it was in a gay mood of flags flying, bands playing, crowds cheering. The battle song of the Spanish-American War was "The Stars and Stripes Forever." The discomforts of camp life, the losses sustained in the actual military campaign, and above all the disease that was so rampant both in the army installations at home and in the fever-ridden camps in Cuba, somewhat dampened in time the enthusiasm of those who actually took up arms; but the country as a whole suffered not at all from military adventure. The national economy was given a new fillip and the prosperity ushered in with the McKinley administration was greatly strengthened.

In comparison with the gruelling struggle of civil war in 1861–65, with the bloody fighting in Europe of 1917 and 1918, and with the global warfare of the bitter years from 1941 to 1945, the Spanish-American War was little more than a summer skirmish, so brief and glorious that it can hardly be dignified by the name of war in modern terms. Still, the contest with Spain had an epochal significance that gives it an enduring place in history. There could be no return to the past, once the United States had burst the bonds of continental domain and reached out overseas to power and influence in the twentieth-century world.

On Sunday night—May 1, 1898—Commodore George Dewey wrote in his diary:

"Reached Manila at daylight and immediately engaged the Spanish ships and batteries at Cavite. Destroyed eight of the former, including the *Reina Cristina* and *Castilla.* Anchored at noon off Manila."

In this laconic style, the commander of the Asiatic Squadron noted a victory that was hysterically hailed throughout the country as soon as the first fragmentary reports of the far-off battle—not officially confirmed for five days—were received by the American press. "The guns of Dewey at Manila have changed the destiny of the United States," the Washington *Post* declared with an exuberant enthusiasm that was echoed in newspapers throughout the land. "We are face to face with a strange destiny and must accept its responsibilities. An imperial policy."

This surprising consequence of a war undertaken to liberate Cuba grew out of a curious chain of events in which Theodore Roosevelt played a highly important part. As Assistant Secretary of the Navy, he had been largely instrumental in securing the appointment of Commodore Dewey to command the Asiatic Squadron, and the two men were in complete accord as to what the squadron's role would be in the event of hostilities with Spain. Even though such a policy may not yet have been that of the McKinley administration, Dewey recorded in his *Memoirs* that on the assumption of his new post, he made every preparation to be in a position to "strike promptly and successfully at the Spanish force in the Philippines."

As early as September 21, 1897, moreover, Roosevelt told the President just what he thought should be done in the event "things look menacing about Spain." He proposed an expeditionary force for Cuba and naval raids off the coast of Spain, certain that they would soon bring the enemy to terms, and meanwhile "our Asiatic squadron should blockade, and if possible take, Manila."

It was also Roosevelt rather than either President McKinley or Secretary of Navy Long, who gave Dewey the specific orders for such action. On February 25, 1898, while his chief was away from the office, Roosevelt "seized the opportunity" to cable instructions to Dewey that if war came, he should be ready for "offensive operations in the Philippines." By chance Senator Lodge visited the Navy Department that same day. There is no question that he approved of the rather extraordinary step his friend had taken, but in spite of being on hand, he had no actual part in it. Roosevelt was acting solely on his own initiative.

Secretary Long, whom Roosevelt regarded as "a perfect dear" although he was always somewhat scornful of what he considered Long's want of spirit, was astonished on returning to his office the next day to discover what had happened during his absence. Commenting in his diary on Roosevelt's zeal, Long wrote that "the very devil seemed to possess him yesterday afternoon," and added that his assistant came "very near causing more of an explosion than happened to the *Maine*." Still, the controversial order was never canceled; the Asiatic Squadron was to be ready for action.

Commodore Dewey was at Hongkong when the expected war finally did break out, and on April 25 he received his final instructions at once to attack the Spanish fleet at Manila—"you must capture vessels or destroy." There was only the briefest delay before he set out on his memorable mission. Rebellion was incipient in the Philippines—the situation was comparable to that in Cuba—and Dewey waited to confer, rather inconclusively, with representatives of the insurgents. He then made ready for sea and with his squadron of six vessels, led by the flagship *Olympia*, headed for the Philippines, where it was known that a Spanish fleet was stationed, under the command of Admiral Montojo.

On the night of April 30 the American squadron cautiously approached Manila Bay and under cover of darkness slipped through the straits of Boca Grande. Two Spanish cruisers, five gunboats, and some smaller craft were discovered lying in a crescent off Cavite Point, and as day gradually dawned—a light haze lay over the water and there was scarcely a breath of air—the slow procession of American craft drew gradually closer to the Spanish vessels. It was five A.M. and the distance something more than four thousand yards when Dewey quietly gave his famous order: "You may fire when you are ready, Gridley."

The guns belched forth and both from the Spanish ships and the land forts beneath which they hovered came an immediate answering fire. The American ships made a run to westward past the Spanish fleet, turned about, and swept eastward through the gauntlet of enemy fire. This maneuver was repeated, and then once again the American ships started on the westward leg at a distance which had now been reduced to two thousand yards. So heavy was the pall of smoke that hung over the entire scene that Commodore Dewey had no way of knowing whether the fire of his ships had been at all effective, and at the end of the westward run he received a disconcerting report that his ammunition was running low. In these circumstances he ordered the entire squadron to withdraw to enable him to review the situation and provide for a redistribution of ammunition.

Only then, as the cloud of smoke gradually lifted, did Dewey and his officers realize the fearful havoc their concentrated fire had wrought. The scene which met their gaze was an astounding one. The Spanish fleet had been rendered helpless. A number of the ships had caught fire and were being rapidly abandoned by their crews; the others were limping back as best they could toward shore, under the protecting batteries of the land forts. With this evidence before him, and with correction of what soon proved to have been a false report concerning the shortage of ammunition, Commodore Dewey signaled his squadron that the men could be given breakfast, and summoned the captains to a conference aboard the *Olympia*. He now learned that the Spanish fire had not seriously harmed any of the American vessels, and that not a single American sailor had been killed or even badly injured. The crews were hoarse from cheering; as one report stated, "and while we suffer for cough drops and throat doctors, we have no use for liniments or surgeons." Dewey dismissed his officers and "at 11:16 A.M. we stood in to complete our work."

Only the ineffectual shore batteries and one vessel, "the gallant little *Ulloa*," offered any further resistance, and this single survivor of the Spanish fleet soon went down with her colors flying. Boats were dispatched to fire such other ships, now beached on the shore and abandoned by their crews, as had not already been sunk. With a white flag flying from the land forts, there was nothing further to do. "The order to capture or destroy the Spanish squadron," as Dewey later wrote, "had been executed to the letter."

The United States had overthrown Spanish power in the Pacific even before it had begun to fight in the Caribbean. Ten ships had been destroyed, three shore batteries silenced, and the Spanish toll amounted to 381 seamen dead or wounded. Commodore Dewey completely controlled Manila Bay, and only the want of an occupying force prevented him, if he had so desired, from capturing the city. The dispatches that finally got through to Washington giving an official report of this amazing victory stated that reinforcements were necessary so far as future land operations were concerned, but that the American fleet was safe. Its commander awaited further orders.

In the meantime the Atlantic fleet under Admiral Sampson had set about establishing a blockade of Cuba. Plans were also being made and slowly put into effect for a military campaign that would break Spanish power and free the Cuban people.

There was one difficulty, however. An enemy fleet of four armored cruisers and three destroyers, under the command of Admiral Cervera, had sailed from the Cape Verde Islands on April 29, destination unknown. Might it not seek to harass the eastern coast, possibly bombard Boston, New York, or other cities? A so-called flying squadron was held at Hampton Roads to meet any such contingency, but panic flared along the seaboard with the thought that war might be actually brought to the United States itself.

In spite of the view of one correspondent of Senator Lodge, that should a Spanish army land in New York it would be immediately absorbed "and engaged in selling oranges before they got as far as Fourteenth Street," there were tremulous citizens in seaboard areas who envisaged actual invasion. Official Washington was deluged with letters asking for special protection for home communities from Portland to Savannah. Wealthy residents along the coast removed their valuables to points of greater safety, and the New England tourist season was a failure, as vacationers hesitated to expose their families to the perils of Spanish raids.

The danger of any attack by Admiral Cervera disappeared with the discovery that his fleet had reached Cuba and was immobilized by the American blockade, but another momentary panic was created by the rumor that a second Spanish squadron under Admiral Camara—a battleship, an armored cruiser, and six converted cruisers—might strike out across the Atlantic. "Intense excitement was caused at Fort Monmouth last night," read a report in the *New York Times* on June 11, ". . . . by a dispatch that Spanish warships were lurking in the vicinity . . . Quarters were sounded and . . . . the gunners took positions at their posts. . . . Some of the officers were with their families at the hotels, and buglers were dispatched for them. The men scurried out of the hotels half-dressed, and hastened to the fort." This and other alarms and excursions (the *New York Times* reported rumors a week later that "the Spanish warships are headed for Boston") were completely false. Admiral Camara's fleet was actually ordered to the Pacific and became waylaid at the Suez Canal. Until this news was confirmed, however, the uneasy residents of the eastern coast continued to fear the worst.

During these nervous days the expeditionary force for the

proposed invasion of Cuba was gathering at Tampa, Florida, in circumstances of such chaotic confusion that for long it appeared impossible it could ever sail. The Army could hardly have been less prepared. The transportation system almost completely broke down under the strain, there were no adequate food supplies for the troops, and much essential military equipment was lacking. The volunteers had no arms, no tents, no blankets. It was impossible to obtain khaki for uniforms, and in the sweltering heat—which was to become even more sweltering when the expedition finally did reach Cuba—the troops had to wear heavy woolen uniforms. Medical supplies were almost nonexistent. In many instances freight trains were waylaid in the yards without any way of getting the equipment with which they were loaded to the army camps.

The charges of inefficiency and corruption that throughout the war were directed against the War Department grew out of this unhappy situation. In a series of dispatches published in the New York *Herald* and *Harper's Weekly,* the war correspondent Poultney Bigelow (later to become more renowned as a friend of the German Kaiser) strongly assailed what he termed the political jobbery and gross incompetence revealed in conditions at Tampa. "The railway, express, telegraph, steamship, and other corporations," he wrote, "are getting fat out of this war; so are all contractors who deal with politics. . . . If this war should be dragged out for a year or so they would be more than delighted. Meanwhile brave boys in blue will be dying in the heat of Tampa, to say nothing of the Cuban swamps."

His critical attitude was vehemently attacked by a more popular correspondent who was fast becoming a symbol of the patriotism and glory of war. Richard Harding Davis, handsome, dashing, debonair, had an immense appeal for the readers of the New York *Journal* and his accounts of martial adventure were closely attuned to the spirit of the times. He denied that there was anything like political jobbery or even inefficiency at Tampa, quoted General Nelson A. Miles, the commander in chief, as attesting to the "magnificent condition and physical perfectness of our men," and assured his readers that every preparation had been made for the forthcoming Cuban campaign. In his later dispatches it was not always clear whether it was the troops or just Richard Harding Davis who was responsible for the victories won by American arms.

The forces collected at Tampa made up the Fifth Army Corps, under the command of General William R. Shafter, and constituted some 18,000 men including both regulars and volunteers. Among the latter troops the best known were the Rough Riders. They were headed by Colonel Leonard Wood, but the second in command, who had been responsible for their recruitment, was the ebullient Theodore Roosevelt. Along with all other officers and men he chafed at the long delays in getting under way, and it was not indeed until spring was nearly over that arrangements were completed to launch the "great historical expedition" to liberate Cuba.

The confusion that attended every move of the Army continued to characterize the last stages of embarkation. The long-suffering General Shafter, having received a peremptory message from Washington on June 7 that "the President directs you to sail at once with what force you can embark," finally ordered the troops to get aboard the transports with their equipment, as best they might. The rival outfits of regulars and volunteers, bursting with patriotic zeal, struggled for passage room, but the next day a further telegram from Washington canceled the sailing order, and the troops waited still another week aboard the broiling transports. On June 15, the little fleet carrying the expeditionary force at last found itself steaming southward "through a sapphire sea, wind-ripped, under an almost cloudless sky." The landings were made without important incident at Daiquiri and Siboney. The transports' small boats took the men ashore in a mad scramble through the pounding surf; the cavalry horses were shoved overboard and left to swim. Within a matter of hours the Army was landed and the great adventure—the war to free Cuba—had begun.

"The instant I received the order I sprang on my horse and then my 'crowded hour' began." So wrote Roosevelt in *The Rough Riders*, and the order which led him to spring to his horse was the opening of the attack upon the ridges surrounding Santiago, collectively known as San Juan Hill. His account of the stirring events that made up his "crowded hour" was not always strictly accurate, but it was certainly one of the most graphic of eye-witness accounts. There was never very much question, moreover, of the hero of his saga. Mr. Dooley was sagely to remark, to the wry amusement of the hero himself, that Roosevelt might well have titled his book "Alone in Cubia."

The whole operation, as observers in addition to Roosevelt have described it, was something strange and wonderful. General Shafter, a huge, unwieldy man weighing some 300 pounds, and almost prostrated by the heat, was to have about as much trouble with his own command as with the Spaniards. He placed General H. W. Lawton, an able and experienced regular army officer, in charge of the advance, but unfortunately Lawton was outranked by General Joseph Wheeler, commander of the dismounted cavalry division which included the Rough Riders. "Fighting Joe" had fought with the Confederate Army, continued to confuse the enemy with the "damn Yankees," and paid little attention to orders. There was also constant rivalry to be first in action on the part of other officers who were afraid of losing their chance for glory, and headquarters was so often out of touch with what was actually happening that it was completely unable to sychronize the troop movements in the field.

Moreover, as the men moved forward along the muddy road skirting the shore and then struggled through the maze of tropical underbrush lining the Santiago hills, they were accompanied by a crowd of foreign attachés and naval officers from the fleet, and by swarms of newspaper reporters and photographers. Over them hovered an observation balloon which usefully betrayed their position to the Spanish. But while such circumstances made the Americans an easy target for both the sharpshooters hidden in the jungle and the enemy artillery, the troops were not daunted. The spirit of the men, Richard Harding Davis wrote enthusiastically, was magnificent as they advanced in the face of withering enemy fire, each man "wearing his red badge of courage."

Even before the main advance, the Rough Riders, placed under Roosevelt's command when Wood took over a brigade, had taken part in an unplanned action against the Spanish at Las Guasimas—"a brisk fight of 2½ hours before we drove them out of their position"—and had endured their first disconcerting experience of having to fight their way through dense tropical jungle. The dismounted cavalry found the going far more tough than they had expected. However, they had come through their baptism of fire successfully—"there was no flinching"— and in spite of considerable losses, they were still enthusiastic and excited when the orders came for their further advance.

After Roosevelt had ridden down the line "rasping brief directions" to his men, the Rough Riders moved forward under concealed enemy fire in conjunction with the main advance, two divisions having been assigned to the frontal assault on the San Juan hills, and a third directed to attack the fortified Spanish position at nearby El Caney. However, a company of regulars which the Rough Riders were supposed to be supporting had taken cover and blocked their path. When Roosevelt sought to rally these troops, their commanding officer would not accept his orders. "Then let my men through, sir," Roosevelt demanded and rode on. His men followed him—"nobody else could command them as I did," he later wrote—and, waving his sombrero from which streamed a blue polka dot handkerchief, Roosevelt led the charge up a section of the ridge known as Kettle Hill, in the face of a hail of flying shrapnel. "By this time we were all in the spirit of the thing," the indomitable Rough Rider later recalled, "and greatly excited by the charge, the men cheering and running forward between shots."

Forty yards from the summit Roosevelt was stopped by a wire fence. He promptly turned his horse loose, broke through the barrier, and ran ahead. Soon Kettle Hill—"there was the usual confusion, and afterwards confusion as to who exactly had been on the hill first"—was in American hands. The Spanish had taken a heavy toll of lives, but the Rough Riders had successfully performed the task given them and held a position protected from the main fire of the enemy.

On their left flank the infantry was having a somewhat more difficult time in carrying out their assignment to take the adjacent ridges, and the Rough Riders, again to quote Roosevelt's account, "had a splendid view of the charge on the San Juan blockhouse." In the face of stout resistance the American attack appeared to waver and the success of this major assault hung uncertainly in the balance. But with all the drama of a movie scenario, help was near at hand:

"Suddenly, above the cracking of the carbines, rose a peculiar drumming sound, and some of the men cried, 'The Spanish machine guns!' Listening, I made out that it came from the flat ground to the left, and jumped to my feet, smiting my hands on my thigh, and shouting aloud, with exultation, 'It's the Gatlings, men, our Gatlings!' "

With the San Juan blockhouse captured, the general assault was renewed and Roosevelt called upon his troops to take up the charge against a further line of Spanish entrenchments. He leaped over another wire fence and started forward on the double, only to find that but three or four men were following him. The main body of Rough Riders—"so excited, what with shooting and being shot, and shouting and cheering"—had not heard him. They soon rallied and came on with a rush, scattered the Spanish, and won the heights.

The other American forces were also successful in attaining their objectives, for in spite of Roosevelt's picture of the battle, the Rough Riders did not win it singlehanded, and by nightfall orders were given to dig in. The Rough Riders had had nothing to eat and no supplies other than what they had captured from the Spaniards, "but their dinners had fortunately been cooked, and we ate them with relish." The enemy launched a number of counterattacks on the newly won American positions, but both the regulars and the volunteers held firm. Santiago was now closely invested. Even though the Spanish forces in the city totaled some nine thousand men, the capture of the San Juan hills proved to be the decisive battle of the Cuban campaign.

The hardships endured by the entrenched troops—alternating tropical heat and biting cold, heavy downpours of rain—were to be a more severe trial than the dangers of actual fighting. And for a time it was feared that a further counterattack might be made in overwhelming force. "We are within measurable distance of a terrible military disaster," Roosevelt was writing Lodge on July 3; "—we *must* have help—thousands of men, batteries, and *food* and ammunition." The cautious General Shafter, whom Roosevelt considered "criminally incompetent," thought of retiring to safer lines.

The final decision in the land campaign was to await the outcome of the naval operations. In the meantime, and for all his concern over what might happen next, Roosevelt was exulting over the experiences of his "crowded hour," as he remembered, with customary romantic exaggeration, his leadership of the Rough Riders' intrepid charge: plunging ahead through the barbed wire entanglements and victoriously breasting the summit of Kettle Hill. "This has been, aside from Edith," he cheerfully wrote Lodge toward the end of July, "*the* time of my life." And years afterward he recalled: "We had a bully fight at Santiago . . . . the charge itself was great fun."

The morning of July 3 (this was the day Roosevelt wrote of possible impending military disaster) dawned clear and beautiful in Cuba. In a half circle off the harbor, the restless vessels of the Atlantic fleet, including five battleships, still mounted guard over Cervera's fleet at Santiago. There was no expectation that the day would be any different from the many others which had found them maintaining their ceaseless watch to prevent the escape of the six Spanish ships—the flagship *Maria Teresa*, three other armored cruisers, and two torpedo-boat destroyers. It was Sunday. Officers and crews were ordered to wear their whites and prepare for a rigorous formal inspection. The battleship *New York*, having hoisted the signal "Disregard motions of commander in chief," drew off to eastward. It was taking Admiral Sampson to a meeting at Siboney with General Shafter. Admiral Schley was left in command.

Aboard the *Iowa*, Captain "Fighting Bob" Evans was in his cabin talking to his son, a naval cadet, when at 9:31 he heard the general alarm sounded aboard his ship. As he emerged from the companionway, one of the *Iowa's* guns was fired and the signal "enemy's ships coming out" was just being raised; when he reached the bridge, the *Maria Teresa* was swinging into sight in full panoply. The battle hatches of the *Iowa* rattled into place. But as they took their positions "her sturdy crew stopped for a moment to cheer the Spanish ship . . ."

One by one the other enemy vessels followed the flagship. They came out, as Captain Philip of the *Texas* recalled, "as gaily as brides to the altar. Handsome vessels they certainly were, and with flags enough flying for a celebration parade." "A grander sight could hardly be conceived," wrote Captain Cook of the *Brooklyn*. "Here was the culmination of our hopes and the end of our vigil."

The cheers that greeted this happy spectacle on the part of the sturdy crew of the *Iowa* were echoed throughout the American ships. Aboard the *Oregon*, which had made a memorable voyage around Cape Horn from her Pacific station to join the Atlantic fleet, the excitement was especially tense. "Our men jumped about the decks," read an account by Lieutenant Eberle, "waving their caps and cheering, and enthusiastically yelling, 'There they come! There they come!' The officers were more serious, for we expected a day of hot work."

The *Iowa* was the first to engage the enemy and as Captain Evans brought his heavy guns to bear on the *Maria Teresa* she answered in kind. "A torrent of projectiles was sailing over us,"

Evans recorded, "harmlessly exploding in the water beyond."
He tried to maneuver his ship so as to ram the Spanish vessel
but, unable to do so, swung the *Iowa* off to starboard and gave
the *Maria Teresa* his entire broadside at a range of twenty-one
hundred yards. She was soon afire, blazing fiercely. Then having struck her colors, she turned about and limped back toward
the shore with a towering mass of smoke ascending from her
stern.

The engagement had in the meantime become general and
most confused. As the Spanish vessels veered off to the west in
a frantic effort to escape, the American ships moved in to the
attack. It was exceedingly difficult to maneuver at such close
quarters and the task was not made any easier by the dense
clouds of smoke that soon enveloped the entire scene. A collision between the *Texas* and the *Brooklyn* was narrowly
averted; the *Iowa* missed by only the most narrow margin a
direct hit on the auxiliary *Gloucester* (the onetime swanky
yacht, the *Corsair*, of John Pierpont Morgan). But while the
Spanish shells continued to screech harmlessly through the em-
battled air, the American broadsides were having a devastating
effect.

The *Almirante Oquendo* was set ablaze shortly after disaster
had overwhelmed the *Maria Teresa*, the two Spanish destroyers
were sunk before they even had a chance to loose their tor-
pedoes, and within twenty minutes the *Vizcaya* had also been
put out of action. Of the proud vessels that had emerged from
Santiago Harbor with flags so gaily flying, only the *Cristóbal
Colón* was still unharmed, streaking off to sea at thirteen knots
in a desperate dash for freedom.

The *Oregon*, the *Brooklyn*, and the *Texas* took up the pursuit
and were soon joined by the *New York*, which had returned to
the scene at the first sound of firing. As the latter ship swept
by the *Iowa*, which was already lowering her boats to help
rescue the Spanish sailors of the blazing *Vizcaya*, Admiral
Sampson hailed Captain Evans to ask about casualties. The latter gave the proud reply, "not a man hurt aboard the ship."

The *Oregon* led a two-hour chase of the fleeing *Cristóbal Colón* and as the other American battleships headed off the Spaniard's escape, gradually drew within firing range. She then opened up with her thirteen-inch guns, and even before a single hit the *Cristóbal Colón's* captain accepted the hopelessness of his position and struck his colors. The sailors aboard the *Oregon*, stripped to the waist, streaming with perspiration, blackened with powder, broke into ringing cheers. "The thunder of heavy guns," Lieutenant Eberle wrote, "was replaced by the strains of 'The Star Spangled Banner' . . ."

There was one further excitement in the midst of this battle. An unknown warship suddenly loomed over the horizon and the *Iowa* and *Indiana*, interrupted in their rescue operations, quickly cleared for action. Almost at once it was discovered that the unknown ship was not Spanish, but Austrian. After a time one of her officers came aboard the *Indiana* and Captain Taylor reported the following colloquy:

" 'There has been a battle?'
" 'Yes,' I replied.
" 'And the result?' he asked eagerly.
" 'We have defeated them.'
" 'But where is Cervera's fleet now?' he inquired."

Captain Taylor then told him the story of the battle.

" 'Mein Gott!' he [the Austrian officer] exclaimed again. 'Admiral Sampson's fleet has destroyed these great Spanish ships, and without injury to his own squadron! Sir, it is unheard of. I must go to inform my captain.' "

It had been a glorious day—or rather a glorious brief few hours. The battle of Manila Bay all over again, though this time one American, but only one, had been killed. The enemy suffered four hundred killed or wounded, nearly a fifth of their total complement.

Let Captain Evans, whose keen lookouts had first discerned

the *Maria Teresa* leading out the Spanish fleet, have the last word:

"The day closed, as it had opened, beautiful and fair. The battle of Santiago had been fought, the much-dreaded fleet of Admiral Cervera destroyed, and its gallant officers and men were either dead or prisoners, almost without exception. The man behind the gun had indeed proved himself a giant."

The Spanish fleet was in every way very much inferior to that of the United States. It never had a chance, and its officers knew from the first it had no chance. Admiral Cervera, if left to his own devices, would never have challenged such superior forces in what he knew was a futile attempt at escape. A sortie, he reported to the captain general of Cuba, would result in "a horrible and useless hetacomb." But the honor of Spain was at stake. Surrender was unthinkable. Madrid had no hesitation about sacrificing ships and men in a last despairing gesture of defiance.

The nation had been anxious about news from Cuba. Messages from General Shafter, emphasizing the dangerous position of his troops and yet at the same time stating that he had called upon the enemy to surrender, completely mystified Washington. And there had been a first report of a naval battle that had seemed to imply that the Spanish squadron might have escaped. It may well be imagined with what overwhelming enthusiasm the public welcomed, after the battle, an official message from Admiral Sampson in which he grandiloquently declared that "the fleet under my command offers the nation as a Fourth of July present the whole of Cervera's fleet."

There was still the Army to be considered, however, and for nearly two weeks, while the military and naval commanders bickered over what further action should be taken to capture the city of Santiago, the final results of the Cuban campaign seemed to hang in the balance. But there was no real cause for concern. The enemy was powerless. On July 16 the Spanish forces capitulated and Cuba was open to American occupation.

A further campaign had been planned for the conquest of Puerto Rico and an army under General Miles rather belatedly embarked for this undertaking on July 25. It met with virtually no resistance. The Spanish forces had no fight left and a cheering populace greeted the Americans with waving flags. Mr. Dooley characterized the Puerto Rican expedition as "Gineral Miles' Gran' Moonlight Excursion."

There had been little picnic atmosphere, however, about the American lines in the hills circling Santiago during these hot summer weeks. The increasingly bad weather, the continuing want of provisions, the mounting incidence of malaria and dysentery, were shattering for morale. The Rough Riders had a particularly hard time. "The lithe college athletes," Roosevelt reported, "had lost their spring; the tall gaunt hunters and cowpunchers lounged listlessly in their dog tents, which were steaming morasses during the torrential rains, and then ovens when the sun blazed down."

Roosevelt himself kept in good health—"I am as strong as a bull moose," he wrote Lodge on July 10—but of the six hundred men who had landed with him in Cuba, nearly one-half were dead, or in the hospital suffering from wounds, or down with fever and dysentery. Their commander felt helpless: "I cannot get even rice and oatmeal for the sick, who lie on the muddy ground in their soggy blankets raging with fever."

From another source it is clear that Roosevelt was not exaggerating this part of his story. The Red Cross was doing what it could to aid in Cuba, under the leadership of the redoubtable Clara Barton, its founder and guiding spirit. A relief ship, the State of Texas, lay off Siboney and on July 26, Miss Barton noted in her diary: "It is the Rough Riders we go to, and the relief may also be rough but it will be *ready*."

After the battle of the San Juan heights, Miss Barton received an urgent note from the front line that supplies were needed. This quiet little seventy-six-year-old woman, so seemingly frail, promptly commandeered three six-mule army wagons and loaded them with provisions. Then perching herself on one which carried a load of hay, she set off along the twisting jungle trail on her mission of relief. At the advanced camps she began distributing her supplies and cooking up great quantities of gruel which she ladled out to the hungry troops. On one occasion, as Miss Barton recorded it, Roosevelt came to her to ask if he could not buy some supplies for his men:

"You can't buy them, Colonel, not for a million dollars."

He was disappointed. "How can I get them?"

"Just ask for them, Colonel."

In a few minutes Roosevelt was striding back to camp with a heavy sack "filled with the most desirable necessities."

The situation became increasingly worse until finally an outbreak of the dreaded yellow fever created a real crisis. Hundreds of men were smitten and there was little that could be done for them. Although the town of Siboney was evacuated and burned down in an attempt to prevent the epidemic's further spread, the fever continued to take its toll among the troops. The officers, with Roosevelt playing a leading part, drew up a round robin note insisting upon the necessity of bringing the American troops home and gave it out to the press. "This army must be moved at once," the officers bluntly stated, "or it will perish."

Finally recalled in mid-August, the troops were segregated in a special camp at Montauk Point, Long Island. Conditions there were for a time not much better than they had been in Cuba, but as reports of the dire need for fresh food, supplies, and medical care became public, there was an immediate popular response and things rapidly improved. The fever eventually ran its course and this unhappy chapter in the story of the Spanish-American War—which had its counterpart in only a slightly lesser degree in other army camps—came to an end.

The peace protocol signed on August 12 had in the meantime

set the formal seal of victory upon the naval and military campaigns. A nation which had as a whole known only the excitement and little of the tragedy of war was once again at peace.

CHAPTER X

GOD, DESTINY, AND MR. McKINLEY

THE STARTLING VICTORY WON BY DEWEY AT MANILA BAY HAD greatly strengthened the latent imperialist spirit of the nation. The annexation of Hawaii was a first concrete sign of its gathering force, but there were soon other indications that the country was ready to venture into strange new paths. If Cuba could not be kept permanently under American control because of the self-denying ordinance adopted at the outbreak of the war, there were Puerto Rico and the Philippines. Perhaps the most telling cry in favor of retaining these unexpected prizes of war —emotionally far more significant than all the reasoned arguments of the expansionists—was that wherever the American flag had once been raised, it would be weak and cowardly to allow it to be lowered.

While the background of events and the spirit of the times conspired to lead the United States along a colonial course, the pliant instrument for actually bringing new overseas possessions within the American fold was to be President McKinley. As during the critical days in the spring of 1898, he was again under intensive pressure to endorse the "large policy" so importunately demanded by the imperialist party. By this time, however, the President hardly needed to be persuaded of the wisdom of expansion. It may be said that he succumbed to the spirit of the times, but he also helped to build and direct the imperialist impulse along very definite lines. In spite of his earlier opposition to an expansionist policy—his forthright statement that forcible annexation could never be considered: "that, by our code of morality, would be criminal aggression"—he moved ahead step by step during the coming months to the most extreme imperialist position.

So complete was his conversion that McKinley felt none of the qualms over imperialism that had marked his submission to the jingoist demand for war with Spain. Indeed, once the die had been irretrievably cast for Cuban intervention, he had accepted even that unnecessary conflict as foreordained. "The faith of a Christian nation," he soberly stated upon the conclusion of hostilities, "recognizes the hand of Almighty God in the ordeal through which we have passed. Divine favor seemed manifest everywhere. In fighting for humanity's sake we have been signally blessed." In this same spirit he convinced himself that the beneficent destiny that had brought new territories under American control decreed their retention. With his remarkable ability to rationalize, he felt it was hardly a matter of choice. The United States had to accept what was at once a great opportunity and a moral responsibility. McKinley became the willing agency of forces he sincerely believed were divinely inspired.

Some time after the battle of Manila Bay, when the Philippine problem appeared to be overwhelming, the President is reported to have said rather plaintively: "If old Dewey had just sailed away when he smashed the Spanish fleet, what a lot of trouble he would have saved us." In the light of circumstance, such a remark is understandable. Yet it was McKinley who had expressly made impossible any such easy escape from the Philippine problem. Even before the news of the American victory had been officially confirmed, he had decided to send overseas the troops that would enable the United States to capture and hold Manila. Such a move could hardly be considered necessary in the light of the objectives for which the United States had taken up arms against Spain, but on May 4 the President gave the first orders authorizing the dispatch of a Philippine expedition of some 15,000 men, and eleven days later he placed General Wesley Merritt in command of the expeditionary forces already assembling in San Francisco. So McKinley thus early set in motion the train of events that quite as much as Dewey's victory, led to Philippine annexation.

Little wonder that an exuberant Lodge was spiritedly writing to Theodore Roosevelt toward the end of May that he was convinced that "the Administration is now fully committed to the large policy that we both desire," and a few weeks later would add that "the whole policy of annexation is growing rapidly under the irresistible pressure of events." The success of the drive for the acquisition of Hawaii was one reason for Lodge's optimism. Even more important was this movement of troops out and beyond any heretofore imaginable range of American interests.

It was in many ways astonishing how quickly the imperialist-minded seized upon the idea of taking over control of the Philippines. Most Americans would have accepted for themselves McKinley's reported statement that before Manila Bay he "could not have told where those darned islands were within two thousand miles!" Albert J. Beveridge, however, had already suggested the new future beckoning the country. Speaking before the Middlesex Club in Boston four days before Dewey's victory, he dazzled his audience with a dream of empire—American law, American order, American civilization planting themselves on shores hitherto bloody and benighted—and declared emphatically that "the Philippines are logically our first target."

On June 4 Lodge wrote Henry White in London that the Philippines "must be ours . . . We hold the other side of the Pacific, and the value to this country is almost beyond imagination." Some two weeks later Roosevelt, champing at the bit in an army camp at San Antonio, was seeking reassurance from Lodge that the wonderful opportunities opening up before the

United States would not be neglected. "Give my love to Nannie," he wrote, "and do not make peace until we get Porto Rico, while Cuba is made independent and the Philippines at any rate taken from the Spaniards."

As the newspapers seized upon the exciting topic of a possible further extension of national horizons, a few adopted a highly cautious attitude. The Washington *Star* expressed the opinion that the Philippines lay far outside any possible sphere of American influence; the Boston *Herald* warned that the United States could no longer expect the Old World to stay out of the New World, if the New World began injecting itself into the affairs of the Old World. More generally, however, the press took up joyfully the refrain of empire, as in the Washington *Post*'s already quoted comment: "a strange destiny . . . . an imperial policy." The popular attitude was perhaps most neatly summarized by the Philadelphia *Record:* "Our war in Cuba has assumed undreamed of dimensions; . . . . willy nilly we have entered upon our career as a world power."

There were already some suspicions that Germany was showing too great an interest in the Philippine situation. Commodore Dewey reported the presence of a German squadron in Manila Bay and its commander, Vice Admiral von Diedrichs, seemed to be doing his best to invite a quarrel through ignoring the American blockade regulations and otherwise hampering operations. The situation was somewhat reminiscent of that in Samoa a decade earlier, and while it came to nothing, the American public was aroused over the idea that Germany might be seeking to deprive the United States of the spoils of war. "We take no crowding," the Philadelphia *Press* stated. While admitting that opinion on the ultimate American policy toward the Philippines might be divided, the *New York Times* flatly declared that should any other power seek to define or limit American rights, "then, indeed, we should become of one mind —and in action."

The expansionist urge, moreover, was reaching out to quarters which had formerly ignored or strongly protested jingoism and imperialism. It was not only the Mahans, Lodges, Roosevelts, and Beveridges that now favored the acquisition of colonies. Perhaps most importantly, the commercial and industrial interests, so powerful in the Republican party, were swinging over to support a movement they had formerly opposed. For the war with Spain had not interrupted the forward march of prosperity; it was opening up new vistas for commercial expansion and for the control of markets that might absorb the supposed surplus of American manufacturers. Big business was now ready to agree with Lodge that Manila had become the great prize of the war "and the thing which will give us the Eastern trade," and to accept Beveridge's exhortation that, in these new circumstances, "the trade of the world must and shall be ours."

The intrigues and scheming of the powers in China, whose plans to divide that country into foreign spheres of influence appeared to be coming to full fruition, further underscored the importance of an American base for commercial operations off the Asiatic coast. Many persons who had thought the annexation of Hawaii and even American construction and control of an isthmian canal needless and dangerous, were now not only won over to these projects, but even more to the desirability of securing the Philippines.

The *Journal of Commerce*, the *Wall Street Journal*, and the *American Banker*—among other such papers or magazines— listened attentively to the siren call of overseas expansion. They denied that they favored a general policy of annexation, colonization, or imperialism, but dwelt upon the need to establish a position in the Pacific that would uphold American interests and enable the United States to protect not only the existing trade with China "but the enormously greater trade likely to be developed in the next 25 years." Such an opportunity as that now presented, it was repeatedly said, might never again occur. The chance to extend American possessions to the shore of Asia, just as Europe seemed about to take over China, appeared to the *American Banker* to be "a coincidence which has a providential air."

At the same time, support for expansion came from the religious press which almost without exception began to rally around the "imperialism of righteousness." The mounting interest in the evangelization of the world, as demonstrated in the growth of foreign missions, gave an added emphasis to the moral responsibility of the United States in extending the blessings of its civilization to the Filipinos. "Among Christian thoughtful people," Senator Platt of Connecticut reported to McKinley, "the sentiment is akin to that which has maintained the missionary movement."

This point of view was perhaps most authoritatively set forth by Robert E. Speer, secretary of the Board of Foreign Missions of the Presbyterian Church. His thesis was that the western movement upon the East was certain and inevitable. In pressing out upon the rest of the world, the nations of the West were discharging a great duty in the development of areas otherwise left unimproved and cut off from trade and commerce. The "civilized" countries had the right to interfere in backward lands, and should exercise that right. The role of the missionary was not to question this process, but to elevate its character.

Dr. Speer also strongly emphasized the complete sympathy of the missionary movement with everything that made for greater trade. Commercial expansion, he declared, was "a necessary part of the great outward impulse of civilization, the missionary movement welcomes it as an ally." If imperialism could be subject to criticism in some instances (although Dr. Speer did not use the word "imperialism"), the missionary point of view was that "the whole Western movement, with all its evils, must surely be believed, in the will of God, to be working for the world."

Any doubts as to how expansion might affect the United States, the religious papers generally agreed, were to be resolved in the fulfillment of the obligations imposed upon the country by its victory over Spain. "Woe to any nation," warned the *Churchman,* which had at first been somewhat alarmed over the growth of imperialist sentiment, "which hesitates for fear its own interests will be entangled."

The possible contradiction, in substituting the rule of the United States for that of Spain over a people whose overwhelming desire was freedom, did not apparently make much impression in religious circles. After all, the Filipinos had never had liberty. Church people believed that morally and religiously, as one paper said, "we should not shun an opportunity to lift up a barbarous people." McKinley himself expressed even more clearly the attitude of evangelistic churches. "Do we need their consent to perform a great act for humanity?" he asked. "We had it in every aspiration of their minds, in every hope of their hearts." And then he added in the true missionary spirit: "Our flag has never waved over any community but in blessing. I believe the Filipinos will soon recognize the fact that it has not lost its gift of benediction in its world-wide journey to their shores."

As public opinion, expressed in so many quarters, appeared to be swinging more and more in favor of American expansion overseas, other influences were brought to bear on the McKinley administration. Henry Watterson, Democrat though he was, again saw in the imperialistic cause a Heaven-sent opportunity to quiet domestic factionalism: "We escape the menace and peril of socialism and agrarianism . . . by a policy of colonization and conquest." Republican leaders were even more convinced that it was the only issue that could maintain the sense of national unity forged by the Spanish-American War. "This new policy," Senator Lodge stated bluntly, "will knock on the head silver and other matters, which have embarrassed us so much at home."

Thus as in earlier instances of the transfer of interest from domestic matters to foreign affairs, imperialism could be made a rallying point for popular support of the party in power. The Republicans could appeal to patriotism in sustaining their foreign policy, and this was no small matter, with the mid-term elections of 1898—and beyond them the presidential campaign of 1900—looming darkly over the national horizon.

President McKinley hardly needed advice, however. He was very happily swimming with the current, and ready to use all his influence in directing it into the appropriate channels. The question could still be asked whether he was actually displaying any more responsible leadership than he had in the days before intervention in Cuba, but at least he was playing a positive rather than a negative role in the development of national policy.

While the President's first step along such lines was the decision to send to the Philippines the troops necessary to occupy Manila, his instructions to them on one point still further underscored the direction of his thinking. En route they were to take over control of the Spanish-held Ladrone (Mariana) Islands. As the expedition which sailed from San Francisco on May 25 neared Guam, its convoy ship consequently opened fire on the antiquated fort that guarded the island's approaches. There was no answering fire and soon a boat put off from the shore with two Spanish officials. They were profuse with apologies: they had been unable to return the visitors' salute because the local Spanish garrison had no ammunition! It was to their complete surprise that the perturbed officials learned that the United States and Spain were at war, and that the supposed salute was the signal of a bombardment. When the Americans demanded surrender, there was no alternative to submission. In such odd and informal circumstances, the Spanish flag was hauled down and that of the United States run up over the public buildings at Guam.

When word reached this country that the United States had assumed control over the Ladrones, the imperialists rejoiced.

"Why the President should have taken those islands, unless he expects to hold on to the Philippines," Lodge logically concluded, "I cannot conceive."

In his first consideration of the possible peace terms that might be offered Spain, as suggested in a cable on June 3 to Ambassador Hay at London from Secretary of State Day, who had assumed this post upon the resignation of the aged John Sherman, McKinley was already puzzling out how far the United States should go. But he specifically proposed that in addition to securing the freedom of Cuba, any future treaty should at least provide for the cession of Puerto Rico, an island in the Ladrones, and a port in the Philippines. If he was still undecided as to whether additional demands should be made, a possible clue to his thinking is provided by a brief memorandum found among his papers. "While we are conducting war and until its conclusion we must keep all we get," McKinley wrote; "when the war is over we must keep what we want."

Somewhat later in June the activities of the Filipino insurgents, who hoped as did the Cubans that American liberation from Spanish control meant independence, led Day to inform Hay that their interests would have to be given just consideration in any settlement. There is no evidence, however, that McKinley was overly concerned over their aspirations for freedom. He appeared to be more than willing to accept the advice from various quarters that the Filipinos were totally unfit for self-government. By the time Spain was ready to sue for peace in late July, in any event, he had begun to think of American retention of at least an island in the Philippines, if not the entire archipelago. In a cabinet discussion of possible peace terms on the twenty-ninth, there was a virtually even division of opinion among those present between taking over merely a naval base or all the islands. When Secretary Day proposed the formal adoption of the first plan, McKinley was unwilling to put it to a vote. Later asked why he had not done so, he is said by his biographer to have replied: "I was afraid it would be carried."

Rather than make any firm decision at the time, the President wished to keep the subject open. The armistice terms consequently went no further than to provide that the United States would continue to hold Manila pending the future disposition of the islands as a whole. Charles G. Dawes noted in his diary on July 30 that Secretary of the Treasury Gage had given him a digest of this cabinet meeting: "The President has had his way as usual and he is right."

In the meantime a feverish debate over expansion raged in the press. With such exceptions as the Boston *Transcript* and the Philadelphia *Public Ledger,* the Republican papers generally favored "keeping whatever we have got"; Democratic organs, apart from such papers as the *New York Times* and the Brooklyn *Eagle,* appeared strongly opposed to annexation. Nevertheless, early in September a *Literary Digest* poll reported that from 192 replies to a nationwide questionnaire, 84 newspapers favored the retention of the entire Philippine group and 63 proposed at least a naval base. Only a half-dozen wanted the United States to clear out altogether, and not a single paper thought the islands should be returned to Spain.

Something over a month later this same magazine reported on the party platforms adopted at the state political conventions. Here the results were not as conclusive. Nearly one-half of the platforms, including both Republican and Democratic conventions, ignored the Philippines issue altogether. Among those which the *Literary Digest* reported as taking a definite stand, there were sixteen favoring the retention of at least some of the islands, and six (all Democratic) opposing any acquisitions whatsoever.

In spite of such apparent political divisions, the Chicago *Times Herald,* the newspaper closest to the Administration, considered itself justified in stating that "we find that we want the Philippines. . . . This is the dominant American sentiment." And even if this were not entirely true, it was the thesis on which the President was acting. He had left the question open until the peace conference, but the delegates he appointed definitely foreshadowed the demands that were to be made upon Spain.

While Secretary Day, known to be at best a very reluctant convert to the need for any overseas possessions, headed the delegation, three of its other members were open and avowed expansionists. These men were Senator Cushman Davis of Minnesota, who had been a vigorous advocate of the annexation of Hawaii; Senator W. P. Frye of Maine, a blazing jingo who once expressed his desire to acquire Cuba by conquest; and Whitelaw Reid, editor of the New York *Tribune*, whose imperialist ambitions were notorious. The only foe of expansion was George Gray, a Democratic senator from Delaware.

It was the appointment of Reid, the only member of the delegation outside government circles, which most clearly revealed the President's hand. For Reid had already set forth his very pronounced views in articles both at home and abroad, writing for the French press with the utmost candor that "what we shall seize we shall undoubtedly hold." In the delegation's first official meeting at the White House, he reaffirmed his position. In the face of the less determined ideas of his colleagues, Reid stated emphatically that having broken down the existing government in the Philippines, "we could not honorably desert them and should be extremely unwise to turn over the task of controlling them to any other power."

The President's instructions to the peace commission on September 16, not made public at the time, also reveal a further advance in his own thinking. While admitting that the Philippines were on a quite different basis from Puerto Rico or Guam, he clearly suggested that there seemed to be a certain inevitability about their coming into American possession. Not yet ready to make their surrender by Spain a specific demand, he nevertheless stated that as an irreducible minimum the United States could not accept less "than the cession in full right and sovereignty of Luzon."

In justifying his position the President went into considerable explanation of why the United States found it necessary to make such a demand. There had been no original thought of complete or even partial acquisition of the Philippines, he said, but the success of American arms at Manila had imposed upon the nation obligations it could not disregard. The march of events had overruled human action:

"Avowing unreservedly the purpose which has animated all our effort, and still solicitous to adhere to it, we cannot be unmindful that, without any desire or design on our part, the war has brought us new duties and responsibilities which we must meet and discharge as becomes a great nation on whose growth and career from the beginning the Ruler of Nations has plainly written the high command and pledge of civilization."

There can be no question that McKinley was sincere in interpreting the situation in such high-minded terms. He wanted to do what he felt to be right, and his emphasis upon duty and responsibility, his acceptance of the divine will of Providence in marking out America's destiny, conformed to his own moral and religious feelings. Yet he was also the practical politician. He believed in the benefits that the United States might gain from expansion overseas. Having paid his tribute to ethical considerations, he added to his instructions with appealing candor the statement that "incidental to our tenure in the Philippines is the commercial opportunity to which American statesmanship cannot be indifferent."

After the peace commissioners sailed for Paris in mid-September, McKinley agreed to attend a number of peace jubilees—at Omaha, Chicago, and Philadelphia—and also took occasion to deliver a series of talks at what a later generation would call whistle-stops along the route of his swing about the country. His speeches were in the main a justification of administration policy, at home and abroad, with an eye on the mid-term congressional elections. Only indirectly and in the most general terms did he refer to the important negotiations in Paris. But he played shrewdly upon the imperialist theme

—and entirely in terms of those twin gods, duty and destiny.

"This war," the President declared, ". . . . will bring to us, I trust, blessings that are now beyond calculation. It will bring us also burdens, but the American people will never shirk a responsibility . . . The currents of destiny flow through the heart of the people . . . The movements of men, planned and designed by the Master of Men, will never be interrupted by the American people . . . Seeing only the highest good of the nation . . . . pursuing no other path but that of duty . . . We must give to the world the full demonstration of our purpose. Duty determines destiny . . ."

These somewhat ponderous sentiments of moral obligation were interpreted by the friendly Chicago *Times Herald* as clearly indicating that the President was prepared to insist on cession of the entire Philippine archipelago. The question had been left open when the peace commission sailed, the *Times Herald* stated, but public sentiment had crystallized, because of the "logic of events and the demands of humanity." It was perhaps something more than a coincidence that in presenting its annexation arguments, this editorial followed almost exactly the same line of reasoning later employed by McKinley in justifying his own final decision. The Philippines could not be returned to Spanish rule, handed over to any other country, or be left to themselves—"the only humane course is to retain the islands and govern them ourselves." The editorial concluded that it would have been unbecoming for the President to state his views more specifically while the question was still at issue in Paris, "but what he might say with propriety had been said and is in harmony with public sentiment."

The New York *Evening Post* asked, "Who determines duty?" and the *World* wondered about destiny: "What does it mean? Nobody knows. What does Mr. McKinley think it means? Nobody knows, Mr. McKinley probably least of all." Nevertheless, the President returned from his tour convinced that the people were with him and that annexation of all the

Philippines would be popularly supported. On October 25 he wrote the American delegates in Paris that in his opinion the well-considered judgment of the majority of the American people would be "that duty requires we should take the archipelago. I will be ready to give instructions when you reach that point."

The peace commission had already reached such a point. On the very day that the President was writing, it cabled for more complete instructions. The delegates themselves were not entirely of one mind as to what should be done. Nevertheless Reid, Davis, and Frye were fully convinced that the United States should insist upon cession of all the Philippines; Day somewhat ambiguously favored the retention of the islands of Luzon, Mindoro, and Palawan, and only Gray reaffirmed his consistent opposition to the annexation of any of the islands. His grounds were that there was no place for the administration or government of subject people within the American system, and also that the proposed policy, as he cabled from Paris, "introduces us into European politics and the entangling alliances against which Washington and all American statesmen have protested."

What had apparently confirmed the expansionist views of the commission majority, in spite of Gray's arguments, were two considerations: advice from American representatives in the Philippines that the islands were not ready for self-government ("anarchy and civil war will immediately ensue and lead to foreign intervention," reported General F. V. Greene), and the mounting evidence from the European point of view that unless the United States took over the entire archipelago, a highly dangerous, indeed impossible, situation might be created in the western Pacific.

The President scarcely needed further advice. His mind was made up. When at Chicago he had said that "the currents of destiny flow through the heart of the people," he had also asked, "Who will check them? Who will direct them? Who will stop them?" McKinley had a good deal to do with directing them; certainly he was not going to try to stop them. Hay, who had returned from London to become Secretary of State when Day resigned this post to go to Paris, promptly cabled the delegation that it was now the President's view that the cession of Luzon alone could not be justified. The question was either all the Philippines or none of them. Since the latter course was inadmissible, the former was required. And these final and definitive instructions were once again couched in ethical terms. "Territorial expansion should be our least concern," President McKinley declared; "that we shall not shirk the moral obligation of our victory is the greatest."

The Spanish commissioners, not surprisingly, strongly resisted cession of the Philippines. For a time there appeared to be a very real danger that even at the risk of renewed hostilities, they would refuse to meet the new American demand. So tense did the situation become that the United States delegates, including Reid and Frye, suggested that some compromise of the issue might be found. Having made his decision, however, McKinley was adamant. Secretary Hay cabled that the questions of duty and humanity appealed so strongly to the President that he could consider no other answer to the problem than the one he had already given. One concession was made to Spain. The United States offered to pay $20,000,-000 in return for the transfer of the Philippines. There was to be no retreat in principle, however, and this proposition was put forward as an ultimatum. The Spanish commissioners capitulated.

The treaty was signed on December 10, 1898. Spain was forced to relinquish her control over Cuba, surrender both Puerto Rico and Guam to American sovereignty, and to state in the treaty's most significant clause, "Spain cedes to the United States the archipelago known as the Philippine Islands."

Over a year later, talking to a visiting delegation of clergymen, the President carefully explained the steps through which he had arrived at the momentous decision to demand the cession of the Philippines:

"I walked the floor of the White House night after night until mid-night; and I am not ashamed to tell you, gentlemen, that I went down on my knees and prayed Almighty God for light and guidance more than one night. And one night late it came to me this way—I don't know how it was, but it came: (1) That we could not give them back to Spain—that would be cowardly and dishonorable; (2) that we could not turn them over to France or Germany—our commercial rivals in the Orient—that would be bad business and discreditable; (3) that we could not leave them to themselves—they were unfit for self-government—and they would soon have anarchy and misrule over there worse than Spain's was; and (4) that there was nothing left for us to do but to take them all, and to educate the Filipinos, and uplift and civilize and Christianize them, and by God's grace do the very best we could by them, as our fellow men for whom Christ also died. And then I went to bed and went to sleep and slept soundly."

Again there is no warrant to question President McKinley's sincerity. He believed that he was doing what was right and just. Yet the evidence is clear that he advanced steadily toward his final position by a much more logical process than any sudden revelation in the midnight fastness of the White House. It has often been pointed out that, unconsciously or not, McKinley stressed all the conventional arguments in favor of imperialism—national honor, economic advantage, racial superiority, and altruism—in describing his experience. Moreover, it is significant that he did not mention a possible alternative to taking over the Philippines as an American possession; that is, the establishment of a protectorate with the promise of granting the Filipinos immediate self-government and ultimate independence. He had become too much of an imperialist.

The policy that McKinley adopted in projecting American

influence, American power, and American sovereignty to the very shores of Asia was to have incalculable consequences. They were hardly foreseen as the American delegates signed this fateful peace treaty with Spain. The United States was assuming responsibilities that meant a sharp break with the traditions of the past. If they were not commitments in the sense of entangling alliances, they were nonetheless obligations which meant inevitable entanglements. Yet McKinley gave little evidence of understanding the more realistic aspects of the step the United States was taking in the establishment of an overseas empire.

The idea of national mission that he emphasized in so many of his speeches had an historic tradition going back to the earliest days of the Republic, but never before had it been interpreted as demanding the imposition of American rule over subject peoples or involvement in the power rivalries of an imperialistic world. The President's sonorous speeches and public statements helped to convince the American people they should undertake the obligations and responsibilities of colonial rule; they did little to suggest what all this might mean in the context of global politics.

McKinley would appear to have been completely beguiled by that dream of empire in whose realization he ultimately played such an important role. He abandoned the principles of foreign policy that had served the nation since its foundation, and put in their place only vague generalizations. He was a good deal more than a passive instrument in the hands of men and events, but he lacked the constructive imagination fully to realize what the nation's emergence as a world power really involved. The foreign policy legacy he left his countrymen was a confusion of purpose shrouded in moral ambiguities.

CHAPTER XI

THE GREAT DEBATE

ALTHOUGH THE PRESIDENT HAD SET THE COURSE TOWARD ANNEXA-
tion of the Philippines and there appeared to be ever-increasing
evidence of popular support for his program, the country was by
no means unanimously in favor of this radical departure from traditional policy. A powerful and stubborn opposition soon made
itself felt. Even before McKinley submitted the treaty signed
at Paris for senate approval, there had opened a great debate—
in and out of Congress—on the future foreign policy of the
United States. It was to continue through the presidential campaign of 1900, even though the treaty of peace had by then been
ratified and the issue supposedly been settled.

What was to become the anti-imperialist crusade gained momentum rather slowly. A strong rear-guard action had been
fought on Hawaiian annexation, but the enthusiasm and excitement of war gave tremendous weight to the argument that the
United States was entitled to hold whatever territories—other
than Cuba—might be wrested from Spain by American arms.
As the cheers and applause that greeted McKinley's oratorical
bows to duty and destiny so clearly suggested, the martial atmosphere of 1898 was not conducive to sober consideration of
all the implications of overseas extension.

Among the voices calling upon the American people to stop,
look, and listen before they plunged the nation into what the anti-
expansionists so repeatedly called the "trackless sea of imperialism," were far more Democrats than Republicans. In many cases,

however, this was not mere partisanship. Even though political alignments made it natural for Democrats to oppose administration policy, there was real conviction in a position that brought together such otherwise antagonistic party leaders as Grover Cleveland and William Jennings Bryan.

Also there were a number of prominent Republicans, acting firmly on principle, who broke with the Administration in vigorous opposition to McKinley's stand. One of the most respected of such men was Senator Hoar, who now found to his intense discomfiture that in spite of everything he had so profoundly believed when Hawaiian annexation was in dispute, the fear of imperialism was anything but needless alarm. Equally opposed to the new policies was Speaker Reed of the House, who had combated Hawaiian annexation and on the first report of victory at Manila exclaimed abruptly, "Dewey ought to sail right away from that place." His strong party feeling often kept him silent during the debates on foreign affairs, but there was never any doubt of his personal bitterness over the McKinley program. Other Republicans taking a definite and forthright stand against an annexation policy included Senator Hale of Maine and Senator Mason of Illinois.

The anti-imperialist cause also attracted a wide-ranging and disparate group of national leaders outside the ranks of politics. Andrew Carnegie and Samuel Gompers were at one on this issue, if on no other. Among intellectuals, where opposition to acquiring the Philippines was especially strong, could be counted President Eliot of Harvard and President David Starr Jordan of Leland Stanford; also William James, John Burgess, and William Graham Sumner. Most novelists and poets of the day— William Dean Howells, Hamlin Garland, William Vaughn Moody, Mark Twain—refused to be swept long with the imperialist tide.

As early as the summer of 1898, a group of these foes of expansion took the initiative in establishing, in Boston, an Anti-Imperialist League. Lodge casually dismissed this development as "a comic incident," but the idea was to spread throughout the country and something over a year later these separate organizations joined forces in the American Anti-Imperialist League. Its leadership was always highly distinguished; its weakness lay in being unable to attract a sufficiently active popular following.

George S. Boutwell, a Secretary of the Treasury under Grant and one-time Republican senator from Massachusetts, repudiated his party to become president of the Anti-Imperialist League. Territorial expansion into the Pacific, he insisted, would ultimately lead to war. He thought there might well be a clash with Japan, but particularly stressed a more dangerous situation in which Russia, winning dominance over China, would directly challenge the American position in the Pacific.

"No event of the near future can be predicted with more certainty," Boutwell stated, "than this—that China is to be transformed into a war-like power, and that its great resources are to be at the service and under the directing hand of Russia." Here was amazing prescience, if half a century may be deemed the near future. And what Boutwell then feared was that sitting down under the shadow of this mighty power, the United States would have to accept either humiliating subserviency, or alliance with England, and a fruitless war. "For us, independence in policy, peace, and self-assertion will be impossible," he concluded, "if we enter into the islands of the east."

A first frontal attack upon the entire new policy of the McKinley administration came not unexpectedly from Cleveland. He took the occasion of a Founder's Day address at Lawrenceville School on June 21, 1898, to reiterate strongly those views he had so often expressed as President. It was a perversion of the national mission, Cleveland declared, to take such an unnatural step as the extension of national boundaries overseas. It could not be reconciled with the principles and traditions of the American people. He soberly called upon his countrymen to summon up the moral courage to resist the lure of empire.

About the same time, Bryan expressed no less positive views. The war in which the country was engaged, he said, must end as it had begun, in defense of liberty. There was no justification for colonization in what had happened at Manila. He warned the nation against repudiating the principle that government must be by consent of the governed, and against letting itself become entangled in the web of international politics in Europe or Asia. He decried the idea that overseas expansion was this country's inevitable destiny, and emphatically declared that no nation could endure half republic and half colony.

Most of the anti-imperialists followed the line laid down by Cleveland and Bryan. While they invariably pointed out the risks and hazards of involvement in world politics, they emphasized far more heavily the incompatibility of any program of colonialism with the basic tenets of the American constitutional system. Their recurrent appeal was to the conscience of the American people. Whatever the imperialists might say of manifest destiny, of duty and obligation, of naval needs or of commercial advantage, their opponents clung to the fundamental thesis that any imperialist departure from the traditions and principles on which American society was based would be a denial of the heritage of freedom that was the country's greatest possession.

The emphasis upon the moral issue forced the imperialists, in accepting such a challenge, to try to develop what they conceived to be an even greater duty for the nation than safeguarding its own liberties. "The opponents of the treaty," Senator Lodge stated, "have placed their opposition on such high and altruistic grounds that I have preferred to meet them there." But while he then emphasized the obligation devolving upon the United States, whatever the risks involved, to carry to the Philippines the blessings of Anglo-American civilization, he soon came back—in spite of all disclaimers—to the material and practical advantages that would accrue to the United States through overseas expansion. The expansionists made the most of the "imperialism of righteousness" to bolster their cause, but they never forgot the down-to-earth arguments that might strengthen the fervor stimulated by appeals to duty and responsibility.

They elaborated Mahan's thesis of the importance of naval power and the consequent need for overseas bases to support such power. They stressed the threat to American economic interests in the Orient unless the United States took over the Philippines to compensate for the spheres of influence the European powers were carving out in China. Even more tellingly, they developed the argument that had so greatly influenced President McKinley: The Filipinos were not capable of self-government and unless the islands were placed under American control, they would become helpless pawns in the international competition of the Pacific, and some other country—a commercial rival—would take them over.

Among the imperialist orators, none was more impassioned or more eloquent than Beveridge. Politically ambitious, intensely earnest, thoroughly imbued with a sense of personal mission, he promoted the imperialist cause with unexampled zest. His earlier talk before the Middlesex Club in Boston had been in a sense the opening gun of the whole annexationist campaign, but another address—the Republican National Committee was to distribute 300,000 copies of it—reached a far wider audience. This was his famous March of the Flag speech, delivered in Indianapolis on September 16, 1898—the very day that McKinley was giving his first instructions to the peace commissioners. The occasion was a political rally that marked Beveridge's entry into the senatorial race in Indiana, and the setting gave an unusually dramatic quality to what he said. The meeting was preceded by a torchlight parade, with the band playing and Beveridge proudly riding in an open carriage, and throughout the evening a crowd that packed the meeting hall to the rafters repeatedly broke out in thunderous applause and ringing cheers.

Beveridge took the forthright position that the principle of consent of the governed applied only to those capable of self-government, and stated categorically that the Filipinos were incapable of handling their own affairs. Could we then abandon them, he asked, with the wolves of foreign conquest all about them? Brushing aside the problem of the Philippines' distance from the United States by saying that the Navy would make them contiguous, he declared that the United States had no alternative to overseas expansion, in the light of the pressing need for new markets to absorb American goods.

There could be no stopping the march of the flag, Beveridge told his cheering audience. It had advanced from the Mississippi Valley to the mountains, and from Mexico to the borders of Canada; it had advanced into the Oregon Territory and into Texas; it had advanced over the territories of the Southwest to peerless California and the folds of glory blazed from ocean to ocean. Now carrying on the torch handed down by Jefferson, Jackson, Monroe, Seward, Grant, and Harrison, declared the young Indianian, McKinley "plants the flag over the islands of the seas, outposts of commerce, citadels of national defense, and the march of the flag goes on."

And then the glowing peroration: "It is God's great purpose made manifest in the instincts of our race, whose present phase is our personal profit, but whose far-off end is the redemption of the world and the Christianization of mankind."

There was little the anti-imperialists could do to combat such emotional appeals, such frenzied flag-waving. The stern dictates of justice, the entanglements into which overseas expansion would surely lead the nation, the heavy burdens of colonial administration—arguments based on such considerations were pale and pallid.

The signature of the treaty with Spain did not remove the issue from public debate, but focused attention on what the Senate would do. Consideration of the treaty itself was confined to executive session, but the public discussion of a series of resolutions on policy toward the Philippines clearly revealed the Senate's attitude.

One of the more important of these resolutions, introduced by Senator George G. Vest of Missouri just four days before the signing of the peace treaty, sought to put the Senate on record as declaring that the United States could not constitutionally acquire or hold foreign colonies. Vest took the position that there could be no government without consent of the governed, and that, in every previous acquisition of territory by the United States, the necessary provisions had been made for the citizenship of the inhabitants and the ultimate admission of the territory into the Union as a state. Since there was no idea of extending such citizenship to the Filipinos or of granting statehood, Vest declared, there was no legal basis for American annexation of the islands.

Senator Hoar supported this resolution. The Philippine question, he declared, was the most important that the nation had faced since its origin. "Have we the right, as doubtless we have the physical power," he solemnly asked, "to enter upon the government of ten or twelve million subject people without constitutional restraint?" He answered his own question emphatically in the negative. Any such move would be contrary to the principles of the Declaration of Independence and of the Constitution. Certainly it could never have occurred to the fathers of the country, he scathingly added, that their descendants "would be beguiled from these sacred and awful verities that they might strut about in the castoff clothing of pinchbeck emperors and pewter kings; that their descendants would be excited by the smell of gunpowder and the sound of the guns of a single victory as a small boy by a firecracker on some Fourth of July morning." To follow the road advocated by the McKinley administration, Hoar told his fellow senators, would mean "descending from the ancient path of republican liberty which the fathers trod, down into this modern swamp and cesspool of imperialism."

The Vest resolution was defeated in spite of such anti-imperialist support. The administration ranks held firm, and there was sufficient backing from other quarters to clear the way for overseas expansion. And the same fate awaited other resolutions dealing with the Philippine issue. A proposal of Senator Bacon of Georgia that administration and control of the islands should be transferred as soon as possible to an independent Philippine government commanded very considerable support, but the anti-imperialists could not get a majority. Their opponents argued successfully that the United States would provide a just and equitable government for the Filipinos, and parried every effort to place the Senate on record as favoring their independence.

Approval of the treaty itself needed, of course, more than the vote with which the imperialists had rejected the proposed independence resolutions—there would have to be a two-thirds majority. In taking charge of the Administration's policy, Senator Lodge realized that he faced a hard fight. Seeking to avoid too much debate on general principles, he insisted upon immediate approval of the treaty as a matter of practical expediency. The repudiation of the President on such an important issue, he further stated, "is the humiliation of the United States in the eyes of civilized mankind and brands us as a people incapable of great affairs or of taking rank where we belong, as one of the greatest of the great world powers."

Soft-peddling the problem of government without consent of the governed, Lodge expressed his confidence that the United States would fully safeguard the liberties of the Filipinos in carrying out "a great, a difficult, and a noble task."

Senator Spooner, who had been so eloquent in calling for intervention in Cuba, took this same line. The future of the Filipinos could hardly be decided at this time, he said, but no one could doubt that the purpose of the United States in accepting the cession of the Philippines would be "one of benevolence and good will to that people." So too Senator Nelson declared that the United States had "no purpose to enslave or enthrall the people of the Philippine Islands. . . . We come as ministering angels, not as despots." The anti-imperialist argument that annexation could not be reconciled with republican principles was countered with the airy statement that subsequent arrangements for the Philippines "will religiously maintain the best ideals of the Republic, and will be in harmony with justice, generosity, and the highest civilization."

And once again the debates in Washington were reflected in widespread public discussion. The anti-imperialist leagues flooded the country with pamphlets, and their speakers lost no opportunity to condemn colonialism as a national policy. One petition sent to the Senate included such prominent names as those of Cleveland, Carnegie, Gompers, Charles Francis Adams, Jr., Carl Schurz, Moorfield Story, Charles W. Eliot, and William Graham Sumner. The country was warned that imperialism abroad would mean imperialism at home, and emphatically told that the plea of destiny was no more than an admission that no other valid reason could be given for expansion.

As the scheduled time for a senate vote on the treaty approached, the hopes of the anti-imperialists that the treaty might be defeated were sadly dimmed by an unexpected political maneuver on the part of Bryan. He was adamantly opposed to the acquisition of the Philippines—of that there was no question—but he had persuaded himself that this was an issue that the people themselves should decide, rather than the Senate. He took the position that the treaty should be ratified in order to assure peace, and the future disposition of the Philippines left for decision at the polls. This program had first been suggested in midsummer and at the time widely approved by both Democrats and independent Republicans. It had been largely forgotten, however. It was to the consternation of many of his followers that Bryan now suddenly appeared in Washington and advised all Democratic senators to vote in favor of the treaty.

In making this move Bryan cannot be judged wholly insincere. There was validity to the thesis that the United States should take over the Philippines and then decide what should be done with them. But his maneuver was at the time, and also in later years, considered highly suspect. For Bryan undoubtedly believed that with the issue held over to the next presidential election, the Democratic party might well win its way back into power in an anti-imperialist campaign under his own leadership. He believed he had a winning issue and was willing to risk the consequences of approving the acquisition of the Philippines in order that he might then become the champion of their freedom.

"One word from Mr. Bryan," Carnegie later wrote bitterly, "would have saved the country from disaster. I could not be cordial to him for years afterward. He had seemed to me a man who was willing to sacrifice his country and his personal convictions for party advantage."

The fate of the treaty even now remained in doubt. The imperialist faction, made up of most of the Republicans and a few Democrats, was reinforced by seventeen additional Democrats and Populists who were persuaded by Bryan to vote with the Administration. Yet this was still not enough. The assured protreaty vote fell one short of the necessary two-thirds majority.

The final ballot was set for Monday, February 6, 1899, at 3 o'clock. That Sunday startling news arrived from the Philippines. Despairing of any action in Washington that might hold out the hope of independence, the Filipino insurgents had broken out in open revolt against the United States forces occupying Manila. Here was a direct challenge to American authority and a clear demonstration of the intense desire of the Filipinos for freedom. How it affected the senators about to vote remains problematic—Lodge was later to say that it caused no shift in existing alignments—but the outbreak heightened the drama of the final battle over treaty ratification. Half an hour before the scheduled vote, administration supporters were still uncertain of the outcome, and only the roll call itself finally determined the issue. The count then proved to be fifty-seven in favor of the treaty and twenty-seven opposed—a two-thirds majority with one to spare!

"The hardest, closest fight I have ever known," wrote Lodge, and he was proud of it. "We were down in the engine room and do not get flowers," he later wrote Roosevelt in recounting the story of his struggle, "but we did make the ship move."

The Senate had made its decision; the Filipino insurgents had rejected it even before the final vote was taken. But the situation was highly complicated. There must be some re-tracing of our steps to explain the gathering sense of frustration in the islands and the deepening hostility toward the United States that led to this Filipino attack on the American military forces.

When Commodore Dewey conferred with representatives of the insurgents at Hongkong on the eve of the battle of Manila Bay, they were apparently operating on the assumption, as a re-sult of previous conversations with the American consul general at Singapore, that the United States was prepared to support Philippine independence. Dewey had no such understanding. "They were bothering me," he was later to say of the insurgent spokesmen. "I was very busy getting my squadron ready for battle, and these little men were coming on board my ship at Hongkong and taking a good deal of my time, and I did not attach the slightest importance to anything that they could do, and they did nothing." Yet this cavalier dismissal of the Fili-pinos was hardly borne out by his own subsequent acts. After the battle of Manila Bay, the Filipino leader, General Emilio Aguinaldo, was brought to the Philippines, and Dewey en-couraged him to lead a new revolt against Spanish rule. When the insurgents then set up headquarters at Cavite and estab-lished a provisional government, no objections whatsoever were raised. Naturally enough the Filipinos interpreted these moves as a further pledge of American backing for their cause. The general impression prevailed among their leaders that in the Philippines, as in Cuba, the goal of the United States was the liberation of the people from Spanish rule.

The reports of this feeling among the Filipinos soon began to create anxiety in Washington circles where the imperialist tide was so rapidly rising. A serious dilemma was posed. The American military forces arriving in the islands might well need the assistance of the insurgents in capturing Manila, but an alliance would further encourage Filipino hopes for an independence that might not fit into American policy. The orders consequently forthcoming from Washington to General Merritt, in command of the American troops, were not to enter into unauthorized negotiations with the Filipino insurgents, and yet to seek their cooperation and avoid at all costs any rupture with them.

Under these circumstances Aguinaldo began to become increasingly suspicious of the ultimate intentions of the United States, and soon found further reason for his disquietude. General Merritt, on the basis of the most rigid instructions from the President, refused to allow the Filipino insurgents to take part in the operations that on August 13, 1898, enabled the American troops to occupy Manila. McKinley's extension of military occupation to all the islands, and announcement of the terms of the treaty of peace, then confirmed Aguinaldo's worst fears. As the Senate commenced its debate on the treaty, he issued a fiery proclamation assailing what he termed American treachery.

Aguinaldo declared that the United States had betrayed the promises originally made him, said Manila would never have fallen into American hands had it not been invested by the Filipino insurgents before the American troops were strong enough to undertake its capture, and poured all his scorn on McKinley's statement that the Americans had come "not as invaders or conquerors, but as friends." He stated emphatically that his people were ready to resist by force any attempt to subjugate them.

As the tension increased between the American and Filipino forces under these unhappy conditions, only a spark was needed to precipitate actual hostilities. It was provided by an American sentry's firing upon a Filipino patrol. The revolt which broke out on February 4, 1899, was then further encouraged by another vitriolic proclamation in which Aguinaldo again bitterly assailed American policy:

"This is the nation where honor is yet unknown, in a word, a nation hated by all other nations! A nation which knows not honor, has not an atom of feeling! Are these our protectors? Bet-

ter death than be related to a people whose evil is inborn! Away
with the wretches! Destruction to the Americans! Down with
the United States!"

To the further developments in the Philippines we shall return later, but this was the immediate background to the continuing debate in the United States on imperialism.

The American people, so far as public opinion was reflected
in the press, were at once horrified by these unfortunate consequences of the Administration's Philippine policy and yet
convinced that under the circumstances the uprising had to be
forcefully suppressed. A number of newspapers declared that
while military action was necessary to restore order, there
could be no condoning the slaughter of Filipinos in a war of
conquest: the end would have to be establishment of an independent republic. More generally, however, the press called
for the complete blotting out of every vestige of opposition to
American rule before anything further could be considered.
Although the country had no stomach for fighting in the Philippines, there indeed seemed to be no alternative if the islands
were to be pacified. National prestige would not permit yielding
at any point.

"We must dismiss all thought of optimistic propagandas,
awake from the visions of Utopia," cried the Washington *Star*.
"These Filipinos must be taught obedience and must be forced
to observe, even if they cannot comprehend, the practices of
civilization. And to that end every resource at our disposal,
every energy we can command, should be employed without
thought or hesitation."

As the fighting in the islands spread, with many other editorials reflecting the attitude of the Washington *Star*, the anti-
imperialists denounced ever more bitterly a policy which led
to bloodshed and war. In seeking to subdue the insurgents by
military force, they found the United States doing in the Philippines just what the nation had taken up arms to prevent the
Spaniards from doing in Cuba. Imperialism was reaping its

inevitable reward. "The story of our attempted conquest of the Philippines," an enraged Carl Schurz would write Charles Francis Adams, "is a story of deceit, false pretense, brutal treachery to friends, unconstitutional assumption of power, betrayal of the fundamental principles of our democracy, wanton sacrifice of our soldiers in an unjust cause, cruel slaughter of innocent people . . ." In bitter comment on the ironic shift in the nation's position, William Graham Sumner gave to his attack on the new imperialism the sardonic title of "The Spanish Conquest of the United States." Agreeing with Schurz that by its new policies the United States was forfeiting its moral credit with the world, he reiterated that imperialism never could be reconciled with the traditions and principles of the American people.

Finley Peter Dunne also was caustic in his comments on a policy that had supposedly been initiated as a generous father's welcome of misguided children but had somehow taken a quite different turn.

"An' there it stands, Hinnissy," he had Mr. Dooley say, "with th' indulgent parent kneelin' on th' stomach iv his adopted child, while a dillygation fr'm Boston bastes him with an umbrella. There it stands, an' how will it come out I dinnaw. I'm not much iv an expansionist mesilf."

William Vaughn Moody sought to awaken the country to the dangers of imperialism in his *Ode in Time of Hesitation*. Appealing to the traditions of a proud republic that "hath not stooped to cheat and scramble in the market place of war," he wrote:

> "Tempt not our weakness, our cupidity!
> For save we let the island men go free,
> Those baffled and dislaureled ghosts
> Will curse us from the lamentable coasts
> Where walk the frustrate dead.
> O ye who lead,
> Take heed!
> Blindness we may forgive, but baseness we will smite."

In the face of the repeated arguments of the Lodges and Beveridges that American policy was as morally sound as it was practically wise, and that to grant self-government to a people who had no fitness for it would be "to dower them with a curse instead of a blessing," these anti-imperialists continued to keep up a drum fire of attacks on the Administration. It was in 1901, indeed, that one of the fiercest of all their assaults appeared, when Mark Twain, who had heretofore kept silent, expressed his embittered disillusionment with imperialism in an article in the *North American Review* under the title "To the Person Sitting in Darkness."

Mark Twain now had nothing but scorn for what he called the Blessings-of-Civilization Trust. "Would it not be prudent," he asked, "to get our Civilization tools together and see how much stock is left on hand in the way of Glass Beads and Theology, and Maxim Guns and Hymn Books, and Trade Gin and Torches of Progress and Enlightenment . . . . and balance the books and arrive at the profit and loss . . . ?" He admitted that, wisely administered, the Blessings-of-Civilization Trust was "a Daisy," with more money, more territory, more sovereignty and other rewards than any other game being played, but he thought Christendom had been doing rather badly and was going to suffer for it. "She has been so eager to get every stake that appeared on the green cloth," he wrote, "that the People who Sit in Darkness have noticed it—they have noticed it and begun to show alarm. They have become suspicious of the Blessings of Civilization. More—they have begun to examine them. This is not well . . ."

So thought and felt the anti-imperialists, and as the dispatches from the Philippines told of American troops combating the Filipino insurgents very much as the Spanish had fought the Cuban rebels, there was no question that American public opinion was disturbed. But the country was settling back to the ways of peace; the Philippines were very far away. Moreover, what now could be done? When President McKinley appointed William Howard Taft to head the second Philippine

Commission in April 1900, Taft stated that he did not approve of American policy and did not want to see the United States hold the islands. "Neither do I," a disillusioned President is reputed to have replied, "but that isn't the question. We've got them."

In the meantime, a presidential campaign was getting under way and the colonial issue as a whole, regardless of the immediate fighting, once again entered into politics. The Republican platform upheld the imperialist program, the Democratic platform condemned it. While the controversy had always had strong partisan implications, it now became almost completely political. Nominating McKinley and Bryan as their respective standard-bearers, the two parties drew even sharper their basic differences.

With Bryan incessantly repeating the old refrain that the nation could not endure half republic and half colony, the Democrats declared the Philippine question to be the fundamental issue in the campaign. But while the Republicans defended their record all along the line, they were still not willing to let the Democrats build imperialism up too much. It had become very troublesome. Seeking to divert attention from what was actually taking place in the Philippines, the party managers stressed over and above everything else domestic prosperity. With only a passing glance at foreign and colonial policies, McKinley's persistent theme was that the return of the Democrats to power would revive free silver and endanger the economic progress being made under the Republicans.

It was once again Mark Hanna who was the driving force behind the party. He accepted imperialism in the blunt, realistic spirit that governed his attitude on every public question. He had become convinced that possession of the Philippines would serve to promote trade with China, and disregarding all the talk of duty, responsibility, and destiny, he stated: "If it is commercialism to want the possession of a strategic point giving the American people an opportunity to maintain a foothold in the markets of that great Eastern country, for God's sake let us have commercialism." But knowing that imperialism did not necessarily mean votes, he too stood on the domestic record. "There is only one issue in the campaign, my friends," Hanna told the country, "that is, let well enough alone."

Economic recovery decided the election. While the Democrats struggled valiantly to arouse greater interest in Bryan's demand for an end to imperialism, the Republicans' shrewd personification of McKinley as the "advance agent of prosperity" won the votes. The American people might be uncomfortable over what was happening to the Filipinos in "civilizing 'em with a krag," but they were highly satisfied with rising farm prices, increased production, and mounting employment on the home front. Their response to the campaign was to reelect McKinley with an overwhelming popular majority and to strengthen Republican control in both houses of Congress.

The results of the election could not possibly be interpreted as a mandate for imperialism. The Republican victory was no more than a re-affirmation of the conservative policies that had triumphed in the previous McKinley-Bryan campaign in 1896. Yet it meant endorsement of the imperialist program by default. It gave a further sanction—whatever the real feelings of the American people—to the overseas expansion that had been accepted with senate approval of the peace treaty with Spain.

Only one question remained: was there any validity to the anti-imperialist charge that the possession and government of such territory as the Philippines was unconstitutional? The Supreme Court grappled with this issue in a series of important decisions. There was no easy way to reconcile the principle of consent of the governed with American rule of a subject people and give Congress the powers it needed. But a way was found.

The Supreme Court developed the thesis that while the Constitution followed the flag, it did not necessarily carry with it a guarantee for Filipinos or Puerto Ricans of all the rights guaranteed the American people. The court made a distinction between what it called incorporated and unincorporated territories. The fundamental rights of life, liberty, and property extended to all territories, but in such unincorporated territories as Puerto Rico and the Philippines there was no need to go any further.

There was, for example, the constitutional provision that all duties, imposts, and excises should be uniform throughout the United States. This could be embarrassing for tariff-minded Republicans anxious to protect domestic producers against the competition of imports from the new territories. Through the decisions in the insular cases, the Supreme Court decreed that Congress could impose a tariff on Filipino and Puerto Rican imports, since no fundamental rights, as distinct from formal rights, were in any way involved.

The Supreme Court's definition of the new possessions as territory appurtenant and belonging to the United States, but not a part of the United States, had a certain mystical quality. Yet the import of the decision was clear. The United States could own and govern overseas colonies in the interests of the American empire.

The *World's Work* stated what it believed had happened, in its issue of July 1901: "Public opinion expressed at the polls, Congressional action, and now the decision of the Supreme Court have established the policy of expansion." Finley Peter Dunne was even more to the point when he had Mr. Dooley say in one of his most felicitous phrases that "whether the Constitution follows the flag or not, th' Supreme Court follows th' illiction returns."

Imperialism had won out all along the line. The United States had expanded overseas and acquired foreign colonies. It now faced the immense problem of what to do with these new territories, and how further to conduct a foreign policy that broke so sharply with all the traditions of the past. It was deeply enmeshed in world politics.

Subsequent events were nevertheless to show that, for all

the enthusiasm engendered by the Spanish-American War and the first intoxication of empire, the American people were not yet so fully freed of their isolationist habit of mind as their contemporary attitude suggested. There was actually to be a rapid retreat from the expansionism of these days, rather than any further advance. But that was in the future. On the threshold of the new century, the triumphant imperialists rather than the agonizing little band of anti-imperialists, seemed to have envisioned America's destiny. The Power that ruled the Pacific, Beveridge had declared, would rule the world, and with the Philippines in its possession, that "Power is and will forever be the American Republic."

CHAPTER XII

ESTABLISHING AN EMPIRE

SO IT WAS THAT THROUGH THE EVENTS OF 1898 THE UNITED States acquired Hawaii, Guam, and Puerto Rico as colonies or dependencies; assumed the responsibility of assuring the independence of Cuba through forcing Spain to relinquish her sovereignty over that island; and in the Philippines undertook to establish its authority in an archipelago whose people were in revolt against American rule. As the great debate continued to rage over the validity of its colonial policy, the McKinley administration was confronted with the arduous task of providing for the government of these new possessions.

There were no very great difficulties in the case of the smaller islands. Hawaii became an incorporated territory through the Organic Act of 1900, and its increasingly predominant white population took over the self-government of the islands in full enjoyment of the rights of American citizenship. Guam remained a naval station administered directly by the Navy Department. Puerto Rico, under the terms of the Foraker Act, was made an unincorporated territory with an elected legislature and an executive council and governor appointed by the President of the United States. In contrast to the relative ease of these arrangements, however, Cuba and the Philippine Islands—from quite different points of view—involved important and confused issues.

Indeed, the entire pattern of colonial and foreign activity in which the United States found itself engaged at the turn of the century was immensely complicated, standing out in striking contrast to the virtual freedom from such problems that the nation had experienced prior to the war with Spain. For fighting an insurrection in the Philippines and making provision for a new government in Cuba did not mark the limits of new and unexpected overseas interests. As we shall subsequently see, these years also witnessed further involvements in Latin America, centering about the proposed transisthmian canal, and the adoption of an interventionist policy in eastern Asia based upon the principle of the Open Door in China. The public hardly knew what to expect as the newspapers heralded these new developments involving a nation that had formerly cared so little for what went on outside its own continental borders.

Popular interest, as reflected in the press, alternately flared up and subsided as particular events caught the imagination. Yet even when the headlines told of some new shift in foreign and colonial policies, or recounted what briefly might appear to be critical situations abroad, these newspaper stories were still generally overshadowed by those that told of domestic developments. The American people could be only momentarily diverted from the developing battles over trusts and railroad regulation, the always absorbing interplay of domestic politics, and other incidents on the home front. But if many people were already looking back rather nostalgically to the days before the lure of overseas expansion had led the country along such strange and unfamiliar paths, those charged with the formulation of policy could not escape their responsibilities. Once the nation had shown its willingness to accept the terms of peace concluded under President McKinley's direction at Paris, there was no alternative to doing whatever could be done to establish the American empire upon a firm and stable basis.

There was never any idea—and it was sustaining proof of the underlying idealism that had led to war with Spain—of rescinding the pledge of Cuban freedom implicit in the Teller Amendment of 1898. While President McKinley declared authoritatively in December 1899 that "the new Cuba . . . . must needs be bound to us by ties of singular intimacy and strength if its enduring welfare is to be assured," he was fully determined to fulfill the American promise that government and control of the island would be restored as speedily as possible to the Cuban people.

The European powers did not put much stock in this self-denying attitude toward the fruits of victory. The general expressions of foreign opinion, as reported in the American press, were almost universally based on the theory that the United States would of course annex Cuba, as well as Puerto Rico, and in all probability seek further colonies both in the Caribbean and the Pacific. A cartoon in one German paper graphically reflected this feeling. It showed Uncle Sam reaching out with wide arms to encircle the globe and saying: "I can't quite reach around—but that may come later." The English *Saturday Review*, warning its readers that it was not safe "to count upon the honeyed expressions of American Senators, who vow their States will never turn megalomaniac," saw the United States trying to extend the Monroe Doctrine throughout the globe.

The military occupation of Cuba after the close of hostilities seemed to give some substance to such European misgivings. Its purpose, however, was to help the Cuban people get on their own feet and to prepare the way for self-government and independence. The United States at once undertook far-reaching administrative reforms, set up a more effective judiciary, initiated an extensive program of public works, provided a new educational system and, perhaps most importantly, launched an island-wide campaign to foster better health conditions and provide modern sanitation.

From December 1899 until May 1902 the military governor of Cuba was General Leonard Wood, the one-time leader of the Rough Riders under whom Roosevelt had served during the war. A self-willed and forceful man, who inclined to the autocratic and had an unusual penchant for controversy, he nevertheless proved himself to be an exceptionally able colonial administrator. It was the judgment of Cuba's foremost historian that Wood worked with complete sincerity, as well as energy and vision, to prepare the Cuban people for democratic government.

The most dramatic phase of the American occupation, and one which throughout received General Wood's full support, was the campaign to raise the standards of public health and to eradicate the scourge of yellow fever. The conditions that confronted the military authorities were appalling. Havana was described in one contemporary report as "a miasma of odors, a hotbed of disease, not only of yellow fever, but typhoid, malaria, dysentery, and the maladies usually associated with filth." Major William C. Gorgas, an army doctor with twenty years' experience, was the health officer in charge of sanitation and succeeded in doing a great deal to clean up Havana and other cities. Nevertheless yellow fever, with some fourteen hundred cases reported in 1900, defied all efforts for its control.

A special commission made up of four army surgeons— Walter Reed, James Carroll, Jesse W. Lazear, and Aristides Agramonte—was consequently appointed to study the disease. Exploring the thesis already propounded by a Cuban physician, Dr. Carlos J. Finley, that the yellow fever bacillus was transmitted not through personal contact but by the bite of the Stegomyia mosquito, these men heroically subjected themselves to various tests and experiments which included letting themselves be bitten by this mosquito. The experiments, which caused the death of Dr. Lazear, clearly demonstrated that the Stegomyia was the host of the yellow fever bacillus and the probable agency in the spread of the disease.

The question still remained whether infection might not be brought about in other ways than by a mosquito bite, and consequently further tests were made. Three American soldiers voluntarily lived for twenty days in a small house in which everything, including the bed clothes and the pajamas worn by the volunteer guinea pigs, had been contaminated by the vomitings and excrement of yellow fever victims. No one of the three volunteers contracted the disease. The evidence appeared to be conclusive that there was no transmittal through personal contact.

Armed with the now certain knowledge that the Stegomyia mosquito was the real key to the yellow fever epidemic, Major Gorgas promptly launched an amazingly thorough campaign for this particular mosquito's eradication. It was generally found in settled communities. In addition to draining swamps and water courses, the military authorities consequently called upon the housewives of Havana and other cities to account for every container that could possibly provide a breeding place. Cisterns and wells were screened and all open water covered with a film of oil to kill the larvae. The Stegomyia mosquito was virtually eliminated from Cuba through these measures and the incidence of yellow fever precipitately declined until, within a few years, the disease had to all intents and purposes disappeared.

The improved sanitation introduced under Major Gorgas also helped to reduce other diseases, including malaria, and the general improvement in health conditions throughout Cuba was perhaps the outstanding contribution of the American occupation. Moreover, the work of the yellow fever commission, as directed by Major Walter Reed, reached out far beyond Cuba. Without its discoveries and the consequent control of yellow fever, such later operations as the construction of the Panama Canal might well have been impossible.

The McKinley administration was concerned not only with the reconstruction of Cuba and with training her people for self-government. It wished to establish those "ties of singular intimacy" that would enable the United States to assure the continued stability of an independent government when the occupation forces were withdrawn. This was felt to be essential, both in the interests of Cuba and in those of the United States, and inevitably became an important political issue.

The man most responsible for the development of American policy in Cuba on these broader grounds, and also for the administration of the recently acquired possessions in the Pacific, was the new Secretary of War. In July 1899 the President had appointed Elihu Root to succeed the thoroughly incompetent Russell A. Alger, and for the next few years Root devoted his great talents, apart from his program for completely reorganizing the Army, to the task of working out the relationships among the component parts of the American empire. A brilliant lawyer, keen and incisive, and an imaginative and creative administrator, Root was to prove himself a statesman of the highest order. Rather cold and austere, sometimes described as a thinking machine, he had at the same time very human qualities and his severity was tempered by a ready wit.

Countless stories reveal his sense of humor, and many of them show how much Root enjoyed directing his ironic shafts against Roosevelt. For while he greatly admired the man who in 1901 was to become his chief and was always on the most friendly personal terms with him, the Secretary of War could not restrain himself when he felt President Roosevelt was becoming too pontifical. "The thing I most admire about you, Theodore," Root is reported to have commented on one such occasion, "is your discovery of the Ten Commandments." Another story relates to William Howard Taft. When Taft was first in the Philippines (already weighing some 300 pounds), he reported to the Secretary of War about a long horseback trip he had taken in the islands. Root at once cabled: "Fine. How's the horse?"

Root had not originally been imperialist-minded, but he had come to believe early in 1898 in the necessity for intervention in Cuba (warning a friend in the cabinet on April 2 that "the President should lead and not be pushed"), and he was prepared to accept in full the new responsibilities devolving upon the United States as a result of victory over Spain. Although he believed that Cuba was entitled to independence, he was just as fully convinced that the United States should retain the right of intervention should the new island republic prove unable to keep its own house in order. His ideas on Cuban-American relations were first embodied in instructions to General Wood, and then more definitely set forth in an amendment to the army appropriation bill of 1901 proposed by Senator Orville Platt of Connecticut. The most important provisions of this amendment were that the United States should be empowered to intervene for the protection of life, liberty, and property whenever the future Cuban government failed to provide such protection, and should be further granted the right to maintain American naval stations in the island. Moreover, it was stipulated that these conditions should be incorporated in the Cuban constitution.

The delegates at the national convention charged with drawing up the Cuban constitution at first refused to incorporate these provisions. There was widespread opposition to any concessions that could be construed as a violation of Cuban sovereignty, and a commission sent to Washington argued strongly against granting the United States the right of intervention. Secretary Root, however, held his ground. Through a skillful mixture of firmness and persuasion—in which firmness perhaps somewhat dominated persuasion—he won his point. The Cuban delegates gave in and on June 12, 1901, the national convention finally adopted a constitution in which the provisions of the Platt Amendment were incorporated. Two years later, moreover, these special rights—that of intervention as well as maintenance of a naval base—were included in the Cuban-American treaty of May 22, 1903.

If Root's position revealed a fundamentally conservative approach to colonial issues, he was completely realistic in the circumstances of the time. Under the Platt Amendment the status of Cuba became for the time being that of a semi-protectorate, but in assuming as it did the responsibility of assuring the independence of the new nation, the United States had somehow to have the authority to act should Cuba be dangerously threatened from either without or within. The proof of American good faith clearly lay in how the United States operated under the terms of the Platt Amendment in future years.

A still skeptical Europe continued to regard these developments as no more than a screen for an assertive imperialism. The Paris *Temps* declared: "Of the independence of Cuba nothing remains; of the promises of the United States equally little." The Cubans would have to reconcile themselves to the fact, it later added, that they had only "exchanged the yoke of Spain for the tutelage of the United States." In Berlin, the *Kreuz-Zeitung* interpreted the Platt Amendment as "the beginning of absolute control by the Americans," while the *Frankfurter Zeitung* flatly stated that "annexation is not far away." English newspapers were generally less critical but the *Saturday Review,* again commenting sarcastically on the American people's "admiration of their own faithfulness and magnanimity," pointed out that Cuba in most respects remained "undisguisedly under the thumb of Washington."

The United States did continue to exercise an often decisive influence in Cuban affairs; it intervened under the terms of the Platt Amendment on several occasions. But even though the island's status when it first became self-governing was subject to the restraints that the United States had insisted should be incorporated in the Cuban constitution, and the dominance of American economic interests was a further restriction upon its complete freedom, this was still a far cry from the annexation that had once been the imperialists' bright dream and the universal expectation of other nations. The withdrawal of the bulk of American occupation forces in 1902 meant that the United

States had fulfilled the pledge made on taking up arms against Spain. It had taken over Puerto Rico and established a new sphere of influence in the Caribbean, but it had stopped short of Cuban annexation.

Helping the Cuban people to set up an independent government was an easier task than persuading the Filipinos to accept American rule. The insurrection which had broken out on the eve of ratification of the peace treaty was to prove far more costly to the United States, in both lives and money, than the war with Spain.

It was not entirely suppressed until long months after Cuba had become an independent, self-governing nation. There was from every point of view something cruelly ironical in the contrasting picture in the early 1900s between what was taking place in Cuba and the melancholy course of events in the Philippines. In theory, the seemingly irreconcilable contradiction in policy was bridged by the concept of "benevolent assimilation" as applied to the Philippines. For all its promise of eventual self-government, however, this program first demanded complete submission to American authority. The Filipinos could never understand why they should be treated differently from the Cubans.

As early as January 1899, President McKinley sent a special commission to Manila under the chairmanship of Dr. Jacob Gould Schurman, president of Cornell, to investigate the entire situation, and the next year he put William Howard Taft, at this time a judge in Ohio, in charge of a second civilian commission. The authority in the islands was vested for the time being in the Army, however, and the task of putting down the Filipino revolt was the difficult assignment of General Elwell S. Otis. He made the double mistake of underestimating the strength of the resistance movement, and yet at the same time moving much too cautiously against it. General Arthur MacArthur (the father of an even more noted American general) soon succeeded Otis, and his more vigorous tactics led to the prompt capture of the Filipino capital. Truce negotiations were then begun in the spring of 1899 and for a time there were hopes that they would lead to peace. But no agreement could be reached. The insurgents again took up arms and, while too weak to renew organized resistance on Luzon, they fled to the forested hills of the smaller islands where the American forces found themselves involved in bloody guerilla warfare that seemed to have no end. It was to prove necessary to increase General MacArthur's command to some 75,000 troops, as fighting continued in the dense tropical jungles.

General Aguinaldo, the Filipino leader, showed no signs of being willing to surrender. This active, energetic patriot, a fiery little man weighing no more than 115 pounds, was dedicated to the cause of Philippine independence. He was variously judged in the United States. The anti-imperialists accepted him as a selfless national leader; the more rabid imperialists considered him "a shifty Oriental, with all an Oriental's vanity and with the treachery inherent in his Malay blood." How difficult it was for some American people to evaluate a Filipino—rebel or patriot—was reflected in a proposal made after the close of hostilities. A commercial showman proposed to the War Department to "lease" Aguinaldo for a nationwide tour, the profits to be divided between the exhibitor and the United States Government!

As the savage warfare went on, reports continued to filter home that American troops as well as Filipinos were resorting to terroristic tactics. In their pursuit of the guerillas into the hills, the Americans were said to be burning and destroying native villages, indiscriminately slaughtering their inhabitants. The charge was also made that captured natives were sometimes subjected to the water cure—tying them down and pouring water down their throats—to force them to divulge military information.

The congressional investigation to which these reports of atrocities later led showed that most of the charges brought against the American troops were either untrue or grossly exaggerated. Under the gruelling cross-examination of Senator Beveridge, many of the witnesses broke down and admitted that their information was based on hearsay and rumor. Nevertheless there was indisputable evidence of some atrocities and of occasional use of the water cure. The American troops were fighting fire with fire. Taft might speak of "the little brown brother," but this was not the view of the men fighting in the hot, steamy jungles and seeing their buddies ambushed, killed, and mutilated by the Filipinos. As a popular song of the day expressed it:

> He may be a brother of Big Bill Taft;
> But he ain't no brother of mine.

Jungle fighting could not easily be patterned on the accepted rules of civilized warfare, but the proved atrocities nevertheless horrified the American conscience.

The ultimate result of the campaign was inevitable. The Filipinos were gradually worn down by the unceasing and relentless pressure of superior and far better equipped American forces. They were driven farther and farther into the hills, and in March 1901 Aguinaldo was finally captured. While there was still to be sporadic fighting for another two years, the loss of their leader really broke the back of the insurgents' resistance, and the scattered guerilla bands one by one surrendered to the American forces. Aguinaldo himself accepted what he could no longer prevent, swore allegiance to the United States, and was in time to become a loyal friend of his former enemies. The long and bloody revolt came to an end; the Philippines were at length pacified.

Upon the return of the first Philippine Commission in December 1899, Dr. Schurman had reported that in his judgment the islands were not ready for complete self-government, but he did advocate that they should be given some form of territorial status rather than be maintained as a colony. He believed that civilian control should replace military rule as soon as possible in spite of the continuing guerilla warfare.

President McKinley approved the report and was ready to go as far as he could in carrying out its recommendations. The second commission, headed by Taft, was consequently instructed to arrange for the transfer of government from the military as rapidly as possible.

Taft found it very difficult to deal with General MacArthur, who was firmly convinced that the Filipinos needed bayonet treatment for at least a decade. He was not to be diverted, however, from his assignment. Acting on instructions from Secretary Root, who in the Philippines as in Cuba was the major architect of American policy, he assumed over-all authority in the islands on July 4, 1900. With the great body of Filipinos now willing to accept American rule, Taft felt certain they would react favorably to a friendly, conciliatory program. Two months after his first assumption of authority, his civilian commission was formally installed as the islands' government.

Congress confirmed these measures, assuming all military, civil, and judicial jurisdiction in the Philippines through an amendment to the army appropriation bill introduced in March 1901 —the month Aguinaldo was captured. This bill also provided for the election of a Filipino assembly to serve as the lower house in a legislature, in which the American commission would serve as the upper house, and for appointment of a civil governor —a post first filled by Taft—with broad executive powers.

The Philippine Organic Act, adopted in July 1902, thereupon formalized these measures for a bicameral legislature and an appointed governor; provided for two resident Philippine commissioners in Washington; declared a full amnesty for all insurgents, and established the status of the islands as an unincorporated territory of the United States. With only minor modifications, this settlement of the political and constitutional problems relating to the Philippines remained in effect until the extension of additional rights and privileges some fourteen years later through the Jones Act.

"So far from having 'sapped the foundations' of free popular government at home by the course taken in the Philippines,"

Roosevelt was to state in reviewing these achievements in his acceptance of the presidential nomination in 1904, "we have been spreading its knowledge, and teaching its practice, among peoples to whom it had never before been anything but an empty name." He quoted with admiration McKinley's earlier statement that "our flag has not lost its gift of benediction in its world-wide journey to these shores." There was justification for this pride in colonial administration. The United States was doing an effective job in the Philippines. Still, it was to be another forty years before their people finally attained their persistent dream of complete freedom.

While the United States was helping to set up an independent government in Cuba and limited self-government in the Philippines, possession was taken of another Pacific island. This was American Samoa.

The tripartite control over the Samoan Islands adopted at the Berlin Conference a decade earlier was still as unsatisfactory as when Cleveland had so severely criticized it in 1893. The commissioners sent out by the United States, Great Britain, and Germany had finally succeeded in quelling the recurrent island warfare, and had persuaded the native chiefs and warriors to return to their homes, but no one of the foreign envoys had any confidence in the existing system. "I cannot forbear to impress upon my Government," the American commissioner reported in 1899, "not only the propriety but the necessity of dissolving the partnership of nations which has no precedent for its creation nor reason for its continuance."

Yet in spite of a desire to give up tripartite control, the United States was unwilling to withdraw from Samoa altogether. The relinquishment of American rights to Pago Pago, President McKinley stated, "was not to be thought of as regards the needs of our Navy or the interests of our growing commerce with the East."

The United States consequently accepted happily a German proposal that the tripartite protectorate be abandoned and the Samoan Islands divided up. Negotiations were initiated to this end and an agreement was reached on December 2, 1899. The United States obtained the island of Tutuila with the harbor of Pago Pago, which was all that it really wanted; Germany took over the remaining islands, and Great Britain was compensated through the cession by Germany of the Tonga Islands, part of the Solomons, and certain other territorial adjustments.

The convention embodying this agreement was approved by the Senate without much debate in the midst of more excited controversy over other aspects of colonial policy. Senator Pettigrew commented bitterly: "We blot out, then, a sovereign nation, a people with whom we have treaty relations, and divide the spoils." The proponents of Samoan annexation, however, hardly deigned to answer his charges. Secretary Hay was convinced that the United States had gained more than either Great Britain or Germany in the new arrangement. Pago Pago was "absolutely indispensable to us," he declared, and in conjunction with the other new Pacific possessions, its retention as a naval base indicated that American interests in the Pacific were "destined to infinite development."

The public hardly knew what was happening in regard to Samoa and cared little about the disposition of the islands. Its earlier concern had been largely in reaction to what was reported to have been the aggressive policies of Germany. When the press commented at all on the settlement with Germany and England, it was to stress the benefit to the country of finally being free of "the preposterous Samoan entanglement." While the New York *Tribune* reflected administration sentiment in calling attention to the enhanced value of Pago Pago, with the further development of trade and commerce in the Pacific, the *Times* expressed a more general view in going no further than to state its gratification that at long last "we have dissolved our partnership with Germany."

From one point of view it was less surprising that the United States annexed so distant an island as Samoa as part of its "Pacific work" than that it did not seize the opportunity to acquire other naval bases in the Pacific. No attempt was made to secure Spanish-held islands in the Marianas or Carolines, other than Guam. There was some talk among naval officers of the desirability of additional island outposts, but when Spain sold her Pacific holdings to Germany, the United States made no protest whatsoever. Captain Mahan himself was later to write that he had not been interested in further expansion and refused "a suggestion to use my supposed influence against her [Germany's] acquisition of the Carolines."

The future implications of such forbearance could hardly be foreseen. At the close of World War I, both the Carolines and the Marianas were made mandates of the League of Nations—with Japan the mandatory power. Upon the outbreak of Pacific war in 1941, Guam was consequently an unprotected hostage in enemy territory and fell an easy victim to Japanese attack. Before they could carry the war to the western Pacific, the United States naval forces were confronted with the terrible task of breaking through the island ramparts Japan had secretly built up as a defensive shield for her far eastern expansion.

Here then was the new empire of which the expansionists had dreamed, with the long arm of American power encircling the Caribbean and stretching out across the Pacific to the shores of eastern Asia. Had it all been the inevitable working out of "a cosmic tendency" against which men and nations were helpless? Could wiser councils and more determined leadership have somehow kept the United States off its imperial course?

The analysis earlier suggested may be repeated. A ground-swell of imperialist sentiment was zealously built up by an eager band of militant expansionists, who skillfully directed it along lines which at least temporarily caught the popular fancy. It was compounded of a sense of racial superiority, economic ambition, international rivalry, and an assertive nationalism. There was neither the will nor perhaps even the wish on the part of the President, charged with the formulation of foreign policy, to withstand such pressures. Imperialism was not inevitable in the form that it assumed, but the forces underlying the movement of 1898 had gathered what seemed to be an almost irresistible momentum.

Yet if the immediate consequences of the Spanish-American War appeared to be a denial of every basic principle of republicanism, there was more substance than the anti-imperialists would ever admit to the expansionists' claims that in acquiring overseas colonies, the United States would speedily extend to them the benefits of a democratic way of life. The colonial policies followed by the United States were liberal and beneficent; their end result was to be complete self-government or independence for the possessions so cavalierly acquired in the excitement and enthusiasm of 1898. The nation succumbed—unhappily, in the light of the traditions of an earlier day—to the imperialist spirit of the times, but it would ultimately redeem itself.

And if this had not been the road through which the United States entered global politics, some other path would have been found. It had become a great power through its own inherent strength, with or without colonies. Under no circumstances could it have long continued to stand aloof from the rest of the world in the pattern of twentieth century life. The acquisition of new territory was not inevitable, but there was no escaping the larger results that flowed from national expansion.

CHAPTER XIII

THE OPEN DOOR POLICY

ON AUGUST 24, 1899, SECRETARY OF STATE HAY WROTE FROM New Hampshire, where he was resting from the heat and burden of a Washington summer, to William Rockhill, currently serving as a State Department advisor on far eastern affairs:

"If you have time between now and next Wednesday to set down your views on this question—in the form of a draft instruction to Mr. Choate, Mr. White, Mr. Tower, and Gen. Porter —I would be greatly obliged. . . . I am taking a good deal for granted—your presence in Washington, your leisure, and your inclination to give us a *coup d'épaule*. But if it should not be convenient, all right."

The question at issue was a pronouncement of policy in regard to the Open Door in China. In this seemingly casual fashion there was set in motion a train of events (for it proved convenient for Rockhill to carry out the task assigned to him in writing instructions for the American ambassadors at Europe's capitals) that led to the formulation of an American position in foreign affairs second in importance only to the Monroe Doctrine.

The concept of an Open Door in China has a long history. From the earliest days of foreign trade with Canton at the close of the eighteenth century, the American merchants doing business in that thriving oriental port insisted upon their right to enjoy privileges equal to those extended to the merchants of any other country. They asked for the support of their government, and they were to receive it. The commercial treaties negotiated with China invariably included a most-favored nation clause—that is, the extension to the United States of all privileges granted the most-favored nation. Here, in effect, was the genesis of the Open Door doctrine as a guarantee of equality of opportunity for all nations seeking a share of China's trade and commerce.

The first contacts between the United States and China were touched with romance, and awakened visions of the riches and wealth to be gained from oriental trade never to be wholly dimmed by later disappointments. The barks and brigantines and other little sailing vessels that made their long voyages around Cape Horn and across the broad reaches of the Pacific were never of more than a few hundred tons' burden, and were manned by youthful crews of adventurous men and boys. Sometimes these vessels sailed directly to Canton with their holds laden with boxes of silver dollars, casks of ginseng, hogsheads of tobacco, sugar, and good New England rum. More often they stopped en route somewhere along the rocky coast of Northwest America and traded cargoes of muskets, blankets, rum, and trinkets for the rich and glossy sea otter furs collected by the coast Indians and so much in demand by Chinese mandarins. No matter what they took to Canton, however, they returned to the United States heavily laden with tea, and also nankeens, silk shawls, embroideries, lacquer, and chinaware. Many a vessel in the old China trade made profits for its owners representing a complete recovery of their original investment in a single voyage.

At the time of the Anglo-Chinese war in the early 1840s——the so-called Opium War—the American merchants in the China trade first became fearful that, in the terms of peace, Great Britain would insist upon special privileges that would deprive them of their valuable market. As a consequence the United States dispatched a diplomatic mission to China in 1844, and Caleb Cushing negotiated the Treaty of Wanghia. The Imperial Government agreed that, in any port opened up for trade, the Americans would enjoy all those rights and privileges which might be granted to Great Britain or any other nation. And in each successive development in the foreign relations of China, the United States continued to insist upon this equality in all commercial matters.

By the close of the 1890s, trade with China had by no means developed as early enthusiasts had anticipated. It actually amounted to no more than something like two per cent of the total of United States foreign commerce. Yet the vision of the tremendous potentialities of the China market persisted and in commercial circles, especially among the firms exporting cotton goods, there remained the belief that nothing was more important than keeping this market open. The considerable role that the desire to promote far eastern commercial interests had played in overseas expansion has already been noted. The forthright statements made by Senators Hanna and Beveridge upon the importance of the China market in absorbing the surplus of American manufactures clearly reflected the views of the business community. Lodge's declaration that it was from this Eastern trade "we must draw our future prosperity" found a ready response among merchants and exporters. Articles appearing in both popular and business magazines in 1898 strongly emphasized the potential value of commerce with China, and the imperative necessity of giving it adequate protection.

Among the most significant of such articles was one by Charles A. Conant, published in the *Forum*, which closely analyzed the new "struggle for commercial empire" and emphatically maintained that the United States could not afford to adhere in such circumstances to a policy of isolation. Nothing was said about the potentialities of further expansion within the country or of the opportunities for investment funds in promoting industry at home. The domestic market for finished goods, Conant said, had "long since been more than supplied." It had become an economic necessity to look abroad, and China was the one part of the world where the United States could find a satisfactory outlet for both manufactures and capital. If it hesitated to safeguard its interests, the nation was lost. "As the result of an accident in Havana harbor," Conant concluded, "the path of destiny has suddenly been opened for us in the East."

The contemporary division of the huge, unwieldy Chinese Empire into foreign spheres of influence and the furious scramble of the European powers for special concessions, as we have already seen, again created very real alarm among economic writers as to what might happen to American trade. The controlling influence exercised by Great Britain in the Yangtze Valley, the position occupied by Germany in Shantung, and especially Russian encroachments in Manchuria, appeared imminently to threaten national trade interests. Commercial circles insisted ever more strongly upon a vigorous China policy, if the economic advantages supposed to flow from the occupation of the Philippines were to be realized.

The original agitation for specific action to maintain the Open Door nevertheless came from British rather than American sources. For while England held a favored position in the Yangtze, she wanted to block any further extension of German and Russian influence that might lead to discriminatory treatment against British trade in other parts of China. So often was this issue debated in Parliament that a speaker in August 1898 referred to the Open Door as "that famous phrase that has been quoted and requoted *ad nauseam.*" Hoping to enlist American cooperation in some move to ensure trade equality, the British Foreign Office, in March 1898, sounded out the United States on the possibility of joint action.

The McKinley administration rejected all such overtures. Throughout 1898 it was absorbed in the problems of war and peace with Spain, and furthermore the President did not believe that American interests were actually threatened by the establishment of foreign spheres of influence in China. In his annual message to Congress in December, McKinley expressly stated that there did not appear to be any prospect that American commerce would be prejudiced by discriminatory treatment. The assurances that he had received from the powers to this effect, he said, "obviated the need of our country becoming an actor in the scene."

However, as the prospects for trade with China—in spite of McKinley's reassuring words—seemed in fact to be increasingly endangered by the European powers' policies, the pressure on the administration for some sort of action rapidly mounted. The press widely interpreted the establishment of foreign spheres of influence as "a conscious or an instinctive move of all Europe against all America, in competition for the markets of the world." It was charged, as in editorials in the *New York Times,* that American interests in China were not being "intelligently represented or adequately appreciated by the State Department," and that the McKinley administration did not appear willing to "lift a finger to protect our interests in the East."

This campaign was further re-enforced, after a second British request for cooperation was rejected early in 1899, by the persuasive speeches and writings of Lord Charles Beresford, a representative of the Associated Chambers of Commerce of Great Britain. On a tour throughout the United States, Beresford urged not only the advantage but the virtual necessity, in the common interests of the United States and Great Britain, for some concerted move whereby the powers would by mutual agreement undertake to maintain "free and equal commercial relations for all time in the Orient." He favored the strongest possible ties between the United States and Great Britain as the only means whereby this program could be carried through, and China herself saved from a complete breakup. And even though this propaganda did not succeed in bringing about joint action, it played its part in popularizing the idea of the Open Door among those interested in far eastern problems.

Even more telling pressure for a vigorous China policy now came from the American Asiatic Association, the spearhead of a group of textile companies importantly concerned with the Eastern trade in cotton goods. It deluged the State Department with memorials and petitions urging that something be done, and brought such direct influence as it could upon the Secretary of State himself. And the Association soon began to feel it was getting somewhere. A notice to its membership as early as March 1899 stated that the McKinley administration finally appeared to be convinced that action of some sort was necessary, and that what now appeared most important was to concentrate upon "the education of the people, the press, and the politicians."

These were the considerations, primarily economic in character and growing out of America's historic interest in the China trade, that provided the background for Hay's request that Rockhill set down his views on the Open Door.

Rockhill had discussed policy toward China with the Secretary of State during the early summer of 1899, and it was the ideas that he had already presented in meetings and correspondence which now led Hay to ask for the further elaboration of his views. These ideas in turn had been suggested to Rockhill by a close friend, Alfred Hippisley, an Englishman in the employ of the Chinese Imperial Maritime Customs Service, who had happened to be visiting that summer in Baltimore. But although he was an Englishman, Hippisley was in no sense speaking for the British Government. His primary concern appears to have been China, and the maintenance of her independence in the face of threatened partition. He found in Rockhill someone equally sympathetic to the idea that anything done to support the Open Door should so far as possible sustain China's political integrity as well as protect American trade, and the two men further agreed that instead of acting in concert with Great Britain, the United States should itself take the initiative in promoting any new policy. Indeed, by this time England was no longer interested in joint action with the United States. She had reversed her earlier position and was now seeking to safeguard her interests by exacting additional concessions from China—such as the lease of Kowloon—and in further consolidating her position in the Yangtze. How completely independent of any British influence was the project being developed by Hippisley and Rockhill is further suggested by the fact that, throughout this hot August, the British ambassador was happily and unconcernedly vacationing at Newport. Moreover, in writing Hay on one occasion, Rockhill explicitly stated that the best policy for the United States was "not a British one—for England is as great an offender in China as Russia itself."

The Rockhill-Hippisley plan called for the United States to ask all the powers engaged in trade with China, which would of course include Great Britain, to declare themselves in favor of commercial equality throughout the empire. They did not propose any interference with existing spheres of influence, which would be specifically recognized. This program was limited to an undertaking on the part of each power concerned to forswear any discrimination against another's nationals in enforcement of the commercial regulations for which it was responsible, and to acknowledge the right of the Chinese government to collect all customs duties on the existing treaty tariff.

Rockhill and Hippisley would have liked to go a good deal further. "You know what my views are about the position the United States should take in China," Rockhill wrote Hippisley on August 3; "I would like to see it make a declaration in some form or other, which would be understood by China as a pledge on our part to assist in maintaining the integrity of the Empire." But both men realized that any such commitment on the part of the United States was politically unrealistic and had no chance whatsoever of obtaining administration support. They felt they had to restrict their policy to upholding the Open Door for trade rather than venturing any further afield and therefore, as Hippisley said, held their proposals down to what they felt to be the irreducible minimum in enlisting Secretary Hay's support.

Rockhill and Hippisley were not at first too sanguine about winning approval for their plan. While he was still the American ambassador in London, Hay had favored cooperation with Great Britain in China and had reluctantly given it up only because of what he believed to be the "senseless prejudices" of his countrymen against anything that might be construed as an Anglo-American alliance. If such cooperation was impractical, he was apparently quite willing to let the matter drop. Although naturally opposed to the dismemberment of China, his concern with the Open Door would appear to have been secondary to his deep interest in an Anglo-American rapprochement. Moreover, President McKinley was still unconvinced of the need to take any action on the matter, and there is no evidence that the idea of a more positive policy in China entered significantly into his thinking at this time.

The pressures being exercised by those associations and firms

which had a direct economic interest in China were nevertheless intensified at the very time that Rockhill and Hippisley were
pushing their own particular program. Hay could not help being influenced by these developments, and he was also fully
aware of the broader implications of the United States assuming a position of leadership in Asia. Two developments in mid-
August, moreover, once again brought far eastern affairs into the
limelight. Jacob Gould Schurman, returning from the Philippines, gave out a widely publicized interview in which he
heavily stressed the importance of the China trade, and the Russian Government announced that it was opening up its concession at Talienwan, in Manchuria, as a free port. Such evidence
of both the need for action in China and of possible Russian acceptance of the Open Door principle, Hippisley enthusiastically wrote Rockhill, should certainly persuade the McKinley
administration to act.

Hippisley also shrewdly suggested, for the benefit of Hay,
that the Administration could win a real political advantage
by making a move certain of winning popular support. "The
public need know nothing of the steps taken by the Sec. of
State," he wrote, "till the negotiations have been consummated,
and the announcement then that the U.S. had secured China's
independence and so served the cause of peace and civilization
would be a trump card for the admin. and crush all the life out
of the anti-imperialism agitation of Bryan, Croker & Co."

Hippisley was in effect saying, with a keen understanding of
the popular temper, that if the Open Door policy were presented
as a move to secure China's independence, as well as to protect trade and commerce, it would appeal to the idealistic spirit
of America, whatever its economic implications. It might well
serve to convince the public that the Administration's policies,
under such heavy attack so far as the Philippines were concerned, were not those of selfish aggrandizement. Here was a
way in which the new-found power of the United States could
be exerted in defense of the freedom of a great and friendly people.

Rockhill was more cautious. He was still waiting to hear from Hay in answer to the various memoranda he had already submitted to him, and was reluctant to make any further move. He was indeed thinking of a no more drastic step than publication of an article outlining his and Hippisley's proposals. And it was just at this point that there appeared, almost from the blue, that unexpected letter from the Secretary of State asking him to set forth his views in the form of draft instructions to the American ambassadors to the great powers.

The notes promptly drawn up by Rockhill in compliance with this request conformed almost word for word with the suggestions already made in the Rockhill-Hippisley memoranda, and they were approved by Hay, with the concurrence of President McKinley, virtually without change. The State Department forwarded them on September 6, 1899, to Great Britain, Germany, and Russia, and then somewhat later to Japan, France, and Italy.

These notes—to recapitulate—specifically asked for assurances from the powers that, within their respective spheres of influence in China, they would not interfere with any treaty port or vested interest; would apply the Chinese treaty tariff to all merchandise and allow all duties to be collected by the Chinese Government; and would in no way discriminate in favor of their own nationals in respect to harbor dues or railroad charges.

The request made by the United States, with its acceptance of existing spheres of foreign influence in China, could hardly have been a more moderate one. Nevertheless, in pursuing even so limited a goal in support of the Open Door, the United States was stepping out of its traditional role of non-interference in affairs outside its borders. It was attempting to exercise the leverage found in its new world position to influence the powers' policy in eastern Asia. If overseas expansion had marked the abandonment of the physical isolation of the nineteenth century, here was a further demonstration that the United States would no longer stand aloof from world affairs.

The American people—as Hippisley had suggested—were not informed of the contents of the Open Door notes or of their actual dispatch. Some two months after they had been sent, the *Literary Digest* referred to a "widely credited report" of some move to insure the Open Door which had been little thought of in this country, and on December 17 the *New York Times* noted rather obscurely that it had learned from "an authentic source" that Germany—but no other power—had been asked to give assurances on the Open Door. It was not until two weeks later, although still without official confirmation, that the *Times* ran a front-page story stating that negotiations had been completed by Secretary Hay to obtain from all the powers a common understanding for "a continued open-door policy." On January 3, 1900, the further announcement was made that Hay had stated at a cabinet meeting that his negotiations had been "eminently successful," and favorable responses to his notes on China policy had been received from all the powers except Italy, whose answer was expected momentarily.

The editorial pages of the country's newspapers at once broke out in paeans of praise for what they universally hailed as a tremendous diplomatic victory for the United States. The *New York Times* declared that Hay had performed a signal public service and had succeeded "in repairing the huge blunder of his predecessor" in refusing to take any part in the British effort in behalf of the Open Door. The Chicago *Times* said that "there had never been a more brilliant and important achievement in diplomacy," and the Philadelphia *Press* asserted that here was "a larger achievement and more important triumph" than the Spanish-American War. The *Review of Reviews* also emphasized "one of the greatest achievements ever won by our diplomacy." John Hay became overnight a national hero who was said to have succeeded, singlehandedly, in guaranteeing the position of the United States in eastern Asia and carrying to completion a noble work of peace.

There was amazing exaggeration in these comments, from

every point of view. Hay had not actually succeeded in winning the powers' assent to even the modest provisions of his Open Door notes. The negotiations had revealed a very marked reluctance on their part—including that of Great Britain—to commit themselves to trade equality within their spheres of influence. They had insisted on reservations, and in each case had made their consent provisional on that of the other countries. Only by the broadest interpretation could Russia's reply be considered approval at all.

Hay was attempting to build up the moral pressures that would persuade the powers that they had to go along with American policy, and he therefore sought, by announcing the acceptance of his plan, to give to its somewhat dubious results the éclat of success. On March 20, 1900—three months after these preliminary announcements—he took the bold step of declaring that the replies to his notes were "final and definitive." He put the powers on record in the eyes of the world as having fully committed themselves to the Open Door.

In the continued chorus of approval and congratulations for his diplomacy, there were a few dissenting voices. Only one important newspaper, however, appears to have looked beneath the surface. The Springfield *Republican* found something "rather funny" in believing that the powers' bland assurances of accepting the Open Door really amounted to very much. It soberly warned that the United States had gone far toward placing itself in a position where, if it were to be consistent, "it must guarantee by military force the political integrity of China, or share in its possible partition."

The general popular attitude reflected two somewhat paradoxical reactions to Hay's diplomacy. The one was pride and gratification that the United States had stepped out on the international stage and made its influence felt. It was a great power. The other was satisfaction that the nation's influence was not being exercised for further imperialist goals, but to block the partition of China and safeguard the independence of her people. The note again and again stressed in editorial comment (including that of the strongly anti-expansionist *Nation*) was the service the United States had performed in allaying imperialistic rivalries and strengthening world peace.

Yet nothing had happened since the first announcement of the negotiations to close the gap between the great expectations aroused by Hay's diplomacy and the reality of its somewhat meager results. If Rockhill professed to believe that, at least for the time being, American policy had assured the powers' acceptance of the integrity of the Chinese Empire, he was expressing little more than a pious hope. The United States had acknowledged rather than challenged the division of China into spheres of foreign influence; it obtained no more than the vaguest of pledges for commercial equality within such foreign spheres. That was all.

Even as Secretary Hay was announcing that the powers had definitely approved the Open Door policy, circumstances had arisen within China that were to put this policy to the test and underscore even more dangerously what Henry Adams described as "the inevitable struggle for the control of China, which, in his view, must decide the control of the world." The outbreak of the Boxer Rebellion, the perilous siege of the foreign legations in Peking, the interallied military expedition for their relief—these dramatic events in the summer of 1900 for a time placed in perilous jeopardy the whole future of China and even the peace of the world.

The Boxer Rebellion was a bitter protest on the part of the Chinese against Western encroachments, a first wave of that intense anti-imperialist, anti-foreign feeling that was recurrently to sweep over the Middle Kingdom in the early 1900s and then be still further emphasized by Nationalists and Communists. It was a popular movement in which the people, despairing of protection for their interests on the part of a corrupt and decadent government, sought in vengeful fury to drive the "foreign devils" into the sea. Interference with native customs by Western enterprise, especially in railroad building, and by Western missionaries seeking to impose their own ways, had awakened the superstitious fears of ignorant peasants. Armed bands made up of members of such secret societies as the Fists of Righteous Harmony—hence the name Boxers— roamed the countryside of northern China, at first destroying the property and taking the lives of Chinese converts to Christianity, and soon attacking the foreign missions themselves with fire and sword.

"Peking, Tientsin, and Paoting-fu," one observer described the situation in the spring of 1900, "are encircled by bands of maddened and fanatical people whose numbers are swollen by an excited crowd of vagabonds, and who, being maintained by leaders in high position, rob, pillage, burn, and kill as they pass. For the moment their activity is directed against Chinese converts, Catholic and Protestant. . . . They do not conceal their objective to get rid of all foreigners . . . . by means of a destruction of religious missions and a general insurrection against European and American residents . . . . and on their flags they now assert they act by imperial command."

The crafty and imperious Empress Dowager Tzu Hsi was indeed more than ready to encourage this phase of the Boxer Rebellion. For the uprising had its anti-dynastic as well as anti-foreign implications, and she was anxious to do everything she could to divert against the Western barbarians, attacks that might otherwise be made upon the Manchus. At heart she was also just as anti-foreign as the Boxer leaders themselves and deeply affected by their superstitious ideas. When the powers protested the danger to foreign lives and property as the rebellion grew in fury, she answered evasively, and actually did little or nothing to maintain public order.

The situation came to a crisis in June 1900 when powerful Boxer bands, armed with swords and spears, overran Peking and began to riot and pillage throughout the city. Over two thousand Chinese converts were massacred, many westerners assaulted, and both the chancellor of the Japanese legation and the German minister were assassinated. Finally the Boxer bands placed the foreign legations under siege. The Empress Dowager made no move to intervene. The life of the imperial court went on undisturbed with the ladies in waiting happily picnicking in the palace gardens within sound of the firing on the legations. And while Tzu Hsi professed that there was nothing the government could do, she was secretly encouraging the Boxer attack.

When the first news of the uprisings reached the United States, Secretary Hay instructed the American minister in Peking, E. H. Conger, to take whatever measures were feasible "to protect with energy American interests." He further warned the minister, however, that he was always to act independently rather than in cooperation with the other powers; and above all "there must be no alliances."

As the Boxers advanced on the Chinese capital, Conger sought further instructions. "It is possible we may be besieged in Peking, with railroads and telegraphs cut," he cabled. "In that case, I ask, as my colleagues are doing, that necessary instructions be given Admiral [in command of the American naval forces in Asiatic waters] to concert with other chiefs of squadron at Taku to take necessary measures warranted by the situation to eventually deliver Peking." A few days later he requested authority to participate in any other steps the representatives of the other powers agreed upon and concluded, "Answer quick." Hay gave the necessary permission.

With the actual siege of the legations, a curtain of isolation descended about Peking. All communications with the outside world were cut off and the wildest rumors of what might be happening began to percolate through the treaty ports. A dispatch to the New York *World* of July 16 gave a fantastic description of the foreigners vainly trying to fight their way out through the cordon drawn about the legations and killing their own women and children to prevent their falling into the hands of the Boxers.

"Heavy guns bombarded all night until the buildings were demolished and in flames," read this sensational report. "Many foreigners were roasted in the ruins. The Boxers rushed upon them and hacked and stabbed both dead and wounded, cutting off their heads and carrying these through the streets on their rifles, shouting furiously."

There was not a word of truth in this dispatch. Without Cuban atrocities to make headlines, the *World* was doing the best it could with manufactured stories from China. Nevertheless other newspapers carried very similar accounts that presented frightening if imaginary pictures of the increasingly grave situation in which the besieged foreigners found themselves. As the rumors multiplied the belief became general, both in this country and abroad, that the legations could not possibly survive the attack being made upon them. In London preparations were made for a great memorial service in St. Paul's to honor the heroism of Peking's supposedly annihilated foreign community.

Just at this juncture in affairs—four days after the sensational *World* report—the dramatic news arrived that although the legations were in the last extremity, they were still holding out. Secretary Hay made public a message that he had received in a roundabout way from the American minister in Peking. "For one month," Conger reported, "we have been besieged in British legation under continued shot and shell from Chinese troops. Quick relief only can prevent general massacre." The entire Western world breathed easier. The members of the foreign community were at least still alive.

Preparations for their relief were already made. Since early June there had been considerable discussion of what measures might be taken in China, with the State Department under heavy pressure from missionary groups to send troops, and an infantry regiment was transferred from Manila to Tientsin in the middle of the month. The question of whether American relief forces should cooperate with those of the other powers or operate independently was for a time hotly debated, but the obvious course was joint action. A first small contingent of foreign troops seeking to advance into the interior was repulsed by the Boxers, but by the end of July sufficient men and equipment were assembled to cope with the situation. The allied expeditionary force, made up of 19,000 troops primarily consisting of Japanese and Russians but including 2500 Americans, set out on the route from Tientsin to Peking on August 4.

As the allies slowly advanced, the world waited fearfully. The role of the old Empress Dowager was decisive. If she gave the word for a general assault, the legations in Peking could not possibly hold out and the relief expedition itself would be in the gravest danger. Torn by doubts and indecision, Tzu Hsi did nothing at all. Then as it grew increasingly clear that the Boxers themselves were unable to offer any effective resistance to the allied advance, she turned her back on the entire affair. Disguising herself as a peasant, Tzu Hsi fled the capital with a handful of her officials.

Thus abandoned by the government, the Boxer leaders called off the siege of the legations, in fear of foreign retribution. They too fled Peking, and their peasant followers melted away into the countryside. Advancing on the capital without further opposition, the allied expedition lifted the siege on August 14. There had been heavy casualties among the 473 civilians and 451 military personnel who for eight perilous weeks had been under intermittent Boxer attack. Some 73 had been killed, another 179 wounded. Nevertheless a general massacre had been averted and the day was saved.

The United States was primarily concerned throughout these weeks of suspense with the rescue of its nationals in Peking, and public opinion fully supported the decision to take part in the allied relief expedition. At the same time, Secretary Hay did not ignore the broader implications of the crisis and was determined to do what he could to prevent the Boxer Rebellion from being made the occasion for further moves toward the partition of China. At stake were the principles underlying his new Open Door policy and the entire position of the United States in eastern Asia.

To secure the broader aims of American policy, Hay consequently sent on July 3—while the fate of the foreigners in Peking was still in doubt—a circular message to the several powers. The United States was determined, the Secretary of State declared, to seek a solution of the crisis that would bring about permanent peace in China, preserve Chinese territorial integrity, safeguard all treaty rights, and maintain the principle of equal and impartial trade in all parts of the Chinese Empire. Here was the logical projection of his notes in 1899. If the Open Door were to be maintained in China, it could only be done through safeguarding China's own political independence. Hay did not specifically ask the powers to accept this policy for themselves. He made clear beyond a shadow of doubt, however, the position the United States was taking. Here was a fair warning that in the settlement of the Boxer troubles, the influence of the United States would be exerted in opposition to any foreign encroachment on Chinese territory.

Once again public opinion found in Hay's action a gratifying expression of American idealism. Among other papers, the *New York Times* stated that the administration had won a new title to the confidence of the people by its wise and statesmanlike policy. The United States would have no part in any attempt to usurp authority in China and would oppose the efforts of any other nation to do so. The anti-imperialist foes of the McKinley administration—and this was the election year in which expansion was being so heatedly debated—could hardly find fault with a program that contrasted so sharply with the harsh campaign still being waged against the Filipinos.

When negotiations were begun in Peking to determine what compensation China should make for the losses the powers had suffered in lives and property, and what guarantees could be provided against further anti-foreign attacks, the United States was to stand alone in its pacific and moderate policy. "There is . . . . not a single power we can reply upon," Hay complained bitterly on one occasion, "for our policy of abstention from plunder and the Open Door." In November he became so discouraged over any possibility of a general agreement that he appeared ready to abandon his basic premises and seek a territorial concession in China for the United States. The American minister was instructed to ask for cession of a naval base at Samsah Bay, in the province of Fukien.

Ironically enough it was Japan, considering Fukien as falling within the Japanese sphere of interest, which formally reminded the United States of its stated policy not to make the Boxer troubles a pretext for seeking any territorial cessions from China. Hay soon dropped the whole idea. There is not much reason to believe that he ever took it very seriously, but went as far as he did only under pressure from the War and Navy Departments.

Rockhill had in the meantime been sent out to China as a special commissioner, and in the early autumn supplanted Conger as minister in Peking. Some time earlier he had confidently written that the American stand had "put a stop to the grab policy . . . . [and] shown the Peking Government that the integrity of the country is not menaced." But as the protracted negotiations among the powers dragged on, he became increasingly discouraged. His attitude, like that of Hay, reflected a profound disillusionment with what he thought had been accomplished through the Open Door policy. He was soon "sick and tired of the whole business." As he later wrote his friend Hippisley:

"England has her agreement with Germany, Russia has her alliance with France, the Triple Alliance comes in here, and every other combination you know of is working here just as it is in Europe. I trust it may be a long time before the United States gets into another muddle of this description."

What both Hay and Rockhill were beginning to realize was that through the projection of its interests to eastern Asia— the Philippine Islands, the Open Door policy, and now its declaration in favor of China's territorial integrity—the United

States was inextricably involved in world politics. No alliances had been formed; no hard and fast commitments assumed. Yet the country could not escape the problems and complexities of its new world role. Here were the lasting fruits of the Spanish-American War and overseas expansion.

The United States nevertheless held to its position in the negotiations in Peking and exercised such influence as it could to prevent any alienation of Chinese territory and to moderate the demands of the other powers for an indemnity. As Hay wrote Henry White: "We want no territory and should regret to see China despoiled. Above all we want the Open Door." The situation, however, became increasingly complicated. President McKinley was anxious to liquidate the entire affair, for he was now under heavy criticism for maintaining troops overseas, and certainly had no desire to become further involved in the China tangle. At the same time, the complete withdrawal of American forces would have weakened the position the United States was seeking to maintain. "The talk of the papers about 'our pre-eminent moral position giving us the authority to dictate to the world,'" the Secretary of State exclaimed in a moment of exasperation, "is mere flap-doodle."

On the broad principle of the continued exercise of American influence in support of the Open Door and China's territorial integrity, Hay did not feel that there should be any retreat. He had accepted overseas expansion; he believed in an extended world role. "The United States of today cannot go back to what the country was fifty or a hundred years ago," he declared. "Whether we will or not, whether for better or for worse, we must go forward." However much he despaired of getting full support for the Open Door from the other powers, he did not for a moment contemplate any withdrawal from eastern Asia.

In the end, the views of the United States generally prevailed in the settlements concluded between the powers and the Chinese Government. The protocols of September 1901 provided for the punishment of the Boxer leaders, imposed upon China an indemnity for the loss of foreign lives and property, and granted the powers the right to maintain troops in both Tientsin and Peking, together with authority to keep communications open between these two cities. But while the indemnity was outrageously heavy (some $333,000,000 in all, of which the United States claimed only $25,000,000, most of which it subsequently remitted), the salient fact remained that the powers did not obtain any territorial cessions. It is true that they retained all their former special privileges, and Russia materially strengthened her position in Manchuria. In theory, if not altogether in practice, however, China's integrity was upheld. Once again the danger of any actual partition of the crumbling empire was successfully averted.

American policy was not the decisive influence in these developments. The situation was really saved because the powers could not agree upon any division of the huge, sprawling country, and other contemporary developments accentuated rather than alleviated the irreconcilable imperialistic rivalries of the day. British involvement in the Boer War, the mounting Anglo-German naval competition, the new ambitions of Czarist Russia—these were the factors on the international scene that made for a stalemate in eastern Asia and for the consequent acceptance of American principles in the Boxer settlement.

Nevertheless the United States had taken its stand as an avowed champion of China's independence. And this stand won wide backing because it was believed to conform to the basic concepts governing the nation's foreign policy. The public was persuaded that it was in the national interest, especially in view of such far-flung possessions in the Pacific, that America should not be excluded from eastern Asia. The promotion of foreign trade with China was accepted as a paramount economic need, while support for the independence of the Chinese people satisfied that idealistic sense of mission which was then and has remained so highly significant in popular attitudes.

Under these circumstances the Open Door policy, for all the

retreats and concessions that might be made when it came under direct attack, gradually gathered a tremendous momentum and force in itself. Here was the basis for the refusal of the United States, even at the risk of the war from which it so often backed away, to sacrifice China to the militaristic ambitions of Japan in 1941.

CHAPTER XIV

THEODORE ROOSEVELT AND WORLD POWER

THEODORE ROOSEVELT BECAME THE TWENTY-FIFTH PRESIDENT OF the United States on September 15, 1901. He had rushed to the bedside of the dying McKinley, who had been shot by a crazed assassin while visiting the Pan-American Exposition in Buffalo, but the President was dead when he arrived. The Cabinet was assembled, and upon taking the oath of office under these dramatic circumstances, Roosevelt stated with due solemnity that it would be his intention and endeavor "to continue, absolutely unbroken, the policy of President McKinley, for the peace and prosperity and honor of our beloved country." This was the young new chief executive's immediate reaction to the responsibilities so unexpectedly thrust upon him. Actually his administration was to usher in a new era in American history that in many ways broke sharply and decisively with the past.

Roosevelt surely was thinking primarily of domestic policies when he took the oath of office. The business community, whose interests were so faithfully reflected in McKinleyism, had shown considerable apprehension over his position in the line of presidential succession. The adolescent cowboy, the impetuous Rough Rider, the boss-defying governor was not considered altogether safe. It was Mark Hanna who demanded despairingly of his friends during the 1900 convention, "Don't any of you realize that there's only one life between this mad-man and the White House?" Roosevelt naturally wanted to give the country every assurance of his moderation and caution.

If such domestic issues as railroad regulation, the control of trusts, labor relations, and conservation were largely to dominate the political scene, matters of foreign policy were at the same time of very real importance. The program of the Mc-Kinley administration appeared to be reaching some sort of completion in September 1901. The establishment of civilian government in the Philippines marked the final stage in the pacification of the islands; an uneasy Cuba had accepted the Platt Amendment, and this same month, the powers at long last concluded the Boxer protocol settling their claims against China. The question remained, however, whether a new administration would seek to renew the imperialist advance of the past few years, or in what other way exercise the power inherent in the position that the United States had now attained in world affairs.

It might appear as if the future had already been blocked out. Had not the Republican spokesmen of 1900 dwelt enthusiastically on the nation's imperial destiny? Had not Senator Beveridge emphatically declared that the power which ruled the Pacific would rule the world, and with the Philippines that power would be the American Republic? His exuberant enthusiasm had awakened many echoes. From a quite different point of view—in gloomy foreboding rather than happy anticipation—the anti-imperialists were saying very much the same thing as Beveridge. "We shall want new conquests to protect that which we already possess," Carl Schurz somberly warned of the consequence of this further drive for power.

". . . . It has always been so under such circumstances, and always will be."

Yet the mood of the nation was already changing. Even more rapid and unexpected than the rise of expansionist fervor among the American people was the speed of its decline. The "explosive imperialism" of 1898 proved to be short lived. The historical concept of expansion as symbolized by the Western movement had given way to sharp disillusionment when it was realized that the new possessions could not be correlated with free land but meant rather the burden and costs of colonial administration. The high expectations of rapidly expanding markets in the new possessions and of a thriving trade with China showed no signs of being realized. The moral fervor of a national mission to carry abroad democracy was sadly dimmed by the unhappy consequences of military conquest in the Philippines. In the very process of securing overseas empire, indeed, the victory of the imperialists was tempered by many indications that the ideals for which the anti-imperialists stood were re-asserting themselves. It was highly significant that the Open Door policy was hailed as a return to fundamental principles because it upheld China's independence in the face of the other powers' imperialistic aggression.

A stubborn Cleveland had been at once fatalistic as to the present and hopeful for the future in commenting in 1898 on what he called "the fatal un-American idea of imperialism and expansion." Writing to John P. Irish, he said that the spirit of the times represented "a new and startling phase in our national character," and presciently added that it was "a craze, which like a fever must have its course." Even Cleveland must have been surprised, however, at how rapidly the fever actually did run its course as the enthusiasm and excitement of war days gave way so quickly to mounting apathy toward overseas dominion.

Imperialism had flourished in part as escapism from the seemingly insoluble problems born of the depression of the

1890s and as a rallying cry for Republican solidarity, but changing economic conditions placed a different complexion on affairs at the opening of the new century. With the return of
prosperity and bright hopes for still further economic advance,
foreign adventure no longer had the appeal it once had. The
American people became far more concerned with what could
be done at home to ensure further progress and to promote the
general well being of the nation. Their major interests were
once again domestic.

Moreover it was with revived hope and confidence rather
than in the bleak despair of farm revolt and labor strikes that
the country took up those progressive reforms that characterized the era opening with Roosevelt's assumption of the presidency. If a shadow had fallen across the American dream with
the domination over government of selfish interests, nowhere
was there any real doubt that political democracy and social
justice were attainable if the people put their minds to it. In
such circumstances, building an overseas empire seemed to
be an unfortunate diversion, a dissipation of energies that
might better be employed in strengthening the forces of democracy at home.

"Here we stand today," declared Senator McLaurin of Tennessee as early as January 1899, "with great issues of financial
reform, labor, and trust questions all sidetracked . . . It is
wiser and better to look at domestic politics first, and not avoid
grave questions at home in order to join in the international
game of land-grabbing." This was the sentiment, rather than
further exaltation of martial virtues and the duty of expansion,
that gained more and more pre-eminence. The fading strains
of imperialist oratory were soon to echo hollowly even in the
halls of Congress.

By March 1902 the fervidly anti-imperialist *Nation* was
cheerfully reporting what it declared to be the "full tide" of
reaction. "For a few months Imperialism seemed to cast a
glamour over the minds of Americans," wrote its editors; "but
its charm diminished on examination, and its feeble and dis-

credited operation has now well-nigh completed the disillusionment. From being weary of it, the people will soon come to think the best thing to do will be simply to 'write off' the losses incurred by that folly, and begin a fresh account."

The disillusionment of so many of the expansionists themselves, however, is more impressive evidence of what was taking place than is the rejoicing of the *Nation*. Senator Beveridge was almost alone among the imperialist band of 1898 in seeking to keep up the march of the flag. He still wanted Cuba and other island bases in the Caribbean. Harping on a too-familiar theme, he again declared that the United States could not escape its moral obligation to extend Anglo-Saxon rule to the inferior races.

"If anyone cherishes the delusion that the American Government will ever be withdrawn from our possessions," Beveridge stated, "let him consult the religious conviction of this Christian people."

But these were no longer the ideas of Henry Adams and John Hay, of Henry Cabot Lodge and Theodore Roosevelt, or even those of Alfred Thayer Mahan. Indeed, after about 1906, Beveridge himself gave up the battle for American empire in his growing absorption in domestic issues. The Philippines, his biographer has written, became in Beveridge's life "as remote as one of the possessions of ancient Rome."

Henry Adams was writing his brother Brooks in 1901 that the world would probably "break its damn neck within five and twenty years." He was inclined "to abandon China, Philippines, and everything else . . . . to let England sink; to let Germany and Russia try to run the machine, and to stand on our own internal resources alone." "I incline strongly now to anti-imperialism," he continued, "and very strongly to anti-militarism."

Lodge was neither so pessimistic nor so philosophic, but he too recognized that something had gone awry with American imperialism. Writing in May 1903 he sadly admitted that the people "have lost all interest in it." He himself felt that the

United States should seek to extend its influence, but by other methods than territorial expansion: "I do not want to annex any more islands."

Mahan would continue to concern himself with problems of naval strategy, but in a muted tone. Whatever he might have thought at the close of the century, he was soon warning his readers that "it is not to the interest of the United States to propose to herself the object of supremacy in the Pacific." He deplored the mounting indifference and apathy toward foreign policy, but realistically accepted it. To point the moral, he told the story of the experienced congressman advising a new representative to avoid service upon "a fancy committee like that of Foreign Affairs" because his constituents cared nothing about international questions.

And what of Roosevelt? The exuberant colonel of the Rough Riders, who had so excitedly written Lodge from the sweltering heat of Tampa that there should be no talk of peace until "we get both Porto Rico and the Philippines," was expressing himself in a quite different vein a few years later. While he still stated publicly that expansion was the duty of all civilized nations, the only means whereby they could uphold "law, order, and righteousness," he wrote Frederic Coudert in July 1901 that he now had very real doubts about the American position in the Pacific. The United States had done its duty in taking over the Philippines, he said, but he varied in his feelings "whether we were to be considered fortunate or unfortunate in having to hold them, and I most earnestly hope that the trend of events will so speedily as may be justify us in leaving them." He was perfectly clear in his own mind, he added, that the United States did not want to expand over another people capable of self-government unless they wanted union with the United States—"and not necessarily even then."

Six years later, in a long letter to William Howard Taft, from which an often quoted phrase is his statement that the Philippines had become "our heel of Achilles," he went further into the whole question. In the excitement of war the American people had thought they wanted to take the Philippines and believed they would be a valuable possession, Roosevelt wrote, but they had soon come to consider them of no value. "And I am bound to say," he continued, "that in the physical sense, I don't see where they are of any value to us or where they are likely to be of any value." If some sort of international guarantee could be obtained for their security, Roosevelt said, he would be very glad to see the islands fully independent.

This was certainly a far cry from his earlier view that in seeking American domination of the Pacific, the opportunity to acquire the Philippines had come at such an opportune time as to appear providential. But on one point Roosevelt remained true to his original convictions: he would not consider for a moment any forced surrender of the islands. "I would rather see this nation fight all her life," he told Taft, "than to see her give them up to Japan or any other nation under duress."

It was of course true that territorial imperialism was losing its impetus everywhere, in the case of the European powers as well as that of the United States. Africa had been partitioned, the islands of the sea were all neatly appropriated, opportunities for expansion in Asia seemed effectively blocked. Still, the United States could conceivably have added to its territories if that had been the will of the American people. Secretary Hay tried to purchase the Virgin Islands from Denmark in 1902, but when a proposed treaty of annexation was rejected by the Danes, the Administration did not press the matter in the face of almost complete public indifference. And it was a sign of the times to find Roosevelt expressing the opinion, when trouble arose somewhat later with Santo Domingo, a persistent goal of earlier expansionists, that he had about as much desire to annex this Caribbean island "as a gorged boa constrictor might have to swallow a porcupine wrong-end to."

The retreat from imperialism did not mean that the United States immediately surrendered its overseas possessions. The road to ultimate self-government or independence for the territories wrested from Spain was long and arduous. Moreover, the United States was to intervene in the affairs of other nations, especially in the case of the little republics of the Caribbean, in ways that critics both at home and abroad strongly denounced as financial imperialism.[1] Nevertheless the movement of the 1890s had run its course and the desire for new territory would not again seize upon the American imagination as it had in that restive decade. Looking back upon these days in which he had played such an important role in consolidating the American empire, Elihu Root would write that the American people had never really cared for overseas expansion— "after the war excitement subsided, people sank into indifference."

For all his willingness to recognize that territorial imperialn had perhaps carried the United States too far afield, Roosel't nevertheless would not relegate foreign affairs to the background. He believed deeply that the United States could not avoid the responsibilities inherent in its new role as a world power. It was his lasting conviction that the guns of the Spanish-American War "left us echoes of glory, but they also left us a legacy of duty." He would constantly bewail the lack of popular interest in foreign affairs which marked the reaction from imperialism, and bemoan his difficulties in gaining intelligent support for his own policies.

There were still some attributes of the irrepressible young jingo in the Roosevelt who entered the White House in 1901. The boy was father to the man. He delighted in the image of the "big stick" and was at times to wield it with a happy aban-

[1] ". . . . If you try to divorce imperialism from territorial control," William L. Langer has written in a penetrating article, "A Critique of Imperialism" (*Foreign Affairs*, XIV, October, 1935), "you will get nowhere. . . . Imperialism is, in a sense, synonymous with the appropriation by the western nations of the largest part of the rest of the world. If you take it to be anything else, you will soon be lost in nebulous concepts and bloodless abstractions. If imperialism is to mean any vague interference of traders and bankers in the affairs of other countries, you may as well extend it to cover any form of influence."

don. There was a reckless irresponsibility about his policy on taking over the Panama Canal zone. He did not hesitate to make ridiculously bellicose threats during the negotiations with Great Britain over Alaskan boundaries. He was ready to go to extreme lengths in protesting Russian persecution of the Jews (". . . . The Hebrews—poor dears!" wrote Hay, "all over the country think we are bully boys"). At the time of the Armenian massacres, he talked of wanting to lead a crusade against the Turks. And finally, there was the message peremptorily demanding the release of an alleged American citizen (Roosevelt knew him to be a naturalized Greek) who had been captured by Moroccan bandits—"Perdicaris alive or Raisuli dead."

Although he had a far keener sense than McKinley of the realities of world politics, Roosevelt was not above playing to the gallery and seeking to make political capital out of foreign policy. It was not sheer coincidence that the famous Perdicaris message was sent during the Republican convention of 1904! Moreover the belligerency which had made him so war-minded in the 1890s still found expression in an assertive determination to uphold American honor and American prestige that could not always be easily reconciled with a responsibility for maintaining peace.

This continued concern with taking a strong position on foreign issues also reflected Roosevelt's underlying conviction that too great an absorption in domestic concerns, material gain, and money-making was a denial of America's great heritage as the champion of freedom. If her people followed a policy of "unwarlike and isolated ease," content to huddle within the national borders as "an assemblage of well-to-do hucksters who care nothing for what happens beyond," he repeatedly warned, the nation could easily become the prey of more ambitious powers. His constant refrain was that there was no surer way to court disaster than to be "opulent, aggressive, and unarmed."

As this attitude and his general scorn for the industrial

tycoons of his day suggests, Roosevelt was little affected by specific economic demands in his formulation of foreign policies. The commercial pressure groups that were constantly calling for protection or support in their operations abroad did not exercise a controlling influence while he was in the White House. The President frequently spoke of the needs of an expanding commerce, as he did in his first message to Congress in 1901 calling for the "permanent establishment of a wider market for American goods," and both publicly and privately he often referred to the importance of the China trade. Nevertheless he did not at any time think primarily in terms of markets and investments. They were only means to an end—building up the power of the United States.

No fear of a direct threat to national security entered into his thinking. "Of invasion in any real sense of the word," Mahan had written some years earlier, "we run no risk." And most Americans would have further agreed with a statement by Senator Hale of Maine that a future war involving the United States was "practically impossible." What Roosevelt wanted was a nation strong enough to safeguard its legitimate interests in any part of the world, and able to play its part in maintaining a balance of global power that would assure continued peace for all nations. He further believed strongly in the need for "proper policing of the world" in the interests of law and order, and he sought by all the means at his command to have the United States recognized and accepted as one of the nations carrying out such duties. "Only the warlike power of a civilized people," he said, ". . . can give peace to the world."

Upon receiving the Nobel Peace Prize after his retirement from the presidency, Roosevelt was to suggest some form of world cooperation in preventing war. ". . . It would be a master stroke," he declared in his acceptance speech at Stockholm on May 5, 1910, "if those great Powers honestly bent on peace would form a League of Peace, not only to keep the peace among themselves, but to prevent, by force if necessary, its being broken by others." Yet he never showed any desire to promote such a league while he was in the White House, and far more representative of his thinking as a formulator of foreign policy was a statement made four years earlier: "As yet there is no likelihood of establishing any kind of international power . . . which can effectively check wrongdoing." He was an intense nationalist, and unwilling in any way to accept commitments limiting the nation's complete freedom of action.

In his concept of the world order that the United States should seek to uphold, Roosevelt never thought of peace, as might well be expected, just for its own sake. It had to be peace based upon justice. There was a strongly moralistic undertone to his views on foreign policy and he repeatedly declared, whatever judgment may be returned on some of his actions, that the nation's steady aim should be to raise the standard of conduct in international affairs "just as we strive to raise the standard of individual action." There remained always the question of how such standards of conduct might be defined and what indeed constituted the justice that should govern foreign policy. At the Nobel Peace Prize ceremonies he was to say, "Peace is generally good in itself, but it is never the highest good unless it comes as the handmaiden of righteousness," but he never defined the attributes of this inspired handmaiden. There was this about Roosevelt, however: whatever policy he adopted, whatever line of action he took, he was always convinced that it conformed to the highest ideals of righteousness. There was never any doubt in his own mind that he was living up to the moral standards he set for himself and the nation.

This emphasis upon ethics in the determination of policy conformed to the missionary spirit of the times. In constantly emphasizing that it was the nation's duty and the fulfillment of a solemn obligation to mankind that accounted both for America's taking up arms against Spain and for her overseas expansion, McKinley had sounded an idealistic note that continued to characterize most public statements on national policy. Roosevelt too felt the necessity to justify his actions in such terms. Yet no more than McKinley can he be judged wholly insincere because he sometimes cloaked quite different motives in noble-sounding phrases stressing peace, justice, and righteousness.

There was a constant interplay between selfish national interest and ethical purpose in the determination of foreign policy throughout this period, perhaps more than during any other era. The lines were never very clearly drawn between the "realists" and the "idealists." Later commentators have said that a continuing source of weakness in American policy has been that "intoxication with moral abstractions which as a mass phenomenon started with the Spanish-American War." [2] But such criticism is subject to two major reservations. The first is that it would be very difficult to show that moral abstractions actually played a decisive part in determining policy as compared with what was rightly or wrongly considered the national interest; and the second, that only so far as the American people could be convinced, again rightly or wrongly, that national policy conformed to high moral standards, would they give it their full support.

The heritage of the past, the sense of national mission in promoting liberty, has always to be taken into consideration in formulating policy. Realists who have thought it could be ignored—either in the early 1900s or in later years—have done so at their peril. If idealism by itself did not entirely account for the liberation of Cuba, the annexation of the Philippines or the Open Door in China, the American people would not have supported these developments had they not generally believed—even if it was in part rationalization—that they were great works of peace.

[2] For interesting discussions on this basic issue in foreign policy see the recent writings of such commentators as George F. Kennan, Walter Lippmann, Hans J. Morgenthau and especially Robert E. Osgood, *Ideals and Self-Interest in America's Foreign Relations* (Chicago, 1953).

"The sentiment of a people is the most energetic element in national action," Mahan once wrote with characteristic perspicuity. "Even when material interests are the original originating cause, it is the sentiment to which they give rise, the moral tone which emotion takes, that constitutes the greater force."

Roosevelt, in any event, clearly reflected both the realistic and idealistic approaches to foreign policy. He placed a constant emphasis upon the "peace of righteousness" and the necessity for acting within the restraints of moral law, and yet invariably made the national interest the final touchstone for his decisions. And he realized always that the United States had to operate within a framework of world politics that called for the development of effective force rather than an ingenuous reliance upon wholly moral influence.

Over and above everything else, however, the most significant fact in Roosevelt's attitude toward foreign policy remained his deep-seated conviction that the United States could not possibly avoid the consequences of its inherent power. Again and again he told the American people that it was no longer a question of whether the United States would play a great part in the world. The only question, he constantly emphasized, was whether the nation would play that great part for good or for ill.

"We may either fail greatly or succeed greatly," he stated in December 1902; "but we cannot avoid the endeavor from which either great failure or great success must come. Even if we would, we cannot play a small part. If we should try, all that would follow would be that we should play a large part ignobly or shamefully."

A first and paramount consideration in the light of these views on the national destiny—a lesson which Roosevelt had learned at the feet of Alfred Thayer Mahan—was the importance of building up naval strength to give concrete expression to the country's new world role. Yet again the power the President sought through a great American Navy was to be exercised not alone for safeguarding national security but for promoting peace—the peace of righteousness.

In campaigning so zealously for more and larger battleships, Roosevelt constantly found himself at odds with those who believed that America's role was to provide an example in disarmament, and that her government should be willing to submit all international disputes to arbitration. He was highly skeptical of the validity of any such program, remaining as impatiently scornful of pacifists as he had been in the 1890s, and he insisted upon a more practical attitude. "The American people must either build and maintain an adequate navy," he told Congress again and again, "or else make up their minds definitely to accept a secondary position in international affairs."

The peace movement, with its emphasis upon disarmament and arbitration, was a powerful force in the opening years of the century. It reflected the reformist impulse of the age, so evident in all domestic affairs, and was at the same time a natural reaction to the growth of emphasis on naval strength since the 1880s. Scores of peace societies were organized, intensive propaganda carried on through the churches and schools, and a number of peace conferences held in various parts of the country. One such conference, sponsored by the New York Peace Society in 1907 under the direction of Andrew Carnegie, was reputedly attended by ten mayors, nineteen members of Congress, four Supreme Court justices, two presidential candidates, thirty labor leaders, forty bishops, sixty newspaper editors, and twenty-seven millionaires! Although this enthusiastic news release may have exaggerated things, there was no question that the peace movement had a very real impact upon the American people. Church members, social reformers, intellectuals, philanthropists threw themselves into it enthusiastically and became so optimistic that many pacifists firmly believed that victory for their cause was almost within their grasp.

The movement had received an early impetus from the peace conference held at The Hague in 1899, on the initiative of the Russian Czar. But while this meeting provided a public forum for the discussion of international issues, its actual achievements fell far short of the expectations of the peace advocates in the United States. The one substantial accomplishment at The Hague was the establishment of a Permanent Court of Arbitration, providing a panel of jurists to which international disputants might submit such questions as they desired. The conference negotiations made it abundantly clear, however, that no nation was willing to accept arbitration as a means of settling those disputes that might actually lead to war. Moreover, no progress whatsoever was made toward the limitation of armaments. The American naval delegate, Captain Mahan, let it be known that in its new world position the United States would actually have to increase its fleet.

It was significant that the United States even sent a delegate to the conference. It was not many years earlier that Secretary of State Seward had refused the invitation to take part in the Geneva convention that established the International Red Cross on the ground that it was fixed American policy not to become a party to any international agreement. Yet in spite of the evidence provided by The Hague that the United States was prepared as it had never been before to participate in world affairs, there were still definite reservations to official American policy. In approving the conference agreements, the Senate made it clear, albeit in somewhat involved language, that nothing in such conventions should be construed as requiring the United States "to depart from the traditional policy of not intruding upon, interfering with, or entangling itself in the political questions or policy or internal administration of any foreign state."

The insistence upon such reservations suggests that the Senate was seeking to convince itself, and also the country, that the fundamental bases of foreign policy had not changed in the face of all evidence that they definitely were changing.

It protested too much. Nevertheless the theoretical line was clearly drawn between entanglements which could not be avoided, and the acceptance of any positive commitments growing out of such entanglements. However futile history was to prove these efforts to be, the United States was still seeking to maintain its complete freedom of action.

Eight years after this first meeting at The Hague, a second peace conference was held and American delegates also took part in these deliberations. In spite of a renewed drive to strengthen the cause of arbitration and effect some limitation of armaments, it proved no more successful than the initial meeting. Efforts to make over the arbitration tribunal into a more effective world court proved unavailing, and again no steps were taken toward disarmament. A number of minor conventions affecting rules of warfare were adopted. In approving them the United States once more denied that it was in any way departing from its traditional noninterventionist policies.

Roosevelt's attitude toward these conferences was rather ambiguous. He expressed great sympathy for the peace movement in 1904, assuring the president of the American Peace Society "that all we can do will be done to bring nearer the day when the peace of justice shall obtain throughout the world," and he was prepared to take the initiative in calling the second meeting at The Hague. Indeed he appeared to be so generally pacific-minded at this time that Mr. Dooley is found remarking to his friend Mr. Hennessy that he had been authorized "to deny th' infamous rayport that th' Prizidint was iver at San Joon Hill. At th' time iv this gloryous an' lamintable performance, th' good man was down with measles conthracted at th' Internaytional Peace Convintion." But 1904 was an election year. When the second Hague conference was actually held three years later, Roosevelt paid almost no attention to it. "I have not followed things at The Hague," we find him writing Root on July 2, 1907; and some two weeks later, he told another correspondent that, disgusted as he was with "the nonsense chattered by the extreme advocates of peace," it was very difficult for him to take "a proper interest" in the conference proceedings.

Roosevelt was in favor of general arbitration treaties, encouraging their negotiation, but only on a basis of strict exemption of issues involving vital interests and national honor. Any program of compulsory arbitration that would include such questions he considered "a noxious form of silliness which always accompanies the sentimental refusal to look facts in the face." And he continued to be highly dubious, as might well be imagined, of the practicality of any limitation of armaments. What he repeatedly returned to was the danger of weakening the real peace-loving nations and placing them at the mercy of military despotisms. It was important above all, Roosevelt declared, to have "those nations which really stand at the head of civilization show, not merely by words but by action, that they ask peace in the name of justice and not from any weakness." And they must be left free, he added, to act "with sanity, with self-restraint, with power; which must be the prime qualities in any program of reform."

Roosevelt's ideas hardly appealed to the pacifist groups and he returned their violent criticism of his attitude—at least privately—with interest. He sought to explain and justify his views in many friendly letters to Carnegie, whom he constantly reminded that it was an even greater duty to work for justice than for peace, but he nevertheless considered the pacific-minded steel-master representative of "the most objectionable class of peace advocates" because of his unrealistic and utopian ideas. He denounced the "hysterical denunciation and fear of war" on the part of journals like the *Evening Post* and the *Nation,* and his natural political antagonism to William Jennings Bryan was heightened by his rival's pacifism and what he considered the nonsensical ideas set forth in Bryan's famous "Prince of Peace" speech. "Of course I do not dare in public to express my real opinion of Bryan," Roosevelt wrote on one occasion. ". . . . But he is the cheapest faker we have ever had proposed for President."

Far from feeling that there was any danger of militarism

among the American people, as the pacifists vociferously charged, Roosevelt believed that the real peril facing the country was "the growth of a foolish peace spirit which is not merely harmless, but fraught with the possibility of mischief." Perhaps the best indication of his fundamental approach to these problems was his stated conviction, in a letter to Charles W. Eliot in September 1906, that "the United States Navy is an infinitely more potent factor for peace than all the peace societies of every kind and sort, that are to be found in the United States put together."

While fighting this running battle with the peace advocates and antimilitarists, he managed to carry through successfully his program for building up the Navy. His congressional opponents invariably combated his proposed appropriations, but through 1905 he succeeded in adding two battleships to the fleet each year. He then stated that only replacements to keep the fleet at the greatest possible efficiency were necessary. However when trouble with Japan loomed over the horizon, he once again called for new construction. Opposition was perhaps stronger in 1907—the year of the second meeting at The Hague —than at any previous time. But while Bryan might inveigh against a policy that placed "an instrument of brute force above the nation's sense of justice as a guarantee of peace," Roosevelt had his way. Before he relinquished office he could state—as he did with great pride—that during his two administrations he had been able to double the size of the Navy and that it had become second among those of the great powers. There were twenty-five battleships in the American fleet in 1909, and sixteen of them had been constructed during the previous eight years.

The President's personal delight in the growth of the Navy was clearly manifest at a spectacular naval show in Long Island Sound in September 1906. As the great line of ships, including twelve battleships, eight cruisers, and some twenty-four other vessels, passed before the reviewing vessel, Roosevelt's face was wreathed in smiles. Enthusiastically throwing his arms around the shoulders of the congressmen who were standing near him, as one reporter described the scene, he exclaimed: "Any man who fails to be patriotically inspired by such a sight as this is a mighty poor American, and every American who has seen it ought to be a better American for it."

Throughout the long debates over naval appropriations, Roosevelt took the stand that the foreign policies adopted as a consequence of the Spanish-American War "demand the possession of a first-class navy." Everything that the United States had been able to do in putting an end to bloody misrule and civil strife in Cuba, Panama, and the Philippines, and in exerting its pacific influence in China, he declared, was possible "only because, together with the purpose to be just and to keep the peace, we possess a Navy which makes it evident that we will not tamely submit to injustice, or tamely acquiesce in breaking the peace." He denied that in seeking to build up the fleet's strength he was "an alarmist, or an imperialist, or an amateur war lord," for a powerful navy was "not provocative of war. It is the surest guarantee of peace."

In the actual conduct of foreign affairs, Roosevelt acted largely on his own initiative and held the reins of policy-making firmly in his own determined hands. He often ignored his Secretary of State and rarely consulted his cabinet. He operated to a great extent through personal emissaries abroad and close friends among the diplomatic corps in Washington, rather than through officers of the foreign service. He was on particularly cordial terms with Ambassador Jusserand of France, a member of his tennis cabinet, and with Ambassador Speck von Sternberg of Germany, the familiar "Specky" of innumerable letters in his correspondence. The British ambassador, Sir Mortimer Durand, he found conscientious and high-minded, but dull and slow. Durand was quite evidently uncongenial to the effervescent President and in one moment of exasperation Roosevelt wrote of his "utter worthlessness." Continuing to correspond with his old friend Cecil Spring-Rice, unfortunately abroad, Roosevelt again and again expressed the wish that "Springy" was representing his country's interests in Washington.

The most interesting phase of the personal diplomatic correspondence of this prolific letter writer was an exchange of letters with Wilhelm II. Roosevelt thought the Kaiser understood him, and that he understood the Kaiser. They seemed to have formed a mutual admiration society. Yet the President would deny indignantly that he was in any sense taken in by Wilhelm, who, he said, was a friend of peace but jumpy and erratic—an "autocratic zigzag." It always bothered him that the impression should get abroad that he was playing the Kaiser's game. "I know Springy thinks I am inclined to fall under the influence of the German emperor," he told the British ambassador on one occasion, "but he is quite wrong. . . . I don't trust him."

The formulation of national policy during the Roosevelt administration could not under these circumstances have contrasted more sharply with what had gone on during the days of McKinley. There was nothing to compare with the influence of that small group of imperial-minded politicians and publicists, or with the popular pressures generated by jingoist propaganda, which had played such a decisive part in settling the issues of war and peace in 1898. Whereas McKinley had played a role forced on him rather than one which demonstrated independent leadership, Roosevelt himself *made* policy. It was impossible for him either to wait upon events or to delegate authority. It was well to have things of importance, he once wrote, "handled by one man alone."

In generally ignoring the role of the Secretary of State in his recollections of his own conduct of policy, Roosevelt was not always fair. Both Hay and Root were instrumental in carrying through intricate negotiations even if it were true that Roosevelt generally initiated policy. Indeed, there was a note of rancor in the President's personal comment after Hay's death that "in the Department of State his usefulness to me was almost exclusively the usefulness of a fine figurehead." It was a remark hard to reconcile with many earlier tributes. "As Secretary of State you stand alone," Roosevelt had written Hay in July 1903; "I could not spare you."

He was more generous toward Root. He repeatedly—both in public and in private—declared that he did not believe there was anyone doing more for the cause of peace, and freely acknowledged a real debt to Root's advice and counsel. The personal relations between Roosevelt and Hay, and between Roosevelt and Root, account in part for these different judgments. There is also the fact that, in the last year or two, Hay's failing health severely limited his activities.

Roosevelt was always impatient of the role of the Senate in considering treaties, and he was prepared wherever possible to circumvent such control as it might seek to exert over foreign policy. The Senate was helpless, he said, when "any efficient work was to be done." He could be very outspoken in his private correspondence on the inability of senators—and particularly, of course, Democratic senators—to understand what he was trying to do or to appreciate the world role of the United States.

As for public opinion, Roosevelt was impatient with the limitations it might impose upon policy and yet he realized that he could go only so far unless he was able to command effective popular support. Writing Mahan in 1901, he commented that public men could never lead the country "much further than public opinion has prepared the way." It was the indifference and apathy to foreign affairs among the people as a whole that continued to baffle him throughout his administration. He generally had the public behind him in his more dramatic moves on the world stage, although there was always sharp criticism from his political foes, but he never felt he had been able to arouse the American people to a full realization of their responsibilities.

Whatever may be said of his relations with his cabinet, with Congress, or with the public in particular instances, however, it remained true that throughout his years in the White House, Roosevelt almost singlehandedly directed foreign policy. Not only that; he thoroughly enjoyed and believed in the exercise of the powers he took upon himself.

"While President I have *been* President, emphatically," he wrote George Otto Trevelyan on June 19, 1908; "I have used every ounce of power there was in the office . . . . and wherever I could establish a precedent for strength in the executive, as I did for instance in regards external affairs in the case of sending the fleet around the world, taking Panama, settling affairs of Santo Domingo and Cuba . . . . why in all these cases I have felt not merely that my action was right in itself, but that in showing the strength of, or in giving strength to, the executive, I was establishing a precedent of value."

There was never any question of Roosevelt's abiding interest in power—power for himself, power for the national government, power for the United States on a global scale. Moreover, as a man of action—Henry Adams characterized him as "pure act"—he was sometimes rash and impetuous in the exercise of power. This never bothered him. His abiding conviction that everything he did conformed to the highest standards of the moral law was easily sustained because he interpreted justice and righteousness solely on the basis of his own judgment of what constituted these ethical concepts.

Nevertheless, when confronted by a real crisis, Roosevelt could show a measure of moderation and restraint that often belied his impetuous nature and seemed out of character with the noisy belligerency that marked his scorn of the peace-minded. And his thoroughly realistic attitude toward the need for the United States to maintain the power that would cause other nations to listen to its voice in world affairs was securely founded on an idealistic conception of what America's role should be in promoting peace and justice.

"No friendliness with other nations, no good will for them or by them," he told his last Congress, "can take the place of national self-reliance. Fit to hold our own against the strong nations of the earth, our voice for peace will carry to the ends of the earth. Unprepared, and therefore unfit, we must sit dumb and helpless to defend ourselves, protect others, or preserve peace."

Roosevelt could be domineering in his attitude toward smaller nations, was sometimes naive in his calculations of the stakes of power politics, and always supremely egotistic in his estimation of his own role in foreign affairs. Moreover, his constant emphasis upon the need to build up the physical power that would enable the United States to speak with authority in the councils of the nations—his aggressive nationalism— was especially to lend itself to criticism when his career was reviewed in the isolationist and pacifist era between world wars. But greater perspective cannot fail at least to modify many of the strictures once brought against his conduct of foreign policy. A different view of the importance of national power—the concept, indeed, of "the big stick"—provides in the 1950s the basis for a more realistic and favorable appraisal of the general course he followed.

Above all else, Roosevelt was the first President to think in global terms. In Latin America, in eastern Asia, and in Europe, he strove valiantly to have the United States fulfill what he believed to be its international responsibilities.

CHAPTER XV

MAKING LATIN AMERICA BEHAVE

APART FROM ALL OTHER CONSIDERATIONS OF FOREIGN POLICY, there was one part of the world where long tradition as well as more recent events seemed to call for a further assertion of American power and influence. This was Latin America. Cleveland had revived popular support for the Monroe Doctrine at the time of the Venezuela dispute—far more than anything said or done by the imperialists—and the American people had shown their determination to resist any possible extension of European influence in the Western Hemisphere. Differences there might be over the role the United States should play in eastern Asia or in Europe. The ranks were closed when it came to Latin America.

Naturally enough the deep impulses that had built up such universal approval for Cleveland's stand in 1896 were reenforced by success in driving Spain out of the New World and by the establishment of paramount American power in the Caribbean. Possession of Puerto Rico and of a naval base in Cuba, and the immediate prospect of constructing an isthmian canal, provided new and even more compelling reasons for preventing any foreign encroachments in this broadened sphere of national interest. The United States was prepared to demonstrate to all the world that the Monroe Doctrine would be upheld.

There was no longer any threat of a British challenge to this historic policy. The settlement of the quarrel over Venezuela, and her friendly attitude during the Spanish-American War, attested to England's willingness to recognize American interests in the Caribbean. There was a recurrent fear in many quarters, however, that Germany might consider Latin America an open field for her aggressive imperialism. Ever since the distant but angry clash over Samoa—where again Cleveland had played a significant part in awakening a strongly nationistic spirit among his countrymen—the American public had looked with suspicion on Germany's apparent ambition to expand overseas.

"No man who carefully watches the signs of the time," wrote Elihu Root in 1900, with an eye evidently on Germany, a nation which he consistently believed to be the great disturber of world peace, "can fail to see that the American people will within a few years have to either abandon the Monroe Doctrine or fight for it, and we are not going to abandon it."

Roosevelt would never for a moment hesitate as to the vital necessity for upholding this historic policy. While still Vice President, he wrote Lodge that he would do everything in his power to have the United States take the attitude that no European nation, Germany or any other, "should gain a foot of soil in any shape or way in South America, or establish a protectorate under any disguise over any South American country."

His attitude was ultimately to lead to an assertion of American power that paid little attention to the susceptibilities of the Latin Americans themselves. To free the European powers of any temptation to interfere in the affairs of this hemisphere, because Latin American republics repudiated their foreign debts or otherwise disregarded international obligations, Roosevelt proclaimed, in his famous corollary to the Monroe Doctrine, the right of the United States to act in this general area as an international policeman. As a means of blocking any possibility of foreign complications, as he wrote privately with an unconscious admission of how he really felt about most Latin Americans, he would show "those Dagoes that they will have to behave decently."

A first development in Latin America, both an expression of new interests and a cause for further concern over the strategic security of the Caribbean, was final completion of arrangements for building an interoceanic canal. It was a magnificent conception but the circumstances under which the canal got underway reflected unhappily on American policy. For the impatient Roosevelt acted on the assumption that nothing, and particularly what he regarded as the obstructive tactics of the people through whose territory the canal was to be built, should be allowed to stand in the way of this great contribution to civilization. The end justified the means. "I took the Canal Zone and let Congress debate," he later declared in a classic statement; "and while the debate goes on the Canal does also."

Every one of the imperialists of the closing decade of the nineteenth century had urged that the United States undertake this great task of linking the Atlantic and the Pacific. Many militant foes of other forms of overseas expansion agreed that here was a project that this country should make its own. While Cleveland, for example, continued to oppose the view that the United States should exclusively own and operate an isthmian canal, believing that it should be placed under international control and considered a trust for civilization, he nonetheless was in favor of its construction.

In the aftermath of war with Spain, with the strategic value of a canal strongly emphasized by the long voyage which the *Oregon* had been forced to make around Cape Horn, it was inevitable that the project should receive fresh impetus. The McKinley administration was fully committed to it. In his annual message to Congress in December 1898, referring to the investigation already under way by a Nicaraguan Canal Commission headed by Rear Admiral John G. Walker, the President stated emphatically that, as a consequence of the annexation of Hawaii and the further expansion of American commerce and influence in the Pacific, "the construction of such a maritime highway is now more than ever indispensable." Even more significantly, he added that in the light of recent developments American policy imperatively demanded that any canal be completely and exclusively controlled by the United States.

A first problem involved in any further development of the project was an understanding with Great Britain. Half a century earlier the United States had concluded a treaty with England wherein it was agreed that neither nation should ever seek to obtain exclusive control over a possible canal, exercise dominion over any adjacent territory, or fortify a canal zone. Secretary Hay consequently sought a revision of this treaty and after long conversations with the British ambassador, Lord Pauncefote, agreement was reached upon a new pact that fully acknowledged the exclusive right of the United States to build a canal. It was still understood, however, that the canal would not be fortified and would be placed under some form of international control.

Hay was completely satisfied with the new treaty. He felt he had won important concessions from Great Britain. To his amazement and chagrin, however, the Senate would have none of it in its existing form, and was strongly backed by an aroused public opinion. It was hardly surprising in the temper of the times that any restrictions at all upon constructing a canal should be hailed as a British victory and a surrender of American rights.

"If we concede a partnership or participation in the canal, to anybody on earth," one paper declaimed, "the radiant glory which has lately settled upon the brow of the nation will fade, and the violet vision of progress, hope and promise that now spreads before us will be lost to our sight."

The strongly Anglophile Hay took such opposition to his treaty very badly. "I underrated the power of ignorance and spite, acting upon cowardice," he wrote angrily, and was ready to offer his resignation. Among public figures opposing the treaty, however, were such staunch Republicans and friends of Hay as Roosevelt and Lodge. Roosevelt considered the treaty wholly inadmissible. He declared in a public statement that it was better to have no canal rather than one which would not be under complete American control in peace and war. The pressures brought to bear from so many quarters finally persuaded the Secretary of State not to resign but to undertake new negotiations with England.

They did not prove too difficult. In the course of reorienting its entire Caribbean policy, the British Government was actually quite willing to accept the new American proposals, and a second completely revised Hay-Pauncefote treaty was signed on November 18, 1901. It fully recognized the right of the United States to proceed entirely on its own in building and also operating a canal, and by implication freely conceded this country's right to fortify the prospective canal zone. Roosevelt was now President and sent the new treaty to the Senate with his enthusiastic support—somewhat to Hay's amusement. It was approved by a vote of 72 to 6 on December 16.

But just where was the canal to be built? It had long been assumed that Nicaragua, as originally proposed by the Walker Commission, was the logical site, but Congress soon became involved in prolonged controversy over an alternative route in Panama, at this time a province of Colombia. Further investigations were made, official views shifted, and the entire issue became deeply enmeshed in politics. Although a second report by the Walker Commission sustained its first recommendation, and early in January 1902 the House of Representatives endorsed a Nicaraguan Canal with only two dissenting votes, a countercampaign in favor of Panama gathered tremendous momentum. As a consequence of one of the most amazing instances of pressure group activity in all American history, Congress was to alter completely its position.

The impetus behind this campaign for the Panama route came from the stockholders of a French company, successor to an earlier corporation that had, under the direction of Ferdinand de Lesseps, builder of the Suez Canal, made a brave but unsuccessful attempt to cut a canal across the Panamanian isthmus in the 1880s. The New Panama Canal Company, as it was called, still held a concession from Colombia for this project, and the only way it could hope to bail itself out was to sell its rights to the United States. Urging Panama as a far superior route to Nicaragua, it blandly offered to surrender the concession for $109,000,000, and began working on Congress.

The driving force behind the New Panama Canal Company was its onetime chief engineer, Philippe Buneau-Varilla, an impressive, dynamic, full-mustachioed Frenchman whose gall was matched by his persuasive charm. The company's stockholders also enlisted the aid of a cool and calculating New York lawyer, William N. Cromwell, whose real asset was his close links with Mark Hanna and other Republican leaders, through whom he contributed $60,000 to the party campaign fund. These two supersalesmen, although they did not themselves see eye to eye, had a way with them when it came to dealing with Congress.

Their first move was to reduce the asking price of the company's concession to $40,000,000 (which perhaps convinced many congressmen that this must be a bargain); the second, to stress the danger of Nicaragua's volcanos as a perilous hazard to any canal project. Buneau-Varilla sought to drive home this point by distributing to all members of Congress a Nicaraguan stamp picturing a volcano, and fate, to his intense satisfaction, promptly played into his hands by providing an actual volcanic eruption. An impressed Senate took the bait and, reversing the stand of the House, passed an amendment to the pending bill providing for construction of a canal across Panama—and payment of $40,000,000 to the New Panama Canal Company—if a satisfactory treaty could be concluded with Colombia.

The House concurred in this change and Hay took up negotiations with Colombia. The United States was willing to pay $10,000,000 for a perpetual lease on a canal site, together with an annual rental of $250,000, but it further stipulated that Colombia should acquiesce in a direct American payment to the New Panama Canal Company for surrender of its original concession. This was hardly pleasing to Colombia, which felt that the proposed treaty not only infringed on her sovereign rights, but allotted a major share of the monetary award to a private company. Her minister refused to sign the treaty. However, he was soon recalled on orders from Bogota, and under very confused circumstances the Colombian chargé d'affaires affixed his signature to the pact early in January 1903. The United States Senate promptly approved this Hay-Herrán Treaty, with no more concern, it was reported, than

might be aroused over making an appropriation for a battleship. However, after bitter and acrimonious debate, the
Colombian Senate unanimously refused to do so.

Roosevelt was incensed. Here was a great project in the
interests of civilization and these "contemptible little creatures
in Bogota" were ready to block the march of progress because of a petty desire for more money. It was as if a road
agent had tried to hold up a traveler, he declared, and Colombia
deserved no more sympathy or consideration than would be
extended to any inefficient bandit. There could be no dealing
with her officials on such terms—"we may have to give a lesson
to these jack rabbits." It was soon reported—in the summer
of 1903—that the lesson would be the outright seizure of
Panama. An old treaty gave the United States the right to
guarantee free transit across the isthmus, and Roosevelt prepared a message to Congress seeking authorization to intervene
in Panama, in defiance of the Colombian authorities, under
this treaty's terms.

The agents of the New Panama Canal Company in the
meantime saw all their plans—and their $40,000,000—gravely
endangered. If arrangements could not be made with Colombia,
Congress had provided that the site for the canal might be
shifted back again to Nicaragua. The company would be
stranded. At a secret meeting in a room in New York's Waldorf
Astoria, its agents consequently hatched a plot for a revolution
in Panama that would enable that province to establish its
independence and thereupon offer the United States the canal
zone that Colombia seemed determined to withhold.

Rumors of the prospective uprising were rife throughout the
summer ("People of Panama Ready to Revolt," reported the
New York Times as early as August 31) and awoke considerable controversy in the American press. Some papers
maintained that the United States had every right to encourage
Panamanian rebellion because Colombia had no more than
nominal control over the province and its independence was
"a righteous and excellent proposition." Others condemned any

idea of intervention as marking "the moral apostasy of the American people, our abandonment of a place among honorable nations."

Whatever the pros and cons of such arguments, the instigators of the revolt did not directly receive any support from Washington officials. A State Department announcement in September said that the idea that the United States had any interest in unrest in Panama was "too trivial for consideration," and Roosevelt virtuously wrote Albert Shaw that he had "cast aside the proposition made at this time to foment the secession of Panama." Yet there was never any question of the President's sympathy, expressed quite candidly in other private letters, for Panama's independence. Buneau-Varilla, the ringleader in all these intrigues, was too shrewd to press matters when he well knew how the land lay.

"I have no idea what Buneau-Varilla advised the revolutionists," Roosevelt later wrote, ". . . . but it was his business to find out what he thought our government would do. I have no doubt that he was able to make a very accurate guess and to advise his people accordingly. In fact he would have been a very dull man had he not been able to make such a guess."

The revolution broke out according to plan. A stalwart little army made up of railway section hands, the local fire brigade, and a contingent of bribed troops rose up against the Colombian authorities in Panama. When the Bogota government sought to move troops across the isthmus to suppress the rebels, forces from the USS *Nashville*, which happened to have been ordered to Colon at this particular juncture, prevented their transit on the basis of the old isthmian treaty. There was nothing Colombia could do, and the Panamanians joyfully proclaimed their independence.

The pace of events had been rapid, but even then seemed to have lagged somewhat behind the schedule as it had apparently been understood in Washington. On November 3 the acting Assistant Secretary of State cabled the United States consul at Panama: "Uprising on Isthmus reported. Keep

Department promptly and fully informed." The disconcerting reply came back: "No uprising yet. Reported it will be in the night." A few hours later the lost time had been made up and all was well. The consul reported: "Uprising occurred tonight at 6; no bloodshed. Government will be organized tonight."

The next day Roosevelt happened to be writing his son Kermit. He described how he was busy at work over "the boiling cauldron on the Isthmus of Panama" when interrupted by a telegram Kermit had sent him of a football game. He rushed into another room to "read it aloud to mother and sister, and we all cheered in unison when we came to the Rah! Rah! Rah! part of it." Then, the President said, he returned to the Panama business.

For half a century, his letter to Kermit continued after this introduction, the United States had been policing the isthmus in the interest of "the little wildcat republic of Colombia," but he did not intend, in any move in connection with the new insurrection, "to do for her work which is not merely profitless but brings no gratitude." Any interference would be in the interests of Panama and the United States. "There will be some lively times in carrying out this policy," he concluded. "Of course, I may encounter checks, but I think I shall put it through all right. Ever your loving father . . ."

Subsequent events now closely followed the pattern set a decade earlier—if at the time unsuccessfully—in connection with the first move to annex Hawaii. Secretary Hay, who was prepared to support the President, whatever his inner qualms, officially recognized the independence of Panama on November 6 and promptly initiated negotiations for a canal treaty with the newly appointed Panamanian minister in Washington. By some coincidence he happened to be Buneau-Varilla. No difficulties whatsoever were experienced, and within twelve days a treaty was signed. The Republic of Panama ceded the United States a canal zone on exactly the same terms as those which the now unhappy and bitterly protesting Colombia had so cavalierly rejected, and the United States undertook to guarantee Panama its newly won independence.

There was no change in party control in Washington to block this treaty, as had happened when the incoming Cleveland administration had undone the work of President Harrison's envoys in Hawaii in 1893. Roosevelt had the situation well in hand. There were, it is true, outraged cries from his political foes. The *New York Times* warned of "the heady wine of territorial adventure that now fires the blood of the Administration," and declared that "we must either withdraw from this miserable business, or, shutting our ears to the voice of conscience and to the reproaches of civilized mankind, plunge on in the path of scandal, disgrace, and dishonor." Other Democratic papers also had a good deal to say about irresponsibility, indecent haste, jingoism and cowboy diplomacy. But the opposition was ineffectual. Although few papers went as far as the New York *Sun*, which enthusiastically hailed "the new risen star in the galaxy of American commonwealths," the Republican press staunchly upheld administration policy. The Rochester *Times* declared the President should have the support of every patriotic American; the St. Louis *Republic* said the American Government had only done its duty; and the Detroit *News*, with refreshing candor, simply stated: "Let us not be mealy-mouthed about this. We want Panama."

It seemed to be increasingly clear that public opinion as a whole agreed with the President that nothing should be allowed to stand in the way of a project that meant so much for all the world. When Roosevelt sought to prove that he had taken no part in instigating revolt in Panama by releasing to the press the message he had intended to send Congress about the need for taking "the matter into our own hands" through quite another form of direct intervention, his supporters somehow accepted it as demonstrating the President's moderation and restraint. There was some debate in the Senate when the issue came up there, but Roosevelt's supporters were in full control. The treaty was approved on February 23, 1904, with only fourteen adverse votes.

The work on the canal was soon started, and in November 1906 Roosevelt went to Panama to look the situation over and "make the dirt fly." The newspapers reported that he had spent twenty minutes operating a steam shovel, getting thoroughly splattered with mud, and had dutifully visited the laborers' quarters. Construction was under the able direction of Colonel George W. Goethals and was finally completed—at a cost of some $400,000,000—in 1914. The canal was triumphantly opened to the commerce of all nations on the very eve of the outbreak of World War I.

Roosevelt at the time, and in succeeding years, stoutly defended his policy as in every respect conforming to the "highest, finest, and nicest standards of public and governmental ethics." No doubts apparently ever assailed him as to the justification for riding so roughshod over the possible rights of Colombia. That he might have moved somewhat more slowly, seeking a more equitable adjustment of the payments earmarked for the New Panama Canal Company and giving Colombia time to reconsider, seems never to have occurred to a man who insisted always on action. His personal correspondence is full of angry fulminations against Colombia ("no more cruel despotism outside of Turkey"), repeated denials that there was any suggestion of conspiracy in relation to the Panama revolt, and frequent suggestions that he had actually not gone far enough in enforcing American rights. As late as 1911 he reiterated, in an article in the *Outlook* describing in full "How the United States Acquired the Right to Dig the Panama Canal," that the action he had taken was "right in every detail and at every point."

Yet there were times when the righteous Mr. Roosevelt seemed to protest too much. The story is told of a cabinet meeting when he was vigorously defending his policy and caught the twinkling eye of Secretary Root. "Have I answered the charges? Have I defended myself?" Roosevelt demanded. "You certainly have, Mr. President," Root suavely answered. "You have shown that you were accused of seduction and you have conclusively proved that you were guilty of rape."

The whole episode shows Roosevelt at his worst. Here was the impetuous, unthinking jingo demanding action, at whatever cost, and then attempting to cover his unjustified impatience with a cloak of specious morality. There was no reason for such precipitate haste, and no need to follow a policy that so heedlessly offended all Latin Americans. The Panama Canal was a great and important project. Its construction was indeed in the interest of the entire world. The argument could well be made that no one nation, even if its motives had been more beyond reproach than those which influenced the Colombian congress, should be permitted to stand indefinitely in the way of such a grand undertaking. Yet time was not so vital as Roosevelt thought. There could be no escaping the fact that the United States had treated Colombia with shocking disregard of her rights.

The President's political foes nevertheless continued to be faced with something of a dilemma. They could assail his methods in Panama, but they were not in a position to repudiate the results of his policy. The Democrats did not dare make it a partisan issue, for the American people thoroughly approved of the Panama Canal and on the whole they could not feel too squeamish about the way Colombia had been treated. Although they had retreated from the imperialism of 1898 and were often dubious about its consequences, here was an assertion of American power that could be condoned because it was so clearly being exercised in behalf of civilization.

Many persons who in retrospect were to be highly critical of the Panama policy were at the time carried away by the enthusiasm and popular support that Roosevelt could so easily evoke. His followers came to believe that he could do no wrong. Writing a good many years later of the Panama affair, Senator George Norris said that though at the time "doubts assailed me . . . . I followed him step by step."

If the seizure of Panama was the most dramatic incident in the development of Rooseveltian policies toward Latin America, it was still only one of a series of events that affected the general relationships between the United States and the neighboring countries to the south. It was possible at one time for Bryan to complain that "there is a tendency under this administration to allow the Monroe Doctrine to acquire a moth-ballish flavor," but with the Panama Canal giving a new urgency to the need for unquestioned American control over the Caribbean, this situation drastically changed.

A first occasion for concern over possible European encroachments in this area arose while the canal project was still being considered by Congress. Venezuela at the time was under the dictatorial rule of the unprincipled General Castro ("an unspeakably villainous little monkey," Roosevelt later called him), and had completely defaulted on certain debts owed her foreign creditors. In an attempt to enforce collection, Great Britain and Germany (later joined by Italy) prepared, in 1902, after long and futile negotiations, to set up a joint blockade of the Venezuela coast. They officially informed the State Department of these plans, giving every assurance that they had no intention of seizing any territory, and the United States consequently raised no objections to the proposed action. At this time Roosevelt as yet had no idea of this country assuming any responsibility in such controversies. "If any South American state misbehaves toward any European country," he wrote his German diplomatic friend "Specky" von Sternberg, "let the European country spank it." His confidence that the Venezuelan situation would take care of itself was reflected in the statement in his annual message in December 1902 that "there seems not to be the slightest chance of trouble with a foreign power."

When England and Germany actually imposed their blockade in mid-December, and Germany sank two Venezuelan warships, the American public nevertheless became considerably agitated. It had heretofore, as reflected in the press, shown little concern over what was happening and did not seem to think that the Monroe Doctrine was in any way involved. This attitude now changed, and the newspapers generally grew highly critical of Anglo-German policy. The Norfolk *Virginian-Pilot* declared that the naval demonstration in the Caribbean was "an insolent and defiant challenge of the Monroe Doctrine —a cut across the face with a whip." The New York *American* said that it grated American sensibilities "to see an American republic kicked and cuffed by a brace of European monarchies." Other jingoist papers called for the immediate dispatch to the scene of the Spanish-American War's naval hero, Admiral Dewey, with orders to uphold the Monroe Doctrine against all comers.

In the light of this popular reaction, and perhaps fearful himself of how far Germany (there was no fear of England) might go in seeking to enforce Venezuela's payment of her debts, Roosevelt undertook to bring direct pressure upon the Kaiser to accept arbitration of a dispute which, if unresolved, might lead to a German-American clash. Under circumstances that remain very obscure, he apparently called in the German ambassador and warned him that the United States viewed with grave concern his country's attitude, and could never acquiesce in any move to seek territorial concessions from Venezuela in compensation for her default on her debts.

The circumstances are obscure because there is no record of these conversations, and a good many years later, in the excitement of pending war with Germany in 1917, Roosevelt gave a highly colored account of what supposedly went on, for which, also, there is no valid evidence. He declared that he had given the German ambassador an ultimatum, insisting on immediate acceptance of arbitration; and had reminded him that with the Atlantic fleet holding its maneuvers in the Caribbean, Dewey was ready to sail to Venezuela at an hour's notice.

Historians have always been intrigued by the unanswerable question of just what Roosevelt did actually say or do. For while the ultimatum story is extremely unlikely, it does not appear to have been made up entirely out of whole cloth. We now know that the fleet maneuvers in the Caribbean were directed with the possible contingency of action against Germany very much in mind, and Roosevelt may well have emphasized the presence of American naval power in the Caribbean in talking with her ambassador. Moreover, in a letter to Henry White in 1906—nearly four years after the event but still ten years before the disputed account of the affair made during war days—Roosevelt wrote that at the time of "the Venezuelan business" he had told the German ambassador that if Germany took any action that looked like the acquisition of territory, the United States would be obliged to interfere, if necessary by force.

Whatever may or may not have been said by Roosevelt, however, the actual course of events led to a peaceful settlement of the controversy. The Anglo-German blockade had caused the obstreperous General Castro to change his tune. He took the lead in proposing arbitration, and even before Roosevelt had purportedly threatened intervention, Germany and England had agreed in principle to the submission of the dispute to the Hague tribunal. A situation that led Secretary of the Navy Moody to state that the country was "never upon the borders of a greater peril," quickly calmed down.

The press generally hailed the agreement for arbitration as a victory for American diplomacy and a triumphant vindication of the principles of the Monroe Doctrine. There was no further disposition, even though lurking suspicions of German intentions were not entirely dispelled, to play up the incident or call for any further action. The *New York Times*, indeed, commended the press for "the sobriety, the moderation, the circumspection" that had been maintained in spite of some efforts to create a war scare. It thought that the popular reaction clearly denoted that the nation had given over the defiant, jingoist attitude of an earlier day. "We have become generally conscious," it stated, "of our international responsibilities."

Roosevelt was also well satisfied. Far from seeking credit for the result, moreover, he appeared willing at the time to attribute the conciliatory attitude of the creditor nations, and their willingness to accept arbitration, to the experience a decade earlier when Cleveland had so successfully brought pressure upon Great Britain in her former dispute with Venezuela. "I congratulate you heartily," Roosevelt wrote Cleveland on December 26, 1902, "on the rounding out of your policy."

Yet this was not quite the end of the affair. The allied blockade continued, pending final official agreement upon an arbitration protocol, and early in the new year a German gunboat bombarded a small Venezuelan town. A few papers again sounded an alarm—even the *Times* ruefully commented that "we assented to a peaceful blockade. It turned out to be a war." —and Germany was widely criticized for a "brutal and unwarranted" attack that showed a complete indifference to the good opinion of the civilized world. Nevertheless the situation was still viewed by the press as a whole with a calm that led the Baltimore *News* to comment that "the remarkable feature of current discussion has been the absence of jingoism."

It was soon clear, in fact, that whatever might be said of Germany's unprovoked bombardment, she had no intention of repudiating arbitration or of seeking an opportunity to seize any Venezuelan territory. The arrangements for submission of the dispute to the Hague tribunal were completed, and the blockade of Venezuela was lifted in mid-February. Popular interest quickly subsided, in the conviction that the policy followed by the United States had again successfully safeguarded American interests and effectively removed any moth-ballish flavor from the Monroe Doctrine.

"Europe has displayed a nervous anxiety to appease American diplomacy," commented one foreign newspaper, the *Allgemeine Zeitung,* confirming the general impression in this country. ". . . . The close of the Venezuelan dispute is equivalent to a victory of America over Europe."

However satisfactory its final resolution, the Venezuela dispute served to persuade Roosevelt—particularly now that the

Panama Canal project was beginning to get under way—of the need to prevent the occurrence of similar controversies in the future. Writing to Von Sternberg in March, 1903, he said that he had not realized how strongly the public would react to even the temporary landing of foreign troops in Venezuela, and had become convinced that the idea of setting up international controls over any one of the "wretched republics" in Latin America could not be contemplated. "A second attempt of foreign powers to collect their debts by force," he concluded, "would simply not be tolerated here."

Early in 1904 Santo Domingo became a case in point. That little island republic had been ravaged by a series of bloody revolts, had no stable government, and found itself totally unable to meet foreign obligations totaling some $32,000,000. The European powers could well be expected to take some action to force Santo Domingo into line, as they had in the case of Venezuela.

At one time the answer might well have been American annexation. Yet despite the fact that acquisition of the Dominican Republic had been an imperialist goal ever since the days of Johnson and Grant, there was nowhere any support for annexing a new island possession. It was in relation to this problem that Roosevelt expressed his own personal feelings in saying that he had no more desire to take over Santo Domingo than a gorged boa constrictor would have to swallow a porcupine. The criticism of his actions in Panama may have had a part in counseling a policy of greater moderation, but whatever the reason, he moved very cautiously. "If I possibly can," he wrote, "I want to do nothing. . . . If it is absolutely necessary to do something, then I want to do as little as possible."

Nevertheless Roosevelt also felt strongly that the United States had an inescapable obligation to aid and protect the little states in the neighborhood of the Caribbean. He wrote William Bayard Hale that his policy was in no way governed by the desire of aggrandizement, but operated solely on the theory "that it is our duty, when it becomes absolutely inevitable, to

police these countries in the interest of order and civilization."
As the situation in Santo Domingo became more pressing, he
put these ideas in concrete form in an official letter to Secretary
Root, read before a Cuban anniversary dinner in New York in
May 1904.

All that the United States wanted, Roosevelt said, was to see
neighboring countries stable, orderly, and prosperous, and if
they kept order and paid their obligations, they need fear no
interference on the part of the United States. But should they
fail to do so, he warned, something would have to be done.
"Brutal wrongdoing, or an impotence which results in a general
loosening of the ties of civilized society," the President declared, "may finally require intervention by some civilized nation, and in the Western Hemisphere the United States cannot
ignore this duty."

This first statement of what was to become known as the
Roosevelt Corollary to the Monroe Doctrine was generally upheld by Republicans; in other quarters it awoke violent criticism as "a flagrant exhibition of jingoism." Anti-imperialist
papers, recalling Roosevelt's bellicose statements in the past,
vigorously attacked what they interpreted as a policy of trying
to boss the world. They accused the President of seeking to
divert attention from domestic issues in favor of "a career of
rowdy adventure abroad."

Roosevelt professed to be rather amused "at the yell about
my letter" and stoutly maintained his position. If the United
States said "hands off" to the European powers, it could do no
less, he declared, than keep order in the Western Hemisphere
itself. His annual message to Congress in December reaffirmed
this stand. His policy, he told the country, was founded on
the principle that in the New World the "adherence of the
United States to the Monroe Doctrine may force the United
States, however reluctantly, in flagrant cases of such wrongdoing or impotence, to the exercise of an international police
power."

While Roosevelt prepared the way, a specific plan was in the meantime being worked out to meet the increasingly involved situation in the Dominican Republic. President Morales was prevailed upon to ask for American aid, and in January 1905 the two countries concluded an agreement whereby the United States took over control of the Dominican customs houses and the collection of all import duties. This agreement further provided that the United States would guarantee Santo Domingo's territorial integrity, seek an adjustment of all its foreign debts, and after allocating 45 per cent of the customs receipts to the local government, apply the balance on the foreign debt account.

To Roosevelt all this was perfectly simple: it was a good plan and he acted on it. But while the public was largely indifferent to what was happening, Congress was not. The Senate, jealous of its own powers in foreign policy, immediately objected to the assumption of such responsibilities through an executive agreement. "The Secretary of State," declared the *New York Times* in commenting on the reasons for this reaction, "is running around the Senatorial end with the Santo Domingo ball, and depositing it, as a *fait accompli,* behind the Senatorial goal."

In the face of such opposition, Roosevelt felt compelled to recast his program, and the American minister in Santo Domingo was instructed to sign a formal treaty embodying the original agreement. But the Senate still balked. In spite of the President's pleas that it was incompatible with international equity for the United States to refuse to allow other powers to collect their debts and yet refuse, itself, to do anything about the situation, political opposition effectively blocked the treaty's approval.

Roosevelt reacted very much as had Hay when the Senate rejected the first treaty with England in respect to an isthmian canal. The Senate did not know what it was doing, he repeatedly wrote; it was wholly incompetent and was acting with extreme stupidity. But the President had no intention of being blocked. He proceeded to apply his program under a *modus vivendi* which did not require senatorial approval. The United States took over control of the Dominican customs houses, made provision for payment of an adjusted national debt, and successfully restored the little island republic's economic and financial stability. Two years later a new treaty was negotiated, carrying forward the program already in effect. In July 1907, the Senate finally approved it.

Here was a direct and practical application of the new corollary to the Monroe Doctrine. Roosevelt's policy safeguarded the Dominican Republic from any intervention on the part of the European powers, protected American interests in the strategically sensitive area of the Caribbean, and redounded to the benefit of the people of Santo Domingo. Yet it also set up a precedent that was to have far-reaching implications. Through intervention in the internal affairs of a small neighboring country, Roosevelt had in effect set up a new American protectorate. At the time, Latin America was not greatly exercised, but when the policy was extended in later years to justify intervention in other instances, there naturally developed bitter suspicions of Yankee imperialism.

As a result of the earlier developments in Venezuela, indeed, the Argentine foreign minister, Luis M. Drago, had already set forth a counter-doctrine stating that armed intervention should never be permissible as a means of collecting debts. The second Hague conference incorporated this proposal in a convention to which the United States subscribed, but with the reservation, nullifying its value from the Latin American point of view, that intervention would be allowable if the offending country refused arbitration. The Roosevelt Corollary, however justified it might appear under then existing circumstances, consequently continued to sow mistrust among the Latin American nations. But it was not given up until more than two decades later. A State Department policy statement then explicitly declared that an interventionist policy could not be justified under the terms of the Monroe Doctrine which "states a case of the United States *vs.* Europe, not of the United States *vs.* Latin America."

The way was paved, so far as the Western Hemisphere was concerned, for the ultimate repudiation of any nation's right to intervene forcefully in another nation's internal affairs.

The Santo Domingo issue had no more than been settled than Roosevelt was faced with a mounting crisis in Cuba where, under the terms of the Platt Amendment, the United States had an accepted legal right—and obligation—to intervene to preserve law and order. New national elections had been held in the island republic in 1905, but the aftermath was widespread rioting and bloodshed. The government appeared helpless to control the situation, and President Palma appealed to the United States for support. Intervention seemed unavoidable if any sort of stability were to be restored.

The situation was made to order from the point of view of the imperialist-minded who still believed that the United States should annex Cuba. Clinging to his ambitious dreams of 1900, Senator Beveridge took the lead in urging that this final opportunity to secure complete control of Cuba and round out American hegemony in the Caribbean should not be lost. Taking the stump during the mid-term congressional elections in 1906, he constantly stressed this theme, and told Roosevelt that the reaction among those whom he addressed could not have been more favorable. "The statement that, should it become necessary to raise our flag again in Cuba, it will be raised to stay," he wrote, "brings a response very much like the wild enthusiasm that preceded the Spanish War."

Beveridge, however, was now a voice crying in the wilderness. There was no popular backing for any further extension of American empire. If the United States were constrained to intervene under the terms of the Platt Amendment, which was generally recognized as a definite responsibility, newspaper after newspaper insisted that such intervention should be temporary, and that the United States should be ready once again to withdraw from Cuba at the earliest opportunity.

Roosevelt also took this view. He may have obtained a canal

zone by somewhat dubious means, and asserted a new right of intervention in Latin America, but he had no idea of seeking to extend American control over Cuba. He stated repeatedly that he hoped intervention of any sort could be avoided, and hurried Secretary of War Taft off to the island to use all his powers of persuasion to bring about peace among Cuba's warring factions. It was only as a last resort that he authorized the dispatch of troops to restore order. In Panama, he had been precipitate, commented the *New York Times;* with Cuba, he was "deliberate, patient, forbearing."

Clearly regretting the need of even temporary intervention, Roosevelt refused to raise the American flag in Cuba, in spite of Beveridge's urgent pleas, and he assured the Cuban people that the United States wished nothing of them "save that they shall be able to preserve order among themselves and therefore to preserve their independence." He still had a somewhat patronizing air toward the Cuban people—as he had toward all Latin-Americans—and he thought in terms of what the United States might have to do in the exercise of its police power. Yet this was far from the imperialism of 1898.

"I am doing my best," he wrote privately in February 1907, "to persuade the Cubans that if only they will be good they will be happy; I am seeking the very minimum of interference necessary to make them good."

It was to take some doing. The failure of attempts at mediation led to the establishment of a provisional government under American control, and it was to be some three years before the situation permitted the final withdrawal of American troops. At no time, however, did Roosevelt waver in his determination that the occupation should be temporary, and that no move should be made toward annexation. The case could easily be made that through the authority given it under the Platt Amendment and through the heavy pressure of American economic interests, the United States maintained a dominant influence over the island's government, but Cuba retained its political independence.

There were times when it appeared as if Roosevelt would have liked to carry his policy of making Latin Americans behave further than he did. Writing to William Bayard Hale on the eve of his retirement from the presidency—in December 1909—he spoke of having wanted to intervene in Haiti ("simply in the interest of civilization") if he could only have "waked up our people so that they would back a reasonable and intelligent foreign policy which should put a stop to crying disorders at our very doors." He had been able to do what he had, in Cuba, Santo Domingo, and Panama, he told Hale, only by minimizing his interference and by always showing the clearest necessity for it.

In the more general phases of Latin American policy after 1904, however, Roosevelt allowed Root a virtually free hand, and he was subsequently to give his Secretary of State all credit for his constant efforts to relieve Latin America of fear of any possible recrudescence of Yankee imperialism. For while Root's program was founded, in full conformity with Roosevelt's views, on the necessity of maintaining strategic control over the Caribbean and of safeguarding the approaches to the Panama Canal, he tried in every possible way to counteract the adverse effects of intervention. He wanted to win the confidence of the Latin American peoples.

Root toured South America in 1906—the first American Secretary of State to do so—and attended the Third Inter-American Conference in Rio de Janeiro. The long trip was a terrific grind of meetings, receptions, luncheons, dinners, speeches, not made any easier by the lavish hospitality and inevitable warm sweet champagne served at every function. But the long-suffering Root survived, and he both made friends and influenced people. No statesman could wholly disabuse the Latin Americans of their suspicion and mistrust of their powerful neighbor to the north. Their economic dependence upon the United States kept them continually on guard. They could not forget Panama. Nevertheless Root made an important and lasting contribution to hemispheric solidarity.

The burden of his message was that the United States had no aggressive designs against Latin America and sought only the friendship and cooperation of all countries in the Western Hemisphere. "We wish for no victories but those of peace," he told the Pan-American conference; "for no territory except our own; for no sovereignty except the sovereignty over ourselves." And he spoke with sincerity and conviction.

"No European statesman of whom I have heard," Roosevelt once wrote Carnegie in glowing tribute to his Secretary of State, "has done as much for peace in any quarter of the world as Elihu Root has done in the Western Hemisphere during the last three years. No other American has rendered services to the cause of peace in any way comparable to his."

In general terms, the motives behind the Latin American policy of these years were clear. The canal project gave a new and vital significance to the American position in the Caribbean. The treaties or other arrangements concluded with the republics in this area, and the new corollary to the Monroe Doctrine as proclaimed by Roosevelt, were designed to maintain the stability that would avert any risk of European intervention in a part of the world where the United States now had interests whose preservation was essential to its security. Here was a new assertion of power and influence, underscoring and emphasizing the national determination to uphold the Monroe Doctrine. If economic considerations affected the general policy, giving rise in some quarters to charges of a new financial imperialism, they were entirely subordinate to basic strategic considerations that have not changed one whit in succeeding years.

The efforts to carry out such a policy in closer cooperation with Latin America, through abandonment of the idea of intervention in internal affairs and by the negotiation of mutual defense treaties, were still in the future. The United States was acting at this time entirely on its own responsibility and, in many cases, with scant respect for the feelings of the peoples of Latin America. Too often it seemed ready to ride roughshod over the interests of little nations unable to protect themselves. But if the designation "semiprotectorate" may be applied to certain of the Caribbean republics, the controls set up by the United States were exercised in the political and economic interests of the countries concerned, as well as in the interests of the United States. They helped to maintain peace and order. Moreover, for all its major concern with strategic security, American policy did not entirely neglect the traditional goal of seeking to serve the cause of democracy among peoples still prone to settle their problems by war and revolution. In its Latin American policy the United States accepted responsibilities and made commitments that were a challenging expression of its new role as a world power.

CHAPTER XVI

WAR AND PEACE IN ASIA

"They're a divvle iv a sinsitive people thim Japs," we find Mr. Dooley telling his friend Mr. Hennessy in the midst of the crisis in Japanese-American relations in 1907. "Look cross-eyed at thim an' they're into ye'er hair. . . . Thin what happens? The first thing I know a shell loaded with dynamite dhrops into th' lap iv some friend iv mine in San Francisco; a party iv Jap'nese land in Boston an' scalp th' wigs off th' descindants iv John Hancock an' Sam Adams; and Tiddy Rosenfelt is discovered undher a bed with a small language book thryin' to larn to say 'Spare me' in th' Jap'nese tongue."

Underlying the facetious tone of this comment, with the usually rambunctious Teddy Roosevelt found in such an uncharacteristic position, Mr. Dooley was expressing an anxiety that he shared with a good many American people. For the fear of possible hostilities with Japan, however exaggerated in some quarters, had a real basis during Roosevelt's second administration. Moreover, the contemporary predictions that, even if the current crisis were resolved, a Japanese-American war was sooner or later inevitable, came true some thirty-four years afterwards. That is, the conflict avoided in these opening years of the century was only postponed, and the far eastern policy developed by Roosevelt consequently takes on a significance that only Pearl Harbor has adequately demonstrated.

On first coming into office in 1901, Roosevelt was prepared to accept the Open Door in China as the basic foundation of America's position in eastern Asia. Even though Hay had already modified to a considerable degree his early hopes of the efficacy of his policy, the President for a time seemed ready to make up what he considered lost ground in upholding the principles set forth in the original Hay notes in 1899, and in the further statement on American interests in China made during the Boxer Rebellion. The United States, Roosevelt firmly believed, should more actively assert itself in Asia. If the commercial considerations underlying the Open Door still affected every phase of far eastern policy—for economic spokesmen continued to consider China the great outlet for the surplus of American manufactures—Roosevelt as always was thinking primarily in terms of political power rather than of economic advantage.

The threat both to American interests in eastern Asia and to the peace of that part of the world arose in the early 1900s from the aggressively imperialist policy being pursued by Czarist Russia. In what was interpreted as arrogant and treacherous disregard of its commitment to the Open Door policy, Russia was insidiously tightening her hold upon Manchuria and seeking not only to monopolize trade, but to establish political domination throughout the entire region. American firms, largely engaged in the textile business, protested to the State Department and sought some protection for their own trade and for the basic principles of the Open Door.

Hay did not feel that anything could be done. When a deeply concerned Japanese government inquired early in 1901 about American policy, he candidly answered that the United States was not prepared, either singly or in concert with other powers, to enforce its views on the Open Door and China's political integrity "by any demonstration which could present a character of hostility to any other power." He constantly protested Russian encroachments, and sought to strengthen his hand by concluding a new commercial treaty with China. Further than that he would not—and felt he could not—go. Hay was convinced that the American people would not support any direct action, even in concert with England and Japan, in resistance to czarist imperialism.

Roosevelt, deeply absorbed in the Panama affair and other phases of Latin American relations, for a time left these far eastern matters almost entirely in Hay's hands. Although he greatly resented what he called the "fathomless mendacity" of the Russians in diplomatic negotiations, and fulminated against a policy that he said was compounded of brutality, ignorance, and arrogance, he did not quite know what could be done about it. But while, in May 1903, he told his Secretary of State he thought he was handling things in a "most masterly manner," Roosevelt's patience was reaching the breaking point. Two months later he declared it was just as well "to show our teeth." In resisting Russia's advance, he now told Hay, he did not intend to give way, and was ready to "go the very limit I think our people will stand." Further developing this theme, he declared that if he were sure that France and Germany would keep out, he would not in the least mind if this meant "going to 'extremes' with Russia."

What Roosevelt may have meant by this remark remains highly problematic. Did he actually contemplate at this time that the United States might go to war to safeguard its interests in Asia? It is an intriguing idea in the light of all the subsequent developments flowing from the interplay of Russian and Japanese rivalry in Manchuria and Korea. However, Roosevelt had a penchant for such rash statements; they were actually no more than the impulsive expression of his momentary feelings. He made no further references to going to extremes, and no move that suggested active American intervention.

If the United States could afford to be rather indifferent to what happened in Manchuria, for its economic interests there were relatively slight, there was one nation whose vital security was threatened by Russia's advance. This was, of course, Japan. Having recently concluded an alliance with England that gave her assurance of British support if any third power intervened in a quarrel with Russia, she boldly challenged czarist pretensions in both Korea and Manchuria. When negotiations got nowhere, Japan abruptly broke them off in February 1904 and attacked the Russian base at Port Arthur on the Liaotung peninsula in Manchuria. It was a surprise attack, preceding any declaration of war, and caught the Russians wholly unprepared. But unlike the reaction to a very parallel situation thirty-seven years later at Pearl Harbor, the American press found nothing to criticize. "There is no ground for the imputation of treachery," the *New York Times* editorialized. Together with most newspapers, it blithely hailed Japan's initial victory in this new war.

Roosevelt's first moves—for he was now taking over complete control of far eastern policy—were to declare American neutrality and to seek from the two belligerents assurances that they would respect the sovereignty of China and safeguard the principles of the Open Door. But while the two warring powers were quite happy to accept in principle the American program relating to China proper, Russia's refusal to consider Manchuria as falling within the territorial control of the Imperial Government in Peking, made her reply almost meaningless. The ambiguity of the status of Manchuria, already admitted by

Hay, would plague far eastern policy down through the years and affect successive international decisions until the days of Yalta.

In his attitude toward the two belligerents, there was no question where Roosevelt's sympathies lay. His scorn for the Russian Government, which he considered a symbol of tyranny and oppression, was in no way abated. He had become convinced that, if victorious in the war, it would lose no time in "organizing north China against us . . . . as a step toward the domination of the rest of the world." On the other hand, he had a very real admiration for the Japanese, and believed their government to be enlightened and progressive. "They have played our game," he said, "because they have played the game of civilization."

In a letter to his friend Spring-Rice on July 24, 1905, he made another of those characteristically exaggerated statements for which there is no contemporary evidence. He said that, immediately on the outbreak of hostilities, he had notified Germany and France that in the event of any combination of European powers seeking to rob Japan of the fruits of her possible victory over Russia, he would "promptly side with Japan and proceed to whatever length was necessary in her behalf." This suggestion that the President was prepared to make the United States a silent partner in the Anglo-Japanese alliance is significant only as a further revelation of his attitude, and of the degree to which he was himself prepared to direct American foreign policy. In no other instance, as subsequent developments showed, was Roosevelt acting more on his own than in dealing with the situation in eastern Asia in 1904–05. The American minister in Tokyo was to write that he was sure that every instruction either he or his counterpart in St. Petersburg received was written in Roosevelt's own hand—"I do not believe he really consulted anybody."

Roosevelt's underlying sympathy with Japan and his suspicions of Russia coincided with the popular view throughout the United States. Newspaper after newspaper spoke admiringly of the courage of little Nippon in daring to challenge the massive might of the Russian colossus. There were other widespread expressions of the desire to see a Japanese victory. American bankers gave concrete proof of such sentiments in cooperating with English bankers in making loans to the Japanese Government.

After all, it was the United States which had opened up Japan to the Western world just a half century earlier, and there appeared to be good warrant to believe that the bonds of friendship between the two nations assured Japanese backing for American interests in Asia. "Public opinion in this country," one contemporary survey stated categorically, ". . . . supports the position assumed by Japan—that Russia shall give her a free hand in Korea and guarantee Chinese sovereignty in Manchuria." Even if a victorious Japan might not prove oversolicitous about the Open Door policy once Russia was defeated, as the more skeptical suggested, the view generally expressed was that anything was better than victory for czarist imperialism. "The organization and control of the millions of China by Russia," stated the liberal-minded *Arena* in an editorial particularly interesting in the light of developments half a century later, "is far more dangerous to the world than would be their control by Japan."

Nevertheless as the Russo-Japanese War proceeded with its startling succession of Japanese victories on both land and sea, the consequences of a triumph for Japan that would make her completely supreme in eastern Asia began seriously to concern the President. Weighing the possible effect on American interests of such an eventuality, he decided that the best thing for the United States would be the establishment of some sort of a balance of power between Russia and Japan. The integrity of China and the Open Door would be most effectively safeguarded, he repeatedly stated in his correspondence, if the two rival powers were in a position "so that each may have a moderative action on the other"; or, as he phrased it on another occasion, if their strength was so maintained that "each power will be in a sense the guarantor of the other's good conduct."

This new principle of "balanced antagonisms" between Japan and Russia served to convince Roosevelt of the desirability of trying to mediate in the war and of promoting a peace that would stop short of driving Russia entirely out of eastern Asia. But it had a more enduring significance in its continuing influence on American policy. Following World War I, the United States again sought to block further Japanese advance on the Asiatic mainland by preventing the complete dissolution of Russia's control over her maritime provinces; and when, some fifteen years later, Japan attacked in Manchuria, a desire to restore the balance of power in eastern Asia was a motivating factor in American recognition of the Soviet Union. With the defeat of Japan in World War II and the concessions made to Soviet Russia at Yalta, application of the balanced antagonisms principle gave a further ironic twist to American policy. For the United States soon found itself building up the power of the former Japanese enemy as a bastion against further aggression by its onetime Soviet ally. If the triumph of communism gave a new dimension to the perennial "problem of China," the principles that Theodore Roosevelt had enunciated some fifty years earlier still seemed to have their relevancy in mid-century.

The possibility that the President might seek to bring the warring powers to the peace table was first publicly suggested in newspaper headlines on March 31, 1905. Two months later, after the dramatic Japanese naval victory in which Admiral Togo—going into action flying the signal: "The destiny of the Empire depends on this one battle"—decisively smashed the Russian fleet at the battle of Tsushima, there were again newspaper stories that the President was trying to end the war. Finally, on June 11, it was officially announced that both Russia and Japan had accepted the President's proposals and that an armistice was imminent.

Behind these brief announcements was a most complicated story of secret diplomatic maneuvers. Roosevelt had for sev-

eral months been doing everything he could to bring the war
to an end and had repeatedly tried to enlist the help of the
Kaiser. The ambitious Wilhelm, however, was playing his own
political game. A professed concern with Asiatic peace and the
Open Door policy was actually a blind for promoting Germany's own imperialist designs. Moreover, he had originally
egged on the Czar to foreign adventure, and he still hoped to
see Russia so deeply mired in the Far East that her power in
Europe would be weakened. Under these circumstances he was
extremely cool to Roosevelt's overtures that he should exert his
influence in behalf of a Russo-Japanese truce. "The noble gentleman," he commented sarcastically on the margin of one report from his ambassador in Washington, "seems to intend to
horn in on world politics." On another occasion he similarly
annotated a second dispatch: "Teddy is quite a dilettante." It
was only after revolutionary disturbances broke out in Russia
and threatened to inspire antimonarchist agitation in Germany, that the Kaiser finally shifted his position and was willing to use his influence with the Czar in favor of peace negotiations.

Although Roosevelt never fully understood the intricacies of
Wilhelm's devious diplomacy, he was not completely taken in.
For in spite of those letters in which he wrote that he felt that
he and "Bill the Kaiser" fully understood each other, and
proudly said that they were "very intimate," he nevertheless
maintained a skepticism that justified his own repeated disclaimer that he was in any sense under Wilhelm's influence.
His ignorance of the intricacies of German diplomacy, that is,
did not prevent him from realizing how shifting and inconstant
this diplomacy actually was. Roosevelt scoffed at the idea that
he would really follow the lead of "a man who is so jumpy, so
little capable of continuity of action, and therefore, so little
capable of being loyal to his friends or steadfastly hostile to
his enemies."

Whatever the relationship between these two intriguing personalities, however, the course of events finally led to their co-

operation in seeking to persuade Russia and Japan to talk peace. The real opportunity came when, on May 31, the Japanese informed Roosevelt they were prepared to consider negotiations, and asked him to sound out the Russian Government. If the response to his overtures should be favorable, the Japanese further said, they hoped the President would then—"entirely of his own motion and initiative"—invite the two belligerents to a conference.

Roosevelt accepted this invitation to mediate, and sounded out Russia as the Japanese had suggested. The Czar was for a time highly reluctant to consider any move toward peace but, under the combined pressure of the President and a now cooperative Kaiser, he was finally persuaded of the inevitability of Russia's defeat and of the necessity for an end to hostilities. Roosevelt thereupon called for negotiations, and the formal acceptance of his proposal by both powers, as announced on June 11, led to the peace conference which met at Portsmouth, New Hampshire, two months later.

Japan's victories left Russia no alternative other than to accept, as a primary basis for peace, withdrawal from Korea and the surrender of those special interests in southern Manchuria, including control of Port Arthur, that she had earlier wrung from a helpless China. The only issues seriously in dispute were possession of the island of Sakhalin and Japan's demand for an indemnity. Here the position of the two powers remained in deadlock, threatening the breakup of the conference and the renewal of hostilities. Anxious on every count to see his mediation efforts succeed and a peace concluded that would enable Russia and Japan to continue to act as counterchecks on each other's imperial ambitions, Roosevelt was once again ready to intervene. He used every possible means to induce Japan to forego an indemnity and to persuade Russia that continuation of the war was under any circumstances completely futile.

He was at Oyster Bay on Long Island during this conference crisis, which developed in the latter part of August, and he became increasingly unhappy under the stress and strain of what he described as "the last throes of trying to get the Russians and Japanese to make peace." To his son Kermit he wrote on August 25 that "I am having my hair turned gray with the . . . . negotiators."

A constant stream of cables, telegrams, and other messages was passing through his summer office.

"Make clear to His Majesty . . . ," he cabled the American ambassador in St. Petersburg in urging the necessity for peace; "I wish you people could get my views . . . ," he told the British ambassador, seeking support from that quarter in relation to the position of Japan; "I hope your government will try to persuade the Czar . . . ," he advised the French ambassador; "My dear Baron Kaneko," he wrote a Japanese delegate, ". . . It seems to me that it is to the interest of the great empire of Nippon . . . ," and to the Kaiser, requesting his support, he cabled, "Peace can be obtained on the following terms . . ."

Still the conference remained deadlocked, and on August 29 met at what was fearfully believed might be its final session. The atmosphere was tense and heavy with foreboding. Very solemnly the Russian envoy, Count Witte, rose and handed a note to the principal Japanese delegate, Baron Komura. It stated that the Russian Government categorically refused to pay any indemnity, but did agree to cede to Japan the southern half of Sakhalin. For a few seconds there was complete silence in the conference room, Count Witte nervously tearing up some paper that lay beside him, and the Japanese sitting quietly without any hint of their reaction. An eye witness then continues:

"At last Komura, in a well-controlled voice, said that the Japanese Government, having for its aim the restoration of peace and the bringing of the negotiations to a successful conclusion, expressed its consent to Russia's proposal to divide Sakhalin in two, without indemnity being paid. Witte calmly replied that the Japanese proposal was accepted and that the line of demarcation would be reckoned the fiftieth degree."

"Peace Arranged; Japan Gives In," heralded the banner headlines of the *New York Times* the next day. Roosevelt's patient
diplomacy had won out. The following morning it was reported
that nine hundred telegrams of congratulation for his successful peacemaking, including messages from all the crowned
heads of Europe, had been received at the White House. The
press enthusiastically hailed what was called the President's
direct, open diplomacy. "Without regard to party or section,"
Public Opinion summarized such comment, "the papers praise
him for his skill and tact in holding the conference together
till an agreement could be reached." Roosevelt had become,
this magazine continued, "the most popular man in the world
. . . . an international asset." When, a month or more later,
he returned to Washington from Oyster Bay, the peace treaty
having in the meantime been signed on September 5, the *Times*
again reported that his reception by enthusiastic crowds was
"marked by a demonstration . . . . as was never before seen
in the capital."

The only exception to this popular acclaim for Roosevelt was
the attitude of the Japanese. Although the government realized
that continuation of the war would impose an impossible financial drain on the country, the people felt that they had been
robbed of the full fruits of their victory in being denied an indemnity. Roosevelt was blamed. There were anti-American riots
throughout Japan and for a time martial law was maintained
in Tokyo.

The failure of Japan to obtain an indemnity, and the diplomatic victory that Russia appeared to have won at Portsmouth,
for a time obscured the real significance of the Russo-Japanese
War. Yet it had actually resulted in a decisive triumph for Japan
in every way, and set up new power alignments that changed
the entire course of far eastern history.

Japan won complete control over Korea and there was little
question of her ultimate annexation of this nominally independent little country. Even before the close of the war, indeed, an agreement between the United States and Japan fore-

shadowed such action. Taft, now Secretary of War, met Count Katsura, the Japanese Premier, in Tokyo. In return for a pledge of Japanese respect for American sovereignty in the Philippines, Taft declared that the United States had no objections to Japan's assumption of suzerainty over Korea's foreign affairs. Roosevelt fully confirmed the Taft-Katsura Agreement.

Even more significant was the new situation created in Manchuria. In falling heir to former Russian rights and privileges, Japan won a further foothold on the mainland and a position of greatly increased power in eastern Asia as a whole. Through her amazing victory over one of the great nations of Europe, she had demonstrated a measure of strength that would henceforth enable her to play a decisive role in a part of the world where the Western powers had previously thought they could completely have their own way.

The war further marked a turning point in Japanese-American relations. Even though there had been rising mistrust about how a victorious Japan might act, and growing fears of her possible hostility toward the West, the American people had remained sympathetic toward Japan throughout the war. The Russians had received a better press during the peace conference, as a consequence of what was considered the brash cockiness of the Japanese, but still Japan stood high in popular estimation. As for Roosevelt, he wrote Rockhill shortly after the Portsmouth meeting that he had always been sympathetic toward Japan but "I am far stronger pro-Japanese than ever." In spite of all this, however, there was a distinct parting of the ways.

It was no longer possible, after Japan's victory over Russia, to maintain that relationship of friendly guardian and grateful ward that had influenced both the United States and Japan ever since the epochal day when the black ships of Commodore Perry steamed into Tokyo Bay and opened up Japan to the Western world. The two nations now met on equal terms, and they were divided by a new and potentially dangerous rivalry over conflicting interests in eastern Asia. Japan was soon to

show that in her great power status she had little intention of
accepting an American policy of the Open Door. She was determined to build up and extend her influence over Manchuria
and ultimately over all China. The lines were drawn for a contest that was to come to its startling climax at Pearl Harbor.

As the United States and Japan first tried to reach an understanding—as exemplified by the Taft-Katsura Agreement—
which would moderate their incipient rivalry in eastern Asia, a
controversy of quite a different sort than the clash of political
interests began to exacerbate their relations. The immediate incident setting off this dispute was an order of San Francisco's
school board, in October 1906, providing for the segregation of
Japanese school children in that city. Behind this move, however, lay a long record of discriminatory treatment of Japanese
residents in the United States, which reflected the fears of the
people of the West Coast, and particularly of California, over
the social and economic consequences of further immigration.
The segregation order was a climax of earlier instances of anti-
Japanese legislation, boycotts, and rioting, and it awoke a bitter
anti-American reaction on the part of the people of Japan.
Roosevelt found himself confronted with a developing crisis
that threatened everything he was trying to do in resolving
the conflicting political interests of the two nations.

The issue of Japanese-American relations was from now on
the major problem of foreign policy that Roosevelt had to face.
At no other time did he have to deal with anything that invoked
an even remotely comparable danger of possible war. For relations with Japan held potential dynamite. As a proud, spirited
nation, flushed with victory over Russia and rashly confident in
its newly revealed strength, Japan might well have felt driven
to challenge the United States in 1906–07. Her leaders were
concerned over potential conflict in regard to the Open Door in
China, and her people were incensed over the insult to racial
pride in American treatment of Japanese nationals in the United
States. War was not only possible; many foreign observers

thought it inevitable. In the light of their own experience, Europeans were convinced that these two newcomers to the ranks of great powers would have to fight out their differences. *L'Intransigeant*, to quote one Paris newspaper, felt that in memory of their recent victories over Spain and Russia, both the United States and Japan were spoiling for a fight.

Roosevelt fully recognized the dangers in this situation. Forswearing the irresponsible belligerency that he displayed on so many less critical occasions, he pursued a policy that was at once conciliatory and firm. He would make every effort to adjust the differences between the United States and Japan on a realistic basis. The Japanese-American crisis of these years was the outstanding example of his instinctive approach to foreign policy—"speak softly and carry a big stick." While he negotiated patiently with Japan, he always held in reserve the power of the American Navy.

In the first stages of the immigration controversy, the President found himself in the difficult position of being unable to intervene directly in the local situation in San Francisco, since the measures taken by the local school board were entirely beyond the province of the federal government. Moreover, he could not but recognize the justification for the prompt and vigorous protest that the Japanese government submitted. "I am being horribly bothered about the Japanese business," he wrote Kermit on October 27, 1906. "The infernal fools in California, and especially in San Francisco, insult the Japanese recklessly and in the event of war it will be the nation as a whole which will pay the consequences." Nor did he hesitate to express in his annual message to Congress the feelings that he so outspokenly revealed in his personal correspondence. The action taken by the school board, he said, was a "wicked absurdity" that could in no way be justified or condoned by the nation.

The Japanese government applauded his attitude; the West Coast bitterly resented what one paper called "an exhibition of impotent rage." There were renewed outbreaks of anti-Japanese violence in California, and further embittered demonstrations of anti-American sentiment in Japan. The situation grew increasingly ominous as 1906 gave way to 1907. With Tokyo papers declaring that should diplomacy fail, "the only way open to us is an appeal to arms," and with the jingo press in this country excitedly talking of possible hostilities, the crisis seemed very real.

The program Roosevelt adopted was two-pronged. He undertook to use his personal influence in dealing with the situation in California, and at the same time he tried to reach a settlement with Japan which he hoped would obviate further trouble. Summoning San Francisco's mayor and the officials of the school board to a conference at the White House, he persuaded them to rescind their segregation order. He then commenced negotiations with the Japanese Government for an arrangement whereby it would withhold passports from Japanese laborers seeking to enter the United States, and also acknowledge this country's right to bar those seeking American entry from Hawaii or elsewhere. In concluding what was to become known as the Gentlemen's Agreement, an accord that would remain in effect until the Japanese exclusion law of 1924, Roosevelt acknowledged the justice of the Japanese case, but emphatically reaffirmed the right of the United States to determine its own immigration policy.

For a time the situation calmed down, but soon the anti-Japanese elements in California were again on the warpath. It might be, as Roosevelt angrily wrote Lodge, that "the feeling on the Pacific slope . . . . is as foolish as if conceived by the mind of a Hottentot." The rest of the country might not share it, as the Washington *Evening Star* stated in an editorial declaring that the Californians "are open to the emphatic condemnation of the whole people of this country." But all this did not help. The West Coast could still make trouble. Something further had to be done, as anti-American feeling once again flared up in Japan and talk of hostilities was renewed. Even though responsible officials in Tokyo were prepared to accept in good faith

Roosevelt's efforts to combat discrimination and deprecated all talk of war, there could be no telling what might happen under popular pressures.

In July 1907 Roosevelt was writing Root that he was more concerned over the Japanese situation than anything else, and gloomily reporting that the best information in France, England, and Germany "is that we shall have war with Japan and we shall be beaten." He went so far as to send special and secret orders to General Wood in the Philippines to prepare for possible attack by Japan. And a further interesting commentary, even if its authenticity is rather dubious, is a statement a distant cousin of President Roosevelt later made in an article appearing in July 1923 in the magazine *Asia*. "Outside the executive departments in Washington," wrote Franklin Delano Roosevelt, "it has never been known in this country that, during the nervous days in the early summer of 1908 [1907?], the United States hovered on the edge of an ultimatum from Japan."

It is not likely that an ultimatum was ever considered in Tokyo. Nevertheless, under the influence of the yellow press in both countries, with William Randolph Hearst most energetically beating the tom-toms of war, American-Japanese relations were perilously strained. Observing what he moderately described as "a very, very slight undertone of veiled truculence" in the continued Japanese protests over what was happening on the Pacific coast, Roosevelt decided that the time had come for a showdown. While continuing the negotiations to bring the Gentlemen's Agreement into final and definitive form, he completed plans which he had already had in mind for sending the entire battleship fleet on a "practice cruise" to the Pacific as a practical demonstration of American naval power.

This project was one very dear to Roosevelt's heart. As we have seen, he considered his successful campaign to build up the Navy, in the face of opposition from so many quarters, one of his greatest achievements. He had long played with the idea

282 THE IMPERIAL YEARS

of an extensive voyage for the new battleships and the time now seemed opportune. Moreover, as subsequent events revealed, he was actually thinking not only of a Pacific voyage but of a round-the-world trip—through the Suez and the Mediterranean. It would impress upon Japan, the President hoped, the futility of challenging the United States, and thereby strengthen the bases for peace.

As these plans became known during the summer of 1907, they awoke widespread discussion and considerable criticism. Some papers interpreted the proposed voyage as no more and no less than a propaganda stunt to inspire larger congressional appropriations for the Navy, while the President's partisan foes brushed the whole thing aside as a move to make political capital for the Republicans in the forthcoming presidential elections in 1908. But in other quarters, the project was taken more seriously. It was attacked from a strategic point of view as provocative of Japan and highly dangerous. The Navy should be kept in home waters.

Opposition to the voyage was particularly strong in the East, which did not like the idea of the battleship fleet being moved from the Atlantic, and both the *New York Times* and the New York *World* were very outspoken in editorial comment. Roosevelt resented their campaign against him and felt it reflected, as on past occasions, the timidity of the business interests of the country. He was not, however, swayed from his determination to carry the project through. It was very well for these papers to criticize him, he wrote one correspondent, "But *I* am commander in chief!"

The jingo press joyfully interpreted his decision as meaning, in the words of the New York *Sun,* "that the Navy is going to the Pacific Ocean for war with Japan," and welcomed the prospect with customary recklessness. More generally, however, such accusations of belligerency (Root referred to the warmongering yellow press as "leprous vipers") were condemned as a libel upon the President. The country as a whole seemed ready to accept his statements that his purposes were entirely peaceful, and warmly applauded so dramatic an expression of American naval power.

Roosevelt personally reviewed the fleet on the eve of its departure, handing sealed orders to Rear Admiral Evans, the "Fighting Bob" of the Chilean episode more than a decade earlier, and he was delighted with the appearance and performance of the sixteen imposing battleships and other accompanying vessels that represented America's naval might. Officers and crews were in fine fettle. "I tell you our enlisted men are everything," the President enthusiastically said to the reporters, "they are perfectly bully . . ." It was with the good wishes of a proud nation that the fleet set out on December 16 on the first leg of its voyage—down the coast of South America, around the Cape and into the broad reaches of the Pacific.

Any danger that Japan would interpret the voyage as provocative was soon dispelled. Early in March 1908, after the fleet's arrival in the Pacific, it was announced that the Emperor had extended an invitation for a visit to Japan. When, seven months later, following calls in Australia, New Zealand, and the Philippines, the gigantic flotilla steamed into the harbor at Yokohama, the Japanese people gave it a rousing and enthusiastic welcome, with ten thousand school children gaily singing *Hail Columbia, Happy Land*. The crews were given daily shore leave and not a single unpleasant incident was reported. "Japan's Heart Won by American Tars," was the heading over one dispatch from Tokyo. All was sweetness and light, and the continued accounts of what was universally characterized as a confirmation of the basic cordiality in American-Japanese relations, "blunted even the sharpest of editorial quills." The fleet's visit, the correspondent of the *New York Times* cabled, "has dispersed the last semblance of a war cloud and makes us feel ashamed of its former shadow." The occasion could not have been a more pleasant one. In spite of the friendly and sometimes tumultuous welcomes the fleet received at other ports, its reception in Japan was the high point in what had turned out to be a gorgeously triumphal voyage.

There was no question that it coincided with a very marked improvement in Japanese-American relations, even though it cannot be proved that this demonstration of naval power was a basic factor in bringing about such an improvement. Roosevelt professed to believe that this was the case. "Every particle of trouble with the Japanese Government and the Japanese press," he later wrote, "stopped like magic as soon as they found that our fleet had actually sailed, and was obviously in good trim." In his *Autobiography* he would insist that this voyage was "the most important service I rendered peace." Certainly the general consensus of opinion at the time was that the fleet's call at Japan was highly successful. "There is nothing left for the war jingo," wrote the *New York Mail*, "but to close his marionette show and pack up his puppets in moth balls."

A further and more important step in the evolution of Japanese-American relations was taken shortly after the fleet left Yokohama. Secretary Root and Ambassador Takahira had for some time been discussing the far eastern issues over which both nations were concerned. In this new atmosphere of amicability, they signed an agreement, on November 30, 1908, which appeared to resolve all matters in dispute.

The United States and Japan reasserted their intention, in what became known as the Root-Takahira Agreement, to maintain the existing *status quo* in the general area of the Pacific, to reciprocally respect one another's possessions, and to preserve the common interests of the powers in China by upholding through all pacific means at their disposal "the independence and the integrity of China and the principle of equal opportunity for the commerce and industry of all nations in that Empire." This appeared to be a complete avowal on both nations' part of the principles of the Open Door policy, but there was another reading of the agreement that substantially modified so sanguine an interpretation. Japan was in possession of Russia's former rights and privileges in southern Manchuria. Recognition of the *status quo* in the general area of the Pacific could not be easily reconciled with effective application of the Open Door policy in these Chinese provinces.

Here was clearly—and accepted as such in both Japan and China—a highly significant American concession. In frank acknowledgment of what were believed to be the facts of life (Root said there was nothing else we could do except fight Japan), the United States recognized Japan's special position in Manchuria as it had previously accepted her paramountcy in Korea. In return for a more generalized commitment in respect to the Open Door, that is, Roosevelt was ready to admit Japan's claim that, on the basis of propinquity and its relation to Japanese national security, Manchuria was a very special case.

The Root-Takahira Agreement had a somewhat mixed press. Many newspapers hailed it as a practical settlement of existing American-Japanese differences, a wise act of statesmanship, and a significant contribution to far eastern peace. In contrast with such favorable reactions, however, other editorial comment severely criticized the President for again by-passing the Senate through an executive agreement, and declared that he had singlehandedly concluded something very close to an entangling alliance. The New York *Press* vehemently stated that the new accord was "as violent a departure from that course charted for the nation in the wisdom of the Fathers as has ever been initiated. . . ."

Roosevelt took these various steps—the Gentlemen's Agreement on immigration, the dispatch of the battleship fleet around the world, and the Root-Takahira Agreement—in the conviction that the establishment of friendly relations with Japan had become the most vital concern of American foreign policy. And he was acting with a moderation—an emphasis upon speaking softly even more than on carrying a big stick—which contrasted sharply with his more bellicose attitude five years earlier in declaring he was ready to go to "extremes" in resisting Russian aggression in Manchuria. To assure an accord with Japan, he was frankly prepared to retreat from the position originally set forth in the Hay notes on the Open Door.

This new approach to far eastern policy was highly realistic. Japan had fought a war over Manchuria, sacrificing blood and treasure. She considered the maintenance of her position there vital to her security. For the United States on the other hand, what happened in Manchuria, however much commercial firms doing business there might complain of the closing of the Open Door, could only be a matter of secondary concern. Roosevelt was on sound ground in believing that such a concession as recognition of Japan's special interests in this area was not too heavy a price to pay for a general accord that could serve both to secure American possessions in the Pacific and to safeguard the Open Door in China proper.

He made his position very explicit in a long letter that he wrote, on December 22, 1910, to his successor in the White House. Roosevelt told Taft that he thought the Open Door policy an excellent thing—so long as it could be maintained by general diplomatic agreement. He did not feel, however, that its maintenance was sufficiently vital to the United States to allow this country to become involved in its defense should any other power challenge it by force of arms. If he was thus reluctant to take a position that might compel this country to uphold the principles of the Open Door in China by military action, he was even less willing to commit the United States in any way to an adamant stand in regard to Manchuria. It was "peculiarly our interest," Roosevelt emphatically told Taft, "not to take any steps as regards Manchuria which will give the Japanese cause to feel, with or without reason, that we are hostile to them, or a menace—in however slight degree—to their interest."

His advice was not followed in succeeding years. American policy backed and filled in respect to the Open Door. The United States repeatedly protested against Japanese violations of American rights in Manchuria and as constantly retreated from any move to hold Japan firmly to account. Without ever winning acceptance of the Open Door's applicability in this region, the United States succeeded only in impressing upon Japan that character of hostility against which Roosevelt had warned.

Ultimately the lines of division between the two nations would harden. As Japan sought to extend over all China the influence she had so securely established in Manchuria, the United States felt driven to take the firm position over which it had so long hesitated. Circumstances had by then—1941— greatly changed. A good deal more appeared to be at stake in the days of Franklin D. Roosevelt than had been the case when Theodore Roosevelt was ready to retreat in Manchuria. Nevertheless the result was the war that had been successfully averted in the early 1900s.

CHAPTER XVII

AN EVEN KEEL IN EUROPE

THE MAJOR PURPOSE OF LATIN AMERICAN POLICY IN THE YEARS succeeding war with Spain was to strengthen the strategic security of the Caribbean; the goal of far eastern policy remained support of American interests and the Open Door in China through a friendly accommodation with Japan. Theodore Roosevelt also looked further afield. In the belief that the ultimate peace and safety of the United States lay in the preservation of a world balance of power, he was prepared to intervene diplomatically in European affairs in trying to help "keep matters on an even keel." There were precedents for a vigorous policy in both Latin America and eastern Asia, but when the President sent American delegates to the conference on Morocco, held in Algeciras, southern Spain, in 1906, he broke squarely with all past tradition and ventured into fields from which all his predecessors had held studiously aloof.

His activities in South America, and more particularly in eastern Asia, had already introduced Roosevelt to the complicated and changing relationships among the powers. He knew full well that the national rivalries and resultant tensions in Europe found expression in maneuvering throughout the world. If sometimes he seemed caught up in the tangled skein of such intricately interwoven political lines, and not wholly aware of the stakes of power, Roosevelt nevertheless continued to be far better informed, and maintained a much more realistic grasp of world politics, than did most of his contemporaries.

In the early 1900s—in spite of everything said or done about arbitration and progress toward peace—the positions were being taken that provided the critical alignments of 1914. For the two most significant international developments of these years were the continued decline in the century-old supremacy maintained by Great Britain and the challenging rise of an imperial-minded Germany. The rivalry of these two powers, accentuated as Germany sought to expand overseas and build up a navy, was leading to new combinations and new alliances.

On the one hand, there was the Triple Alliance of Germany, Austro-Hungary, and Italy; and on the other, the Dual Alliance of France and Russia. If England still sought to stand aside in the "splendid isolation" of the nineteenth century, the further maneuvers of Germany in seeking to break down the Dual Alliance inevitably forced British statesmen to reconsider their continental ties. The flirtations of the Kaiser with the Czar, and other German intrigues seeking at one time to build up a new continental coalition and at another to weaken the position of France, threatened to make England's isolation more dangerous than splendid.

A first British move related primarily to Asia rather than

Europe. The conclusion of the Anglo-Japanese Alliance, however, was soon followed by other steps more directly affecting the situation on the Continent. An agreement on conflicting colonial problems brought into being a new Anglo-French accord in 1904, and three years later a somewhat comparable Anglo-Russian understanding was reached. The Triple Alliance was soon to be confronted with a Triple Entente, and Europe found itself divided into two rigidly opposed armed camps.

In every instance of their treaty-making, the powers had in mind a double purpose. They were concerned with building up their respective national positions and keeping the way open for the further exploitation of their colonial holdings. But they sought at the same time so to adjust their differences, thereby strengthening their interlocking alliances, as to preserve a balance of competing power that would somehow serve to maintain peace even if it were an armed peace.

The American people were not entirely ignorant of what was taking place. They could not help sensing the relative decline of British power and increase in German strength, and they realized that this might affect the United States. For so far as British imperialism became static or was actually forced back into retreat, it represented no threat to the United States; while German imperialism, increasingly aggressive and reaching out toward new fields of conquest, could directly endanger American interests. Yet by and large very few people tried to find their way through the maze of European politics that provided the backdrop for such developments.

One significant reaction, however, was clear. For all the controversy and friction that would always plague American relations with Great Britain as a normal carry-over from the past, the likelihood of war between the two nations had disappeared after the excitement and furor over the first Venezuelan crisis. This was seen in the friendly accommodation of Anglo-American interests in both the Caribbean and eastern Asia. On the other hand, the recurrent signs of Germany's expansive imperialist ambitions continued to arouse suspicion. From the Samoan episode of the 1880s through the second Venezuela affair in 1902–03, Germany appeared to be testing out United States policy. An actual clash between the two countries was always possible.

If such considerations did not importantly affect the public at large, national leaders charged with the formulation of foreign policy were unable to ignore them. They realized that the United States could not entirely escape involvement in the shifting European alignments. They saw that under existing circumstances American interests and American sympathies brought the United States into closer accord with the emerging Triple Entente than with the Triple Alliance. The historic tradition of nonentanglement in European affairs, and the prevailing faith in the great good of "our power of detachment," obviated any idea of American participation in either international grouping. What was more subtly taking place, however, was the growth of a natural sympathy between the United States and Great Britain, based on a sense of a community of interests, that was to become of increasing importance.

As has been already suggested, this concept of the necessity for a common stand in world affairs on the part of the two Anglo-Saxon powers had originally been advanced in the 1890s and was a first indication—even before the Spanish-American War—of the forces making for the assumption by the United States of broader responsibilities in world affairs. Among other publicists, Alfred Thayer Mahan had suggested the need for what he called "accordant relations" between the United States and Great Britain; Albert Beveridge called for "an English-speaking people's league of God for the permanent peace of this war-worn world"; and many other contemporary writers dwelt upon the advantages of the closest possible understanding with England, if not an outright Anglo-American alliance.

After the turn of the century, John Hay was perhaps the foremost of Anglophiles. In his conduct of foreign policy he had consistently sought to strengthen Anglo-American ties ever since the occasion of a famous speech, while he was still ambassador to Great Britain, in which he eloquently described "a partnership in beneficence" that would help to realize the common aims and aspirations of the two nations. He never wavered from this position. In spite of widespread popular sympathy for the Boers during England's war in South Africa, Hay insisted on a rigid neutrality and did everything possible to hold such anti-British feeling as existed in check. Soon after he became Secretary of State, in a letter to Henry White, he set forth his attitude very explicitly. While recognizing that an Anglo-American alliance would have to remain, under existing circumstances, "an unattainable dream," he declared that "as long as I stay here no action shall be taken contrary to my conviction that the one indispensable feature of our foreign policy should be a firm understanding with England."

Roosevelt was never as strong an Anglophile as Hay and could at times be highly critical, if not resentful, of British policy. Yet he too recognized the basically common interests of the two countries. Although he could never forget that the United States and Great Britain were separate nations, he wrote on one occasion, "the fact remains, in the first place, that we are closer in feeling to her than to any other nation; and in the second place, that probably her interest and ours will run on parallel lines in the future." And some years later he declared that "in keeping ready for possible war I never even take into account a war with England. I treat it as out of the question." This was an attitude differing sharply from that which he maintained toward the other powers, and particularly toward Germany.

Even more symptomatic of the changing climate of opinion was the sharp reversal in the views of Lodge. He completely abandoned his earlier habit of twisting the lion's tail on the slightest provocation, and became a strong supporter of England. Lodge's conversion to an Anglo-American rapprochement gave rise to a shrewd Peter Finley Dunne essay on "The

Decline of National Feeling." We find Mr. Dooley remember-
ing the good old days "whin ye'd hear Hinnery in th' Sinit,
spreadin' fear to th' hear-rts iv th' British aristocracy . . . .";
but now: "Faith, he's changed his chune, an' 'tis 'Sthrangers
wanst, but brothers now,' with him, an' 'Hands acrost th'
sea an' into some wan's pocket'. . . ."

It was against this background that the Moroccan crisis of
1905 developed and Roosevelt was persuaded of the advisability
of taking a hand in its solution. He did so reluctantly. Nevertheless the heightening tension in the relations among the
European powers seemed dangerously threatening to world
peace; or at the very least to be placing in jeopardy the
efforts he was making at this very time to bring the Russo-
Japanese War to an end.

The crisis grew out of Germany's well-founded fears that
the understanding reached between England and France over
their colonial policies in North Africa was not only freezing
her out of this part of the world, but strengthening the new
Anglo-French entente at Germany's expense. Morocco, nominally independent but actually little more than a pawn in
Europe's fascinating game of power politics, thus became the
center of controversy when France sought—as it appeared to
Germany—to extend her control even more fully over the
native Sultan's territories.

The German Chancellor, Von Bülow, decided to challenge
this development and induced a reluctant Kaiser to make an
inflammatory speech at Tangier in which he congratulated the
Sultan on his independence and assured him of Germany's
continuing friendship. The French were furious at what was so
clearly an attack on their position in Morocco, and their foreign
minister, Delcassé, took such a belligerent stand as to suggest
possible war. The sharp German reaction to his provocative
statements led to a ministerial crisis in France, and Delcassé
was dismissed in the hope of easing the tension. But while

this moderated the crisis, it by no means solved it. The dispute centering about Morocco remained.

The United States was not itself in any way involved in this controversy, although it was a signatory of an 1880 commercial treaty providing for the Open Door in Morocco, and Roosevelt was at first prepared to ignore it altogether. He was at the time enjoying one of his periodic trips in the West and his correspondence revolved about his hunting adventures rather than international diplomacy. He wrote Von Sternberg, for example, that he did not feel there was any reason for the United States allowing itself to become entangled in the Moroccan affair, and then concluded his letter with an enthusiastic description of coursing wolves on a nine-mile run and going out after bear. And more important than Morocco, in any event, was the precarious state of his efforts to mediate between Russia and Japan. In an official letter to Taft, who was "holding the lid down" in Washington, the President drew attention to these negotiations and stated emphatically that he did not feel that the United States should in any way interfere or take sides in the dispute between Germany and France. "We have other fish to fry," he said, "and we have no real interest in Morocco."

Yet pressures were building up for the exercise of American influence in helping to resolve the issues at stake in North Africa, and when the Kaiser urged Roosevelt to persuade France that a conference was in order, the President somewhat hesitantly undertook to do so. He did not know that the Anglo-French accord actually provided a free hand for France in Morocco, and that Germany had good reason for her fears of being frozen out. Nor did he apparently understand, as he might well have, that the British Foreign Office was fully supporting France and that the growing hostility between England and Germany was a primary cause for Europe's mounting tension. In a letter to Hay, he almost casually dismissed this phase of the situation. "As funny a case as I have ever seen," he wrote, "of mutual distrust and fear bringing two peoples to the verge of war." He now began to see, however, that trouble in Europe, even if it did not lead to war, might upset his negotiations with Japan and Russia. He decided to do anything he could to help resolve Europe's crisis.

While he was prepared to act as a go-between upon the suggestion of Germany, his private correspondence clearly reveals that he was already thinking in terms of drawing France into closer association with her natural allies. "France ought to be with us and England . . . . in our zone and combination," Lodge was writing. ". . . It would be an evil day for us if Germany were to crush France." And Roosevelt thoroughly agreed.

With all these considerations in mind, the President induced France to accept a Moroccan conference and the Kaiser, who had become fearful he was getting beyond his depth, gratefully said that he would follow the American lead on any issue that came into critical dispute. The meeting was then summoned for January 1906, at Algeciras. Roosevelt announced that on the basis of its treaty relations with Morocco in respect to the Open Door, the United States would be represented, its principal delegate being the veteran diplomat Henry White.

Root, who had become Secretary of State only a few months earlier upon the death of Hay, penned the actual instructions to White. Acting on his professed principle that the main object of diplomacy is "to keep the country out of trouble . . . . in the right way," Root was not particularly concerned over the Moroccan dispute, and he specifically stated that American interests were not sufficient "to justify us in taking a leading part." He consequently called upon White to be careful not to take sides in the controversy and to limit himself to safeguarding legitimate American interests. Nevertheless in a personal letter to White he went somewhat further. "In the broader and really important part that the conference is to play in the politics of Europe," he said, "keep the peace and make it as difficult as possible for any one to pick a quarrel."

About this time Roosevelt was a good deal more explicit in various letters. While he hoped White would play the role of mediator, exercising American influence for peace, he again candidly acknowledged that his sympathies were with France as against Germany. Writing to Joseph H. Choate, whom he had first considered as the American representative at Algeciras, he said that while he wanted to keep "on fairly good terms with Germany," he definitely intended to stand by France. And he confidentially told White to try to maintain cordial relations with all participants in the conference, but to "help France to get what she ought to have."

The American people, as might well be expected, did not become unduly excited over the situation in Morocco or the participation of the United States in the Algeciras conference. There were many other matters to absorb popular attention in the winter of 1905–06. Roosevelt was just hitting his stride as President in his own right and bombarding Congress with his demands for railroad regulation, a pure food and drug act, and conservation measures. The political pot was boiling, as Congress wrangled over his proposals and "Teddy" continued to steal the headlines. The public loved it:

> T.R. is spanking a Senator,
> T.R. is chasing a bear,
> T.R. is busting an awful trust
> And dragging it to its lair.

And there were other news stories. A former governor of Utah was murdered in a bombing outrage; Professor Woodrow Wilson complained that the automobile was dangerously spreading socialistic feeling; Marshall Field died and left an estate estimated at $150,000,000; and Alice Roosevelt to the public's great delight, was married with pomp and ceremony at the White House. Here were events or incidents close at hand; for most Americans, Europe was just about as far away as it had always been.

Even though Algeciras was consequently relegated to the newspapers' back pages, if mentioned at all, there was nevertheless some controversy in both Congress and the press over Roosevelt's action in ignoring isolationist traditions and allowing the United States to become entangled in what appeared to be a completely European political controversy. Although, in his instructions to White, the Secretary of State had said that in signing any agreement the United States should make it unmistakably clear that there would be no departure from its traditional policy of no foreign involvements, Roosevelt's critics were not satisfied.

Senator Bacon of Georgia, who had strongly opposed the annexation of the Philippines in 1898 and was a consistent isolationist, raised the issue in Congress by introducing a resolution calling for full information on White's instructions. A lively and acrimonious debate, generally following partisan lines, took place. The Administration's entire policy was raked over the coals in the course of the discussion, and Algeciras was repeatedly linked with the contemporary fracas over Santo Domingo as an example of the President's arbitrary attitude in conducting foreign affairs. His casual ignoring of senatorial prerogatives accounted for much of the criticism, especially on the part of the Democrats. The feeling was strongly expressed that Roosevelt was developing an entirely new policy upon which the Senate had a right to be consulted.

Lodge vigorously defended the President. In spite of the obvious fact, based on the historical record, that American attendance at a European conference concerned with political issues was a good deal of a novelty, he denied that there was any departure from tradition. It had always been American policy, he said, not only itself to maintain peace but to demand peace of the other powers. "It is not to be supposed for a moment," Lodge said, "that we are never to exert our great moral influence or to use our good offices for the maintenance of the world's peace." Praising Roosevelt's role in the Russo-Japanese negotiations—"one of the great events of modern times"—he called for support of a like effort at peace-making at Algeciras.

Other commentators generally tended to uphold participation in the conference. They did not believe that it meant permanent entanglement in European affairs, and took the line that American influence would be effective at Algeciras, since it reflected a detached and neutral point of view. "The separation of this country from European alliances and intrigues," declared the New York *Tribune*, "makes its judgments and counsels appear more impartial and disinterested, and indeed enables them to be so." Answering charges that Algeciras represented the very sort of meddling in European affairs against which the Founders had warned, the *Sun* asked whether it was a crime to use the prestige and influence of the United States in so good a cause as peace.

The conference duly met at Algeciras and followed a tortuous path in trying to resolve the problems centered about the powers' respective rights and interests in Morocco. The diplomatic complexities were baffling even for the delegates, and completely inexplicable to an American public which actually had so little interest in the proceedings. It soon became apparent, however, that Germany stood entirely alone in her pretensions to any control over Morocco, and had committed a grave blunder in urging that the conference be held. She made no headway in seeking to drive a wedge between England and France, could get no support from a Russia facing revolutionary disturbances at home, and was deserted even by Italy, whose earlier colonial settlements with France made her immune to German blandishments. Only Austria remained true to her ally.

The actual conference meetings, as reported by White, followed a pattern that has since become increasingly familiar at international gatherings, but which in 1906 was very much a

novelty for American diplomats. The delegates of the thirteen
participating nations met at formal sessions in the gold and
white dining room of the Hotel Cristina, profusely decorated
with national flags; but the real work was done in private
dining rooms and in the hotel's corridors and lounges. The
place was overrun with newspaper reporters who continuously
roamed "the parlors and smoking-rooms, pouncing with questions on every hapless delegate." This was confusing for all
concerned. "It is very amusing," White wrote his wife, "how
most of the members of the conference don't in the least know
what is going on."

The American envoy did know. With his broad background
of professional experience, his wide acquaintanceship among
European diplomats, his suave and affable manner, he was an
admirable representative of the United States. No one was
more successful at Algeciras in bringing the right people together for informal conversations, in smoothing over difficulties, and in quietly and persuasively exercising an influence in behalf of moderation. White was himself to feel
that American participation in the conference served a very
useful purpose. "Any opinion we expressed (which I did
privately very often)," he wrote Roosevelt, "was listened to
with serious attention, and often adopted . . . . there were
many occasions . . . . on which my influence privately exercised, with both French and German delegates, has brought
about pacific terminations to crises which seemed on the point
of becoming acute."

At one time the conference really was on the verge of failure.
With Germany obstinately refusing to come to terms with
France, headlines briefly flared in American papers declaring
that the situation was critical and that there were again fears
of war. Within a few days, however, the excitement subsided
and further reports told of the presentation of a compromise
American plan that was believed to be acceptable to both
France and Germany. Within the framework of his original
proposals, and in reliance on the commitment the Kaiser had

made to follow his lead, Roosevelt had intervened. He instructed White to introduce a proposal (which the American delegate himself had devised) for setting up a native police force in Morocco under French and Spanish officers and for establishing a new foreign bank in which all the powers would hold substantially equal shares. This plan in effect preserved the principle of international control in Morocco, and yet gave the substance of power to France. There was some further controversy, but Germany at length came into line and the conferees were able to draw up the necessary diplomatic documents.

The dispatches from Washington dealing with these developments emphasized that Roosevelt was acting entirely on his own responsibility in trying to smooth the troubled European waters. It was once again—as in the Russo-Japanese peace negotiations—personal diplomacy. "Nothing akin to intervention," the *New York Times* reported on March 25, 1906, "has been suggested, or is even contemplated, by the Washington Government." If some people questioned what this policy was, if not intervention, and still wondered why the United States had anything at all to do with affairs in Morocco, the general public still seemed willing to let the President continue his mediatory efforts.

The General Act of Algeciras was signed on April 7, 1906. It recognized the independence of Morocco and the sovereignty of the native sultan, reaffirmed the Open Door for trade, set up the proposed international bank at Tangier, and most importantly, delegated to France and Spain, the authority to provide officers and instruction for the Moroccan police force. This was actually a marked rebuff for Germany. She was no longer in a position to exercise any influence in this critical area of North Africa. Even more significant, England and France were drawn more closely together in common opposition to German ambitions.

Roosevelt was very happy over the outcome of the conference and pleased with his diplomacy. He was especially delighted to receive the cordial thanks for what he had done from both the French and German governments, and while he warmly congratulated White for his part in the affair, he did not hesitate to acknowledge that the important part of the work was his own. The Kaiser might have been interested in the President's comment a month or so later. "In this Algeciras matter," he wrote privately, ". . . . I stood him on his head with great decision."

From Lodge, traveling abroad shortly after the conclusion of the conference, came a final endorsement which reflected both his and Roosevelt's strong nationalist views. "We are the strongest moral force—also physical—now extant," the Massachusetts senator wrote the President on July 25, 1906, "and the peace of the world rests largely with us. So far you have saved the situation."

In signing the General Act of Algeciras, White had incorporated the reservations upon which Root had insisted. American acceptance of the treaty, it was stated, should in no way be construed as marking any departure by the United States from its traditional policy of avoiding all foreign commitments. Convinced himself that "our great interests are on this side of the Atlantic," and ever mindful of the Senate, the Secretary of State had wanted to make assurance doubly sure that no objections would be raised against the pact on the ground that it constituted an entanglement in European politics.

Senator Bacon, still fearful of any foreign involvement whatsoever, nevertheless returned to the attack on administration policies when, later in the year, the treaty came before the Senate for approval. He charged that it did constitute a departure from traditional policy and demanded still further reservations. As the debate raged on the senate floor, and then spilled over into newspaper columns, other critics renewed their assaults upon the President. They again accused him of arbitrarily exceeding his constitutional powers, seeking only personal aggrandizement, and ignoring all the warnings of

Washington and Jefferson against foreign commitments. The treaty was finally approved in December, but only after adoption of the further reservation Bacon had submitted. It somewhat ironically reiterated the proposition that acceptance of the treaty was not a departure from traditional policy "which forbids participation by the United States in the settlement of political questions which are entirely European in their scope."

In the over-all pattern of the international politics of these days, the role played by the United States at Algeciras was perhaps a minor one. The European powers would in all probability have settled the immediate controversy without American assistance. Yet the fact that the United States took part in the conference, and exercised its influence along lines that tended to cement the Anglo-French entente and also to strengthen the ties of England and France with the United States, was significant for the future. Secretary Root was to say that the United States had helped to "preserve world peace because of the power of our detachment," yet in seeking to maintain the balance of power that made for peace, Roosevelt had in truth thrown American weight very definitely on one side of the scales.

Such participation in European affairs, however, was on a very temporary basis. There were to be no further comparable moves on this country's part as the rivalries underlying Europe's power alignments pursued their relentless course toward war. Succeeding Roosevelt in the White House, Taft would have nothing to do with the second Moroccan crisis in 1911, when Germany and France again clashed with even more dangerous repercussions. The United States reverted to a completely independent and aloof stand in its foreign relations. Both the American people and their leaders believed that the nation had well served the cause of peace at Algeciras, but they did not want to accept further responsibilities. They little understood that the conference had in reality settled nothing, and at best only postponed the European conflict that was drawing closer every year. And even less did they realize, when this conflict finally did break out, that American detachment was wholly illusory and would only briefly serve to keep the nation out of war.

CHAPTER XVIII

END OF AN EPOCH

SUCCESSFUL MEDIATION IN THE RUSSO-JAPANESE WAR AND PEACE-making during the Moroccan controversy, together with the round-the-world voyage of the battleship fleet, were Theodore Roosevelt's final significant moves on the world stage. As his term of office drew to an end, his chief concern was the nomination and election of his successor. He felt he had done well for his country, and his career as a statesman appeared to have been crowned with his nomination for the Nobel Peace Prize.

In a long letter at the very close of 1908, he outlined what he thought were his most important achievements in the realm of foreign affairs: in addition to his diplomacy in eastern Asia and at Algeciras ("all worked out by me personally"), he cited the doubling of the Navy; the start of construction on the Panama Canal ("absolutely my own work"); settlement of the affair of Santo Domingo; a policy of good faith toward Cuba; and establishment of more friendly relations with the other countries of Latin America, and also with Japan, by demonstrating that while the United States wanted peace and friendship, "we carry a big stick."

These achievements were substantial—if sometimes obtained at a high cost—and Roosevelt could make further claims. America's international prestige was high; there was universal recognition of her important role in world affairs. Without the assumption of any hard and fast commitments that prejudiced a complete freedom of action, the United States appeared to be set on a course that would enable it to exercise its great influence in support of a stable balance of world power and a righteous peace.

The retirement of Roosevelt from the presidency marked something more, however, than his own relinquishment of the reins of control over foreign policy. In a very real sense it brought to an end a distinctive epoch in the relations of the United States with the outside world. The forces that had given rise to America's dramatic emergence upon the world scene were, as we have seen, largely spent as he left office. Although Roosevelt had periodically aroused popular interest in what he was doing abroad, with his singular flair for the dramatic, and had helped to make the American people intermittently aware of their larger stake in world affairs, he had actually been unable to arouse the continuing, consistent support for his basic ideas that would permit their being carried forward in the future.

It was not only that the retreat from territorial imperialism was virtually complete. Foreign affairs in general were being pushed further and further into the background. If there was no return to the completely casual attitude, interrupted only by occasional outbursts of jingoism, that had characterized the 1880s and early 1890s, the American people were once again becoming generally apathetic toward what went on beyond their own continental borders.

For this Roosevelt himself, somewhat paradoxically, was partly responsible. In spite of all he said and did in building up national power and national prestige, he never drove home one vital lesson. The United States sooner or later had to face up to the fact that its inevitable entanglement in world politics could not be glossed over by reiteration of the popular view that it did not involve any departure from traditional foreign policy. Roosevelt himself perhaps failed to realize, and therefore was incapable of demonstrating to the American people, the basic contradiction in assuming what were in effect commitments, especially in Latin America and eastern Asia, and refusing to acknowledge them frankly.

"Here in the United States," he once told André Tardieu, the French statesman, "what is most lacking to us is to understand that we have interests in the whole world. I wish all Americans would realize that American politics is world politics; that we are and that we shall be involved in all great questions . . . . the whole American people must become accustomed to this idea. They must be made to feel and understand these international interests."

This was all very well, but Roosevelt did not go far enough. He was never completely convincing because he himself always held back, as already suggested in discussing his intense nationalism, from advocating any definite steps along the road to collective action in place of a wholly independent policy.

A sophisticated and informed minority was always deeply concerned over the future course of world politics, even though what Roosevelt said—and so much regretted—about lack of understanding clearly applied to the great majority of his countrymen. Whether or not such people accepted Roosevelt's approach to specific issues, they agreed with him that the United States could not avoid playing a great part in the world. Whatever their other differences, the spokesmen of this small group were convinced that any attempt on the part of the United States to seek escape from its responsibilities by sustaining an outmoded isolationism was both futile and dangerous. They did not accept the prevailing popular idea that international stability was somehow assured and that America need have no concern for the future. They believed that the uneasy balance of power in Europe, as the Moroccan dispute suggested, might well collapse and that war might tragically shatter the general peace of nearly a century. And they further feared that in such an event the United States, however anxious to remain aloof, would sooner or later become directly involved.

Henry Adams, for one, continued to observe the contemporary scene with his habitual pessimism. He was convinced that the efforts of his old friend John Hay to extend American organization to world affairs—an expansion of McKinleyism—had signally failed, and that Roosevelt had nothing more concrete to offer in staving off ultimate catastrophe. If such views led him at times to say there was nothing the United States could do other than revert to its nineteenth century isolation, on other occasions he advocated a new system of alliances with American participation. His interpretation of the trend of international politics at the time of the Algeciras conference foreshadowed the future with remarkable foresight.

"We have got to support France against Germany and fortify the Atlantic system beyond attack," he wrote; "for if Germany breaks down England or France, she becomes the center of a military world, and we are lost. The course of concentration must be decided by force—whether military or industrial matters not much in the end."

In 1917 such considerations were to play their part in bringing about the alignment of the United States with Great Britain and France against imperial Germany; they were again to come into play when Hitler's Germany invaded western Europe and appeared even more dangerously to threaten the former allies. And a final demonstration of the Adams thesis can be found in the formation of the North Atlantic Treaty Organization, although this time West Germany was included within the framework of a fortified Atlantic system that was erected in defense against an even more powerful continental power—Soviet Russia.

Brooks Adams, who, his brother rather sardonically said, "runs about and instructs the great," also continued to hold very definite ideas on foreign policy. He believed strongly in the closest kind of cooperation between the United States and

Great Britain, and was convinced that only through an actual coalition could the two nations maintain either their commerce or their security against the pressures being exerted by the continental powers. He realized, as subsequent mid-century developments were so clearly to demonstrate, that with the decline in British power the United States would have to carry the major burden in seeking to uphold a peaceful world order.

Brooks Adams also remained greatly concerned over the commercial position of the United States, and continued to insist that the one great potential market for the sale of American surplus manufactures was China. This meant, in his opinion, mounting rivalry and possible conflict with Russia in the establishment of a paramount influence in eastern Asia. He was persuaded that unless Russia and Japan were restrained by their own mutual rivalry, the day would come when the United States would find it necessary to uphold the Open Door by force of arms. The views that Brooks Adams expressed along these lines may well have influenced Roosevelt in his own far eastern policy. The two men were in frequent contact, and it was from Brooks Adams that the President borrowed the phrase, in urging the building up of American power, that no greater danger could face the nation than to be "opulent, aggressive, and unarmed."

Another contemporary publicist, the economist H. H. Powers, was fully alive to the implications of the changed world of the twentieth century. "A year ago," he had written in the course of the Spanish-American War, "we wanted no colonies, no alliances, no European nations, no army and not much navy. . . . Today every one of these principles is challenged, if not directly rejected." He believed that this was a logical consequence of national growth and that the United States could no longer avoid becoming closely associated with the other powers and "a party to their titanic struggle" for supremacy.

In later writings he further emphasized such views in the conviction, which he shared with both Henry Adams and

Brooks Adams, that a breakdown in the existing balance of power in Europe was inevitable. In that event the United States might well find itself dangerously confronted by whatever nation emerged victorious from the European war. He thought it would probably be Russia. "Slav and Saxon," he wrote, "it narrows down to these . . . . which will rule the world?"

In such circumstances Powers naturally had little sympathy with those who believed that this country could somehow continue to go its own independent way. "That the ideal of national isolation is a Utopia," he wrote, "is due to no accident of mood or circumstances, but to laws as fundamental as the constitution of a protoplasm."

A. Maurice Low, writing in the *Forum*, stressed these same ideas in relation to both the political and commercial interests of the United States. "Slowly, irresistibly, unconsciously—against their will perhaps, but unable to thwart it," he said, "the American people are being forced into the vortex of European politics." He admitted that the nation lay outside any immediate circle of such activity, but said it could not be indifferent to a shift in the political equilibrium that might enable any single power to win a dominating position in Europe. The United States could not help being affected by any such development, if for no other reason than that politics and commerce had become so indissolubly linked that they could not be separated. Even though American security might not at once be threatened by the collapse of the European balance of power, Low said, the nation's economic well-being would be.

A quite different type of commentator on the passing scene was Homer Lea, a brilliant, embittered, hunchbacked little man who was deeply interested in eastern Asia and for a time an advisor to Sun Yat-sen. He thought exclusively in terms of the stakes of military power. In his first book, *The Valor of Ignorance*, Lea wrote with uncanny accuracy of what he considered to be certain war between the United States and

Japan. He gave vivid descriptions of Japanese attacks upon Hawaii, the Philippines, and California. A second book, *The Day of the Saxon*, forecast another war which would find the United States and Great Britain aligned against Germany. Upon his death, Lea was engaged in gathering material for still a third study in which he depicted a great climactic struggle between the West and Russia. At the time, these books attracted some attention—favorably received by the military-minded, and vigorously attacked by the peace advocates—but they were then quickly forgotten until Pearl Harbor aroused a new interest in their author's prophecies.

Still another perspicacious observer of the international scene, holding views very similar to those of Henry Adams, was the diplomat Lewis Einstein. He saw the gravest danger to the United States in the developing rivalry between England and Germany, and felt that in the face of the power alignments in the European treaty system, nothing could be more futile than any attempt on this country's part to maintain its traditional isolationism. He urged even more directly and specifically than Adams that the United States should uphold England as against Germany, and declared that ultimately this country would have to be ready to come to England's assistance with military force.

These prophecies and warnings reflected the views of a handful of students of international politics. They reached a tiny audience. They had no impact whatsoever on the American people as a whole. Even so far as they may have been read by some national leaders, there was no transmission belt to carry their ideas to a broader public. The overwhelming majority of Americans looked to the past rather than toward a problematic future in considering the nation's place in the world; they saw no reason to change views that were inherent in the old isolationist tradition.

Richard Olney, well versed in the ways of his countrymen through his own experience as Secretary of State under Cleveland, once made a very shrewd analysis of popular attitudes toward foreign affairs. The rule of policy originating with Washington and pre-eminently wise for his time, Olney wrote, had ever since been taught in the schools, lauded on the public platform, preached in the pulpits, and displayed in capitals and italics in innumerable political manuals and popular histories. Under such circumstances, he felt that this rule had become a part of the mental constitution of the generations to which it had descended, and "they accept it without knowing why and they act upon it without the least regard to their wholly new environment." In such a state of mind more than anything else, Olney believed, could be found the real basis for the paralyzing grip of the isolationist tradition.

There were two other related phenomena which contributed to renewed apathy and disinterest toward foreign affairs, in spite of the warnings of those best informed. One was the mounting absorption in domestic matters in this era of progressive reform, and the other, a widespread belief that major wars had become a thing of the past. There was to be no awakening of the public to the larger international issues until the sharp impact of actual events incontrovertibly demonstrated that what happened in Europe or Asia, in any part of the globe, had its effect upon the United States, and might well endanger national security and the American way of life. A symposium on the problems of the twentieth century, published by the New York *World* in 1900, did not even mention international affairs!

The progressives so busily engaged in pushing through those reforms which they hoped would recover political power for the people and eliminate the abuses within the capitalist system, believed in the expansion of trade. It was another means toward achieving their ultimate aim of a stronger, more healthy nation. To this extent at least they were prepared to support the vigorous foreign policy of Theodore Roosevelt. Also, they never entirely lost sight of the old idea that America had a unique mission in the world in promoting the principles of democracy and of a just peace. In their opinion this mission was to be carried out, however, not through direct action or intervention in other nations' affairs, but through the force of precept and example. There were naturally exceptions to any such generalization, yet most of the active progressive leaders remained convinced during these opening years of the century that the United States had more than enough to do at home without going abroad "in search of monsters to destroy." If the nation itself could remain at peace and succeed in strengthening the bases of American democracy, that was the most it could hope to do. The progressives believed with Henry Clay, the spokesman for isolationism nearly a century earlier, that the American contribution to peace and freedom should be to keep the "lamp burning brightly on this western shore as a light to all nations."

A scornful attitude toward Europe, with its balance of power, its rivalries, its arms races, its constant threats of war, continued to stand squarely in the way of anything that could be construed as direct participation in its affairs. Particularly in the Midwest could be found that age-old belief, as expressed by Robert La Follette, that Europe was "cursed with a contagious, a deadly plague." The United States should at all cost, he believed, avoid the close association which might mean the spread of this plague to a nation so far free from entangling alliances, militarism, and the conscription of its young man power into standing armies.

The grass-roots feeling in regard to any sort of foreign adventure or concern with outside affairs was once expressed in even simpler terms by William Allen White. He had accepted the imperialism of 1900, although even then looking back nostalgically to the days when the United States was free of such responsibilities; but reflecting his Midwestern environment he became less and less interested during the passing years in events in other parts of the world. "Every one in this town," he wrote at the time of the flurry of excitement over possible German ambitions in Venezuela, "is busy and earning money and saving it. Everyone is engaged in honest work and is looking after his own family. The *Gazette* contends that this is better than bothering with Venezuela."

It is also symptomatic of general attitudes that when the young Walter Lippmann, later so deeply concerned with everything related to foreign policy, first began to write on public questions, he became so wrapped up in domestic reform that he largely ignored all other issues. "I cannot remember taking any interest whatsoever in foreign affairs until after the outbreak of the First World War," Lippmann later recalled. ". . . . I remained quite innocent of the revolutionary consequences of the Spanish-American War."

The further belief—in such sharp contrast with the views of Henry Adams, Homer Lea, or Lewis Einstein—that the United States need not bother itself with foreign developments, because all danger of a major war was illusory, also found widespread expression during these years. It was repeatedly brought out in the congressional debates on naval appropriations, and was characteristic of much of the thinking of the leaders in the general disarmament movement. William Jennings Bryan, always a dedicated crusader for peace and disarmament, expressed the conviction that the moral influences at work in the world were bringing an end to periods of strife; and Charles W. Eliot also emphasized constantly the new moral climate that he saw influencing the nations. David Starr Jordan went even further: "The day of nations is passing," he wrote, ". . . . Imperialism, like feudalism, belongs to the past."

So too wrote B. O. Flower, editor of the *Arena,* who believed that an international tribunal would soon be established with power to settle all disputes between nations. "Despite all superficial signs to the contrary," he declared in optimistic analysis of the peace movement, ". . . . the face of the civilized world is set toward universal arbitration and the reduction and final destruction of the menace and curse of militarism."

Perhaps it was Andrew Carnegie, however, who revealed

the most ingenuous point of view in his zest for promoting peace. He accepted fully the efficacy of international law and felt that it held out infinite promise for the world because of the very fact that it had no constraining force behind it. "It is a proof," he stated, "of the supreme force of gentleness."

The century-long history of European stability, the settlement of such crises as that created by the dispute over Morocco, and the apparently limited nature of such conflicts as did occur, encouraged this belief that peace was becoming the natural order of mankind. It is impossible in the mid-twentieth century to recapture the prevailing attitude of these years. Yet there it was. Minor wars might be expected in the future, but in directing their efforts to prevent such outbreaks, the peace advocates remained convinced that the great civilized powers would never again resort to military aggression. There was an abiding faith that arbitration treaties and other measures for the settlement of international disputes would effectively prevent any reversion to the barbarism of the past.

The idealism that so generally characterized the progressive movement partially helps to explain why the American people accepted such roseate views of the future course of world politics. An attitude that reflected what many writers called "the spiritual uprising of the nation" was carried over, from the zealous campaign for social justice at home, into the unfamiliar world of international affairs.

Woodrow Wilson, entering upon the presidency in 1913, was to express this feeling when, in his inaugural address, he spoke with high confidence of the "growing cordiality and sense of community interest among the nations." Most of his countrymen would have agreed with his statement that such developments foreshadowed "an age of settled peace and good will."

Over the horizon was a first world war, which would change the entire course of history. Only two short decades later, another and even more devastating global contest would break out. And a world that was still striving to recover from these two wars was then to find itself confronted with the menace of still a third possible struggle, which, should it ever come, might well endanger the very foundations of civilization. The golden age of the nineteenth century—as it so often appeared to be in retrospect—tragically gave way to a new age of conflict.

There may be no reason to believe that if in the early 1900s the anxieties of the tough-minded had made more of an impression on the American people, or if the warnings of anti-isolationist spokesmen had carried more weight, the age of conflict could have been avoided. The imponderables of history cannot be disposed of so easily. Yet the inability of the American people fully to understand or really accept their obligations as a world power, their generally apathetic attitude toward foreign affairs, and their naive belief that peace was assured without any commitment for its support, prevented the United States from exerting the influence on world affairs that might otherwise have been possible. In seeking to maintain an illusory independence, the nation was to find itself at the mercy of events over which it had sacrificed all possible control.

The years which extended from Cleveland's first term through the second term of Theodore Roosevelt found the United States beginning to act as a great power along lines that foreshadowed the role that it would so decisively play in the middle of the twentieth century. They also witnessed the failure of the American people to give to the development of a coherent global policy the wholehearted support that alone might have made such a policy successful. It was the tragedy of the world as well as the tragedy of America that the immense power of the United States—physical and spiritual—could not somehow have been more effectively marshaled in defense of peace and liberty, without mankind having first to undergo all the savagery and cruelty of total war.

BIBLIOGRAPHICAL NOTES

THE BASIC SOURCES FOR THIS BOOK COMPRISE TWO CATEGORIES of material: the contemporary writings that suggest the forces and influences responsible for the formulation of American foreign policies between 1885 and 1909, and the broad range of histories, biographies, and special monographs dealing with this period. In the light of the immensity of this material, the following bibliographical notes are necessarily highly selective.

PRIMARY SOURCES

The contemporary sources—substantiating the book's major thesis—reveal a gradually increasing interest in foreign policy during the 1890s, a high peak of popular discussion at the turn of the century, and a gradual decline in popular concern during the early 1900s. Two newspapers have been heavily drawn upon: the *New York Times* and the Washington *Post*. The author would at this point like to acknowledge his indebtedness to Gerald E. Ridinger, his research assistant at Ohio State University, for his careful survey of these papers for news and comment throughout the entire period under review. Additional contemporary editorial comment has been largely taken from the *Literary Digest* and *Public Opinion*, while the sources of other quoted articles embrace a wide range of magazines, reflecting every possible viewpoint, which in each instance have been noted in the text. Equally if not more important in sampling public opinion are the records of foreign policy debates in the *Congressional Record*.

The statements of presidential policy have been taken from James D. Richardson, *A Compilation of the Messages and Papers of the Presidents* (10 vols., 1896–1909); quotations of diplomatic correspondence from *Papers Relating to the Foreign*

Relations of the United States, 1885–1909, and other official material from a series of senate documents, most notably those dealing with the annexation of Hawaii, the Spanish-American War, and the acquisition of the Philippines.

The letters, diaries, and other autobiographical material of contemporaries have proved invaluable. Outstanding in this category are *The Letters of Theodore Roosevelt,* admirably edited by Elting E. Morison (8 vols., 1951–54). Other important sources were Allan Nevins, ed., *Letters of Grover Cleveland* (1933); *Selections from the Correspondence of Theodore Roosevelt and Henry Cabot Lodge, 1884–1918* (2 vols., 1925); Theodore Roosevelt, *An Autobiography* (1913); *Letters of John Hay and Extracts from Diary* (Microfilm, 1941); William Roscoe Thayer, *The Life and Letters of John Hay* (2 vols., 1915); Mary B. Bryan, ed., *The Memoirs of William Jennings Bryan* (1925); George Frisbie Hoar, *Autobiography of Seventy Years* (2 vols., 1903); and Henry Adams, *The Education of Henry Adams* (1918). More particularized letters will be noted under special topics.

Contemporary books have provided some factual material, but were more important as revealing the spirit of the times. One of the most interesting proved to be Harry Thurston Peck, *Twenty Years of the Republic* (1906). An early attempt to deal with contemporary history and covering exactly the same period as the present volume, this book has freshness and vitality, but nothing could more graphically illustrate how greater perspective changes the interpretation of very recent events. The topical writings of such authors as John Fiske, Josiah Strong, Alfred Thayer Mahan, Brooks Adams, Henry Adams, Rudyard Kipling, and others proved most useful, while special note should be made of the keen observations of Peter Finley Dunne, available in several contemporary volumes of the sayings of Mr. Dooley and conveniently assembled in Elmer Ellis, ed., *Mr. Dooley at His Best* (1938).

GENERAL SECONDARY SOURCES

The general histories of American foreign policy that have valuable sections dealing with the period under discussion include Thomas A. Bailey, *A Diplomatic History of the American People* (1950); Samuel F. Bemis, *The Diplomatic History of the United States* (1950); Julius W. Pratt, *A History of United States Foreign Policy* (1955); Samuel F. Bemis, ed., *The American Secretaries of State and Their Diplomacy* (10 vols., 1927–29); and such more interpretative accounts as Robert E. Osgood, *Ideals and Self-Interest in America's Foreign Relations* (1953); Frank Tannenbaum, *The American Tradition in Foreign Policy* (1955); Foster Rhea Dulles, *America's Rise to World Power* (1955); and George F. Kennan, *American Diplomacy, 1900–1950* (1951).

In this general category of sources there should also be noted Samuel F. Bemis, *The Latin American Policy of the United States* (1943); Dexter Perkins, *The Monroe Doctrine, 1867–1907* (1937); A. Whitney Griswold, *The Far Eastern Policy of the United States* (1938); Foster Rhea Dulles, *America in the Pacific* (1932); Lionel M. Gelber, *The Rise of Anglo-American Friendship: A Study in World Politics, 1898–1906* (1938); A. L. P. Dennis, *Adventures in American Diplomacy, 1894–1907* (1928); Julius W. Pratt, *America's Colonial Experiment* (1950); Harold and Margaret Sprout, *The Rise of American Naval Power, 1776–1918* (1939); G. T. Davis, *A Navy Second to None* (1940).

Biographies have an important place in the secondary literature. *Benjamin Harrison,* by Harry J. Sievers (1952); *Grover Cleveland; A Study in Courage,* by Allan Nevins (1932); *John Hay: From Politics to Poetry* by Tyler Dennett (1933); *Theodore Roosevelt,* by Henry Pringle (1931); *Elihu Root* by Philip K. Jessup (2 vols., 1938) are particularly outstanding. *The Life of William McKinley,* by Charles S. Olcott (2 vols., 1916) is valuable, but a much less objective study. Other useful books on relatively less important figures are John A. Garraty, *Henry Cabot Lodge* (1953); Allan Nevins, *Henry White; Thirty Years of American Diplomacy* (1930); Henry James, *Richard Olney and His Public Service* (1923); David S. Muzzey, *James G. Blaine* (1934); Matilda G. Gresham, *The Life of Walter Quintin Gresham 1832–1895* (2 vols., 1919); Claude Bowers, *Beveridge and the Progressive Era* (1932); William D. Puleston, *Mahan, The Life and Work of Captain Alfred Thayer Mahan* (1939);

Paul A. Varg, *Open Door Diplomat, The Life of W. W. Rockhill* (1952).

The numerous special studies in diplomatic history may be more properly noted in the following sections taking up special topics on a chapter by chapter basis.

CHAPTER I—MR. CLEVELAND TAKES OFFICE

The material for this chapter is drawn from contemporary records of Cleveland's inauguration—primarily the *New York Times* and Washington *Post*—with the quotation of the inaugural address itself taken from Richardson, *Messages and Papers of the Presidents*. The comments by Bryce are from his *American Commonwealth* (2 vols., 1911) and by Carnegie, from *Triumphant Democracy* (1886). For the more general background, see particularly Nevins, *Grover Cleveland;* Peck, *Twenty Years of the Republic;* and Arthur M. Schlesinger, *The Rise of the City* (1933).

CHAPTER II—THE PATTERN OF THE PAST

The general diplomatic histories have provided the basic material for "The Pattern of the Past" with a primary reliance upon the opening chapter of Dulles, *America's Rise to World Power*. The quotations have been drawn from a wide variety of sources including Charles F. Adams, ed., *The Works of John Adams* (10 vols., 1856); Worthington C. Ford, ed., *The Writings of John Quincy Adams* (7 vols., 1911); William H. Seward, *Works* (5 vols., 1884); the report of the Perry expedition as found in *Senate Executive Document 34*, 33d Congress, 2d session; Frederick W. Seward, *Seward at Washington as Senator and Secretary of State* (1891); Rudyard Kipling, *American Notes* (1891); James Bryce, *The American Commonwealth;* Stephen Gwynn, ed., *The Letters and Friendships of Sir Cecil Spring-Rice* (2 vols., 1929); and Richardson, *Messages and Papers of the Presidents*.

CHAPTER III—MR. CLEVELAND'S FOREIGN PROBLEMS

Apart from the contemporary sources—documents, debates recorded in the *Congressional Record*, newspaper and magazine material—the most useful books dealing with the topics in this chapter are Nevins, *Grover Cleveland* and Charles C. Tansill, *The Foreign Policy of Thomas F. Bayard, 1885–1897* (1940). An almost contemporary record is George R. Dulebohn, *Principles of Foreign Policy under the Cleveland Administration* (1901). On the fisheries dispute see specifically Charles B. Elliott, *The United States and the Northeastern Fisheries* (1887); Joseph I. Doran, *Our Fishery Rights in the North Atlantic* (1888), and the more recent and scholarly account, Charles C. Tansill, *Canadian-American Relations, 1875–1911* (1943). The most comprehensive record of the entire Samoan story is George H. Ryden, *The Foreign Policy of the United States in Relation to Samoa* (1933), but see also John B. Henderson, *American Diplomatic Questions* (1901) and Dulles, *America in the Pacific*.

CHAPTER IV—BACKGROUND OF ADVENTURE

The material for this chapter has been drawn almost entirely from contemporary sources. The more important books are Josiah Strong, *Our Country* (1885) and the same author's *Expansion Under New World Conditions* (1900); John Fiske, *Darwinism and Other Essays* (1884); Kipling, *American Notes* and, carrying the account further forward, the writings of Alfred Thayer Mahan: *The Interest of America in Sea Power, Present and Future* (1897), *Lessons of the War with Spain* (1899), and *The Problems of Asia* (1905).

A valuable monographic study on the growth of the spirit of imperialism is Julius W. Pratt, *Expansionists of 1898* (1936). There is also interesting material in Albert K. Weinberg, *Manifest Destiny* (1935); Ralph Gabriel, *The Course of American Democratic Thought* (1940); and Samuel Hofstadter, *Social Darwinism in American Thought, 1860–1915* (1944). See also William E. Livezey, *Mahan on Sea Power* (1947).

CHAPTER V—THE FIRST STIRRINGS OF IMPERIALISM

There is much useful material on the general foreign policies of the Harrison administration in Sievers, *Benjamin Harrison*, in Alice F. Tyler; *The Foreign Policy of James G. Blaine;* and in an interesting article, A. T. Volwiler, "Harrison, Blaine and Foreign Policy," *American Philosophical Proceedings*, LXXIX (1923).

Again see Ryden, *The Foreign Policy of the United States in Relation to Samoa* on this particular issue. In addition to such general volumes as Bemis, *The Latin American Policy of the United States* and Perkins, *The Monroe Doctrine*, Western Hemisphere policy is discussed in A. C. Wilgus, "Blaine and the Pan-American Movement," *Hispanic America Historical Review*, V (1922). The Chilean episode is covered in Henry Clay Evans, Jr., *Chile and Its Relations with the United States* (1927) and William R. Sherman, *The Diplomatic and Commercial Relations of the United States and Chile, 1820–1914* (1926). See also Robley B. Evans, *A Sailor's Log-Book* (1901).

There is an extensive literature on the Hawaiian story. The beginnings of the annexation movement are discussed in Sievers, *Benjamin Harrison;* Tyler, *The Foreign Policy of James G. Blaine;* John W. Foster, *Diplomatic Memoirs* (1909); but the most comprehensive account is Sylvester K. Stevens, *American Expansion in Hawaii, 1842–1898* (1945). See also Pratt, *Expansionists of 1898;* Dulles, *America in the Pacific;* and Ralph S. Kuykendall and Grove Day, *Hawaii: A History* (1948).

CHAPTER VI—MR. CLEVELAND RETURNS

Apart from the books already noted dealing with Cleveland's foreign policies in general, and the sources cited above for Hawaiian and Latin American policy, there is further material in Gresham, *The Life of Walter Q. Gresham;* James, *Richard Olney;* and N. M. Blake, "Background of Cleveland's Venezuela Policy," *American Historical Review*, XLVII (1942).

CHAPTER VII—BEHIND THE SCENES

The material here is drawn entirely from contemporary letters, diaries, and memoirs. Such sources include *The Education of Henry Adams;* Worthington C. Ford, ed., *Letters of Henry Adams* (2 vols., 1938); Harold D. Cater, *Henry Adams and His Friends* (1947); *The Letters and Friendships of Sir Cecil Spring-Rice; The Letters of Theodore Roosevelt, Letters of John Hay,*

Correspondence of Theodore Roosevelt and Henry Cabot Lodge and comparable material extracted from Nevins, *Henry White;* Garraty, *Henry Cabot Lodge;* Varg, *The Life of W. W. Rockhill;* and Puleston, *Mahan.*

CHAPTER VIII——THE RISING TIDE

Apart from the previous sources for the rise of imperialism as noted under Chapter V, there are many and important magazine articles reflecting the sentiment leading to war and overseas expansion. The course of diplomacy is most comprehensively available in State Department, *Correspondence Relating to the War with Spain* (3 vols., 1902) and *Senate Document 62,* 55th Congress, 3rd session. Other contemporary sources not heretofore cited are Lawrence Mayo Shaw, *America of Yesterday: As Reflected in the Journal of John Davis Long* (1923) and Charles G. Dawes, *A Journal of the McKinley Years* (1950).

Secondary sources include Olcott, *The Life of William McKinley;* Pratt, *Expansionists of 1898;* Walter Millis, *The Martial Spirit* (1931); French E. Chadwick, *The Relations of the United States and Spain* (2 vols., 1909, 1911); Marcus M. Wilkerson, *Public Opinion and the Spanish-American War* (1932); Joseph E. Wisan, *The Cuban Crisis as Reflected in the New York Press* (1934); Orestes Ferrara, *The Last Spanish War: Revelations in Diplomacy* (1937).

CHAPTER IX—"A SPLENDID LITTLE WAR"

The most graphic and readable account of the Spanish-American War remains Millis, *The Martial Spirit,* but the sources on which this chapter is based are a highly selective group of contemporary accounts. They include George Dewey, *Autobiography* (1913); Theodore Roosevelt, *Letters, Autobiography* and *The Rough Riders* (1904); Evans, *A Sailor's Log-Book;* Richard Harding Davis, *The Cuban and Puerto Rican Campaign* (1898); Clara Barton, *The Story of the Red Cross* (1904); and the series of accounts of the battle of Santiago appearing in the *Century:* "The Story of the Captains—Personal Narratives of the Naval Engagement Near Santiago de Cuba," *Century Magazine,* LVIII (May 1899). As noted in the text, additional material has also been drawn from contemporary newspapers.

CHAPTER X—GOD, DESTINY AND MR. McKINLEY

The material on President McKinley is taken from *Messages and Papers of the Presidents; Papers Relating to the Foreign Relations of the United States;* Olcott, *The Life of William McKinley,* and the contemporary press. The account of public discussion is derived from a sampling of current newspapers and magazines, including the *Literary Digest,* and debates reported in the *Congressional Record.* Pratt, *Expansionists of 1898* is again most important among secondary sources.

CHAPTER XI—THE GREAT DEBATE

The major sources are once more the contemporary press, current magazines and the *Congressional Record,* but they are supplemented by the pamphlets issued by the Anti-Imperialist League. See also *Memoirs of William Jennings Bryan; Autobiography of Andrew Carnegie* (1920); Hoar, *Autobiography of Seventy Years.* Two highly interesting articles are by F. H. Harrington: "The Anti-Imperialist Movement," *Mississippi Valley Historical Review,* XXII (1935) and "Literary Aspects of Anti-Imperialism," *New England Quarterly,* X (1937); a third is Thomas A. Bailey, "The Election of 1900, A Mandate for Imperialism?" *Mississippi Valley Historical Review,* XXIV (1937).

See also Garraty, *Henry Cabot Lodge* and Bowers, *Beveridge and the Progressive Era.*

CHAPTER XII—ESTABLISHING AN EMPIRE

The reports of the Schurman and Taft commissions to the Philippines found in *Senate Documents No. 138,* 56th Congress, 1st session, and *No. 112,* 56th Congress, 2nd session; the report on yellow fever in *Senate Document No. 882,* 61st Congress, 3rd session; Jacob Gould Schurman, *Philippines Affairs, Retrospect and Prospect* (1902); Elihu Root, *The Military and Colonial Policy of the United States* (1916) are among the more important official records of establishment of a colonial empire.

There is also much material in Olcott, *The Life of William Mc-Kinley;* Jessup, *Elihu Root;* Pringle, *Theodore Roosevelt;* Dennett, *John Hay,* and Hermann Hagedorn, *Leonard Wood, A Biography* (1931).

Further secondary material is very extensive: Julius W. Pratt, *America's Colonial Experiment* (1950); Garel A. Grunder and William E. Livezey, *The Philippines and the United States* (1951); William H. Haas, ed., *The American Empire* (1940); Earl S. Pomeroy, *Pacific Outpost: American Strategy in Guam and Micronesia* (1951); Russell H. Fitzgibbon, *Cuba and the United States, 1900–1935* (1935).

CHAPTER XIII—THE OPEN DOOR POLICY

Apart from the official diplomatic record itself, the best accounts of the origin of the Open Door policy are found in Dennett, *John Hay;* Griswold, *Far Eastern Policy of the United States;* and Varg, *The Life of W. W. Rockhill,* but see also Charles S. Campbell, Jr., *Special Business Interests and the Open Door* (1951); Paul Clements, *The Boxer Rebellion* (1915); Foster Rhea Dulles, *China and America* (1946).

Especially noteworthy among contemporary books and articles are Charles Beresford, *The Break-Up of China* (1899); Mahan, *The Problem of Asia* (1900); Brooks Adams, *America's Economic Supremacy* (1900); Charles A. Conant, "The Struggle for Commercial Empire," *Forum,* XVII (June 1889); William W. Rockhill, "The United States and the Future of China," *Forum,* XXIX (May 1900).

CHAPTER XIV—THEODORE ROOSEVELT AND WORLD POWER

The sources for this chapter are primarily the Roosevelt material: *The Letters of Theodore Roosevelt,* the *Autobiography,* and *The Works of Theodore Roosevelt* (20 vols., 1926). In addition to Pringle, *Theodore Roosevelt,* additional studies include John M. Blum, *The Republican Roosevelt* (1954); Gordon C. O'Gara, *Theodore Roosevelt and the Rise of the Modern Navy* (1943); Tyler Dennett, *Theodore Roosevelt and the*

Russo-Japanese War (1925); Thomas A. Bailey, *Theodore Roosevelt and the Japanese-American Crisis* (1934); and Howard C. Hill, *Roosevelt and the Caribbean* (1927).

For the decline of imperialism and the peace-movement, contemporary magazine articles and congressional debates are most rewarding. There is also material in Merze Tate, *The Disarmament Illusion: The Movement for a Limitation of Armaments to 1907* (1942); Merle Curti, *Peace or War: The American Struggle, 1636–1936* (1936); Joseph H. Choate, *The Two Hague Conferences* (1913). For general background, Harold U. Faulkner, *The Quest for Social Justice, 1898–1914* (1931), and Mark Sullivan, *Our Times, the United States, 1900–1925* (6 vols., 1926–1935).

CHAPTER XV—MAKING LATIN AMERICA BEHAVE

Contemporary material for this chapter supplementing the general sources includes Philippe Bunau-Varilla, *Panama; the Creation, Destruction, and Resurrection* (1914); Theodore Roosevelt, "How the United States Acquired the Right to Dig the Panama Canal," *Outlook,* XCIX (1911); and Albert G. Robinson, *Cuba and Intervention* (1905). In addition to secondary literature already noted for this period, including Dennett, *John Hay,* Jessup, *Elihu Root,* and Perkins, *The Monroe Doctrine,* the following books are especially helpful: Dwight C. Miner, *The Fight for the Panama Route* (1940); Fitzgibbon, *Cuba and the United States;* David A. Lockmiller, *Magoon in Cuba: A History of the Second Intervention, 1906–1909* (1938); Melvin M. Knight, *The Americans in Santo Domingo* (1928); William D. McCain, *The United States and the Republic of Panama* (1937); Wilfred H. Calcott, *The Caribbean Policy of the United States, 1890–1920* (1942); J. F. Rippy, *The Caribbean Danger Zone* (1940); Dana G. Munro, *The United States and the Caribbean* (1934), and Mack Gerstle, *The Land Divided: A History of the Panama Canal and Other Isthmian Canal Projects* (1944).

Among special articles: S. W. Livermore, "Theodore Roosevelt, the American Navy and the Venezuela Crisis of 1902–

1903," *American Historical Review,* LI (1946); J. Fred Rippy, "The Initiation of the Customs Receivership in the Dominican Republic," *Hispanic America Historical Review,* XVII (1937); J. Fred Rippy, "Antecedents of the Roosevelt Corollary of the Monroe Doctrine," *Pacific Historical Review,* IX (1940); Rudolph Dillon, "The Venezuela Arbitration Once More: Facts and Law," *American Law Review,* XXXVIII (1940); John Patterson, "Latin American Reactions to the Panama Revolution of 1903," *Hispanic America Historical Review,* XXIV (1944).

CHAPTER XVI—WAR AND PEACE IN ASIA

New sources in addition to those cited for Chapter XIII, include E. H. Zabriskie, *American-Russian Rivalry in the Far East, 1895–1914* (1946); E. Tupper and G. E. McReynolds, *Japan in American Public Opinion* (1937); T. A. Bailey, "The Root-Takahira Agreement of 1908," *Pacific Historical Review,* IX (1940); and W. B. Thorson, "American Public Opinion and the Portsmouth Peace Conference," *American Historical Review,* LIII (1948).

CHAPTER XVII—AN EVEN KEEL IN EUROPE

The Letters of Theodore Roosevelt, supplemented by the diplomatic record, congressional debates and the contemporary press, constitutes the most important source for the Algeciras conference. There is further valuable information in Nevins, *Henry White.* See also E. H. Anderson, *The First Moroccan Crisis, 1904–1906* (1930); Gelber, *The Rise of Anglo-American Friendship;* Clara E. Schieber, *The Transformation of American Sentiment Toward Germany, 1870–1914* (1923); Richard R. Heindel, *The American Impact Upon Great Britain, 1898–1914* (1940).

CHAPTER XVIII—END OF AN EPOCH

The Letters of Theodore Roosevelt; The Education of Henry Adams; Letters of Henry Adams; Brooks Adams, *America's Economic Supremacy;* Homer Lea, *The Valor of Ignorance;* William Allen White, *Autobiography* (1946); *LaFollette's Auto-*

biography (1913); Walter Lippmann, *U.S. Foreign Policy* (1943); and *Autobiography of Andrew Carnegie,* together with various magazine articles and publications of the American Peace Society, have provided the greater part of the special material for this final chapter.

INDEX

Adams, Brooks, 92, 124, 223, 305-306
Adams, Henry, 62, 91, 210
  anti-imperialist and anti-militarist views, 223-224
  on 1897 change of administration, 105
  direct part in development of imperialism, 94
  frustration and cynicism, 91-92
  interest in foreign affairs, 93-94
  pessimism on U.S. foreign policy, 305
  opinion of Theodore Roosevelt, 240
Adams, John:
  isolationist beliefs, 6
  on U.S. as world leader, 34
Adams, John Quincy, 8
  noninterference policy of, 7
Adams-Hay-Lodge-Roosevelt circle, 103, 106-107
Africa, carving up of, 44
Agricultural utopia:
  and end of frontier, 38
  and isolationist attitude, 15
Aguinaldo, General Emilio, 175-176, 192
  capture of, 193
Alaska, purchase of, 11
Alcohol and tobacco, "devitalization" by, 33
Algeciras, conference and General Act, 294-300
Alger, Horatio, 4
Alger, Russell A., 184
Allgemeine Zeitung, 257
Allied Expeditionary Force, Boxer Rebellion, 214
"Aloha Oe," 63
American, *see also* United States
American Anti-Imperialist League, 166-167

American Asiatic Association, 203
American Banker, The, 152
American Commonwealth, The, 15
American dream, 4
American empire:
  building of, 7-8
  establishing of, 184-198
American idealism, and belief in peace, 312
American Peace Society, 234
American people:
  as "chosen people," 36-37
  failure to accept obligations as world power, 313
American Red Cross, 146
American superiority, sense of, 49
American world mission, idea of, 34
Amusement, *see* Entertainment
Anglo-American friendship, prophecy of, 90
Anglo-Chinese War, 1840's, 200
Anglo-Japanese Alliance, 289
Anglo-Saxon peoples:
  colonizing instinct of, 39
  spiritual Christianity and civil liberty of, 33-34
Anglo-Saxon supremacy concept, 32-33, 35-37, 43, 290
Annexation craze, 78; *see also* Hawaii
Anti-imperialists, 166-168, 171, 222-223
Arbitration Court, the Hague, 233-234, 256
Arena, The, 48, 311
Arthur, Chester A., 1
Asia:
  European imperialism in, 44
  extension of American possessions to, 152
  imperialistic "push" in, 44-45
  threat to American interests in, 267

Asia (cont.):
   U.S. foreign policy in, 266-287
Atlanta Constitution, 20
Atlanta Journal, 85
Atlantic, The, 104

"Balanced antagonisms" principle,
   Russo-Japanese War, 272
Baltimore, USS, 58, 60, 61
Baltimore American, 69
Baltimore News, 257
Barnum and Bailey circus, 5
Barton, Clara, 146-147
Baseball, big-league, 4
Bayard, Thomas F., 19, 21, 23, 26, 27,
   45, 102
   as Anglophile, 83
   on jingoism, 47
Beresford, Lord Charles, 203
Bering Sea, sealing rights dispute, 46
Berlin General Act, 13, 55-56
Beveridge, Albert J., 105, 150
   on Anglo-American "league of
      God," 290
   on Anglo-Saxon superiority, 36, 223
   as imperialist orator, 169-170
   on Open Door policy, 201
   on triumph of imperialism, 183
   urges annexation of Cuba, 262
Bicycling, as universal craze, 4-5
Bigelow, Poultney, 136
Bismarck, Otto von, 28
   avoids controversy over Samoa, 29
   conciliating mood at Samoan con-
      ference, 54
   on role of U.S. in world affairs, 51
Blaine, James G.:
   primary concern of, in Latin-Ameri-
      can relations, 56-62
   reaffirms U.S. interest in Samoan
      autonomy, 54
   as Secretary of State under Harri-
      son, 51-52
   urges moderation in Chilean dis-
      pute, 60-61
"Blessings of Civilization Trust," 179
Blount, James H., 72
   reports against annexation of Ha-
      waii, 74
Boer War, 291
Boston, USS, 66
Boston Herald, 151

Boston Transcript, 115, 157
Boutwell, George S., 167
Boxer Rebellion, 106
   antecedents of, 210
   outbreak of, 210-214
   punishment of leaders and indem-
      nity, 217-218
   British, antagonism toward, 18; see
      also Anglo-Saxon; Great Britain;
      England
British Aggressions in Venezuela, 81
British Guiana, boundary dispute with
   Venezuela, 80-88
British legation, siege of, in Boxer Re-
   bellion, 213
British power, relative decline of, 289
Brooklyn Eagle, 157
Bryan, William Jennings, 254
   advises Democratic senators to op-
      pose Philippine Treaty, 173
   attacks McKinley's foreign policy
      168
   belief in moral outlawry of war, 311
   free-silver dream, 108
   presidential candidate, 180
   Prince of Peace speech, 235
Bryce, James, 4, 15
   on justification for imperialism, 50
   on Nation, 48
Buchanan, James: imperialist views,
   10
Buneau-Varilla, Philippe, 246-247, 249
Bülow, Bernard Heinrich von, 292
Burges, John, 166

Cable cars, 3
California, conquest of, 7
Cameron, J. Donald, 94, 97
Cameron resolution, 94
Canada, retaliatory policy against, 22
Capitalistic development, as decisive
   factor in imperialism, 49-50
Caribbean area: Henry Adams' views
   on, 93-94
   attempts to secure bases in, 52
   England's recognition of American
      rights in, 242
   fleet maneuvers in, during German-
      Venezuela dispute, 255-256
   imperial ideas in, 8
   obtaining new territories in, 79
   and Panama Canal, 245

Carnegie, Andrew, 4, 166
  belief in "supreme force of gentleness," 311-312
Carroll, James, 186
Castro, General Cipriano, 254, 256
Census Bureau, U.S., report on "disappearance" of frontier, 37
Cervera, Admiral Pascual, 130, 134-135
  destruction of fleet under, 141-144
Charleston News and Courier, 60
Chautauqua meetings, 5
Chauvinism:
  era of, 46-48
  of Lodge, 99
Chicago Times, 208
Chicago Times-Herald, 119-120, 157, 160
  urges war with Spain, 124
Chicago Tribune, 73
  on Chilean dispute, 59
Chile: dispute with, 46, 58-60
  ultimatum to, 61
China: beginnings of trade with, 9, 201 ff.
  Boxer Rebellion, 106
  British imperialism in, 45
  Open Door policy, see Open Door policy
  threat of, and U.S. urge to annex Philippines, 152
  trade with, 201 ff.
  as warlike power, 167
China coast: foothold off, 11
Chinese Communists, 210
Chinese Empire, spheres of influence in, 201-202
Chinese immigration: Cleveland administration, 31
  problems created by, 13
Choate, Joseph H., 295
"Christianization of mankind," 170
Churchman, The, 154
Cincinnati Enquirer, 85
Circus troupes, 5
Cities, overcrowding in, 4
Civilization, "blessings" of, 179
Civil War, domestic problems growing out of, 11
Clay, Henry, 310; attitude of toward European affairs, 7

Cleveland, Grover:
  accepts McKinley foreign policy, 109
  accused of "pigheadedness" and wifebeating, 21
  attacked as pro-British, 22
  attacks McKinley's foreign policy, 167
  calls Washington conference on Samoan policy, 26-27
  on commercial expansion, 41
  defeat of, 1888, 50
  disapproves idea of territorial expansion, 16-17
  dismisses Sackville-West, 23
  final message to Congress, 31
  firm stand on Venezuela boundary dispute, 80
  foreign problems of, 17-31
  inaugural address, 3, 6, 17
  message to Congress on Venezuelan boundary dispute, 84-85
  moderation in North Atlantic fisheries dispute, 19-20
  opposes annexation of Hawaii, 64, 71
  opposes territorial expansion, 80
  orders warships to Samoa, 28
  political philosophy, 1-2
  recognizes importance of foreign policy, 16
  refuses to back down in Samoan Islands dispute, 18-19
  refuses to recognize Cuban rebellion, 116
  second term, 70-91
  sees imperialism as un-American, 221
  shame at annexation of Hawaii, 115-116
  support for Monroe Doctrine, 242
  supports expansion of merchant marine and Navy, 41
  upholds Olney in Venezuelan dispute, 83
  upholds U.S. interests in Latin America, 16
  withdraws Berlin General Act from Senate consideration, 13
Colombia:
  disregard of rights of, by Theodore Roosevelt, 250-253

Colombia (cont.):
  negotiations with, in Panama Canal case, 247-248
Columbus Dispatch, 20
Commercial Advertiser, 73
Complacency, in international affairs, 1880's, 14-15
Conant, Charles A., 201
Conger, E. H., 212
Congo Free State, 13
Constitution, U.S., in Philippine annexation, 181-182
Cortelyou, George B., 126
Coudert, Frederic, 224
Country fairs, growth of, 5
Cowles, William Sheffield, 118
Coxey, General Jacob, 71
Cromwell, William N., 247
Cuba:
  acquisition of, 12
  annexation of not sought, 190-191
  blockade of, 134
  demand for intervention in, 117
  independence of, 94, 183-184
  invasion of, 136
  liberation of, 185-186
  movement to secure in 1850's, 8
  revolution in, 98, 107 ff.
  rioting and bloodshed in, 1905, 262
  as semiprotectorate under Platt amendment, 190
  Spanish oppression in, 116
  withdrawal of American troops from, 263
Cuban-American Treaty of 1903, 189
Cuban intervention, as "vote-getter," 120
Curtis, Charles, 120
Cushing, Caleb, 200

Danish West Indies, 12, 101, 108
  acquisition of, urged, 11
Darwin, Charles, on U.S. character as result of natural selection, 33
Davis, Cushman K., 49, 158
Davis, Richard Harding, 136-137, 139
Dawes, Charles G., 157
Day, William R., 110, 125, 156
Day of the Saxon, The, 308
Debs, Eugene V., 71

Democratic party:
  anti-imperialist campaign of Bryan, 173-174, 180
  opposes McKinley's foreign policy, 166
Denver News, 123
Depression, of 1890's, 40, 70
Detroit Evening News, 20, 46, 70
Dewey, Admiral George, 151
  as cause of overseas expansion, 148-149
  denies promise to support Filipinos, 175
  in Venezuelan dispute, 255
  visit to Manila, 130-135
Dole, Sanford B., 75
Dominican Republic, bases in, 52; see also Santo Domingo
Drago, Luis M., 261
Dual Alliance, 288
Dunne, Finley Peter, 31, 138, 146, 178, 182, 234, 266, 290-291

Economic progress, 1870-1890, 3
Education of Henry Adams, The, 92-93, 97
Eliot, Charles William, 166, 173, 236, 311
Empire, American, see American empire
England, see Great Britain
"Entangling alliance," 6, 10, 56, 290
Entertainment, increase of, in 1880's, 4
Europe, scornful attitude toward, 310
European affairs:
  early 1900's, 288 ff.
  "even keel" policy, 287-302
  nonentanglement policy, 6-7, 10, 56, 290
  U.S. involvement sees as inescapable, 290, 307
Ethics, in Theodore Roosevelt's foreign policy, 229-230
Evans, Rear Admiral "Fighting Bob," 58-59, 142, 283
Evolutionary doctrine, and American overseas expansion, 34
Expansion, U.S. (see also Imperialism), 7-8
  Adams-Hay-Lodge-Roosevelt circle and, 104
  Caribbean, see Caribbean area

Expansion, U.S. (*cont.*):
national, 8, 12, 37-38
Pacific, *see* Pacific area
Spanish-American War and, 151-152

Farm problems, 3, 88
Farm revolt, nationwide, 38
Field, Marshall, 295
Fifth Army Corps, confusion in Spanish-American War, 137
Filipino revolt, 174-175
Filipinos (*see also* Philippines):
charge of U.S. treachery by insurgents, 176-177
problems involving, 191-195
unfitness for independence claimed, 156, 169
Finley, Carlos Juan, 186
Fish, Hamilton, 24
Fisheries, North Atlantic, dispute with Great Britain over, 17, 19-23
Fiske, John, 32, 39
Florida, acquisition of, 7
Flower, B. O., 311
Footnote to History, A, 30
Foraker Act, 184
Foreign affairs:
apathetic attitude toward, 313
lack of experience in Secretaries of State, 13
Foreign entanglements, avoidance of, 6, 10, 56, 290
Foreign markets, need for, 39
Foreign policy:
awakening of American people to, 44
Cleveland's, 2 *ff.*
Bryce statement on U.S. contempt for other countries, 15
"Great Debate" of 1900 on, 165-183
McKinley's, 100-111; new role of, 88
popular demand for more positive character in, 32
Foreign relations, emphasis on, 1800-1850, 12
Foreign trade (*see also* Open Door policy):
aggressive search for, 39-40
new importance of, 39
Formosa, 9-10

Foster, John W., 67-68
Forum, The, 98, 201, 307
France:
imperialist policy, in Africa, 44; *see also* Morocco
in Asia, 44-45
French Indo-China, 44
Freneau, Philip, 7
Frontier:
disappearance of, 37-38
westward march of, 12

Garfield, James Abram, 51
Garland, Hamlin, 166
stories of frustration over end of frontier, 38
General Act of Algeciras, 299
General Act of Berlin, 79
Gentlemen's Agreement, Japan, 280, 285
George, Henry, 4
Germany: dispute over Samoan Islands, 17-18
protectorates in Africa, 44
rise of imperialism in, 288
"ultimatum" to, in Venezuelan affair, 255
"war" with Samoa, 28
war with U.S. and Great Britain predicted, 308
Godkin, E. L., 48
Goethals, George Washington, 252
Gompers, Samuel, 166
"Good will," age of, 312
Gorgas, Major William C., 186-187
Great Britain (*see also* British):
boundary dispute with Venezuela, 80-88
difficult relations with, 1880's, 17-18
dispute over North Atlantic fisheries, 17-18
dispute over sealing rights in Bering Sea, 46
empire building in Africa, 44
growing U.S. sympathy with, 1900's, 290
and Open Door policy, 202-203
"Great Debate," on foreign policy, 165-183
Great Plains, westward settlement across, 12

Greenbackism, 11
Greene, General F. V., 161
Greenebaum, Berthold, 25
Gresham, Walter Quintin, 79, 81
Guam: acquisition of, 155-156, 183-
    184
  Japanese conquest of, 197

Hague Tribunal:
  founded, 233
  second peace conference, 234
  settlement of Venezuelan dispute,
    256
Hale, William Bayard, 228, 258, 264
Haiti, coaling station in, 52
Hanna, Mark, 109-110, 118, 127
  accepts imperialism in campaign of
    1900, 180-181
  on Open Door policy, 201
  on Panama Canal, 247
Harper's Weekly, 136
Harrison, Benjamin, 99
  accepts annexation of Hawaii, 67
  bellicose note to Chile, 61
  brings Chilean issue before Con-
    gress, 59
  inaugural address, 31, 51
  overshadowed by Blaine, 51-52
  supports Blaine's "sphere of influ-
    ence" policy, 56
Harvard Crimson, 101
Hawaii:
  annexation of, 11, 12, 43, 52, 62-71,
    96, 98, 109, 111, 114, 115, 183-
    184
  becomes Territory, 183
  commercial and strategic impor-
    tance of, 68
  Committee on Public Safety, 66
  early history, 63-64
  Japanese immigration to, 112
  as "key to Pacific," 64
  as port of call for American mer-
    chantmen, 9
  Provisional Government, 75-76
  Queen Liliuokalani, see Liliuokalani,
    Queen
  treaty of annexation, 9
  U.S. flag lowered by Blount, 72
  U.S. imperialist moves in, 45
  U.S. troops landed in, 67

Hay, John, 62, 91, 110, 156, 196
  Henry Adams' opinion of, 305
  on Boxer Rebellion, 212
  character and policies, 95-96
  circular message on safeguarding
    China's political independence,
    215-216
  exaggerated success of Open Door
    policy, 208-209
  as foremost Anglophile, 290-291
  Open Door policy, 105-106, 198-
    199, 208-209
  on Panama Canal, 244-245
  protests Russian encroachments in
    Asia, 268
  recognizes independence of Pan-
    ama, 250
  value of, to Theodore Roosevelt, 239
Hay-Herran Treaty, 247-248
Hay-Pauncefote Treaty, 244-245
Hayes, Rutherford B., 25
Haymarket riots, 3
Hemisphere solidarity, 264
Hippisley, Alfred, 204-208, 216
Hitler, Adolf, 305
Hoar, George Frisbie, 63, 114, 171
Hoover, Herbert, 120
Howells, William Dean, 166

Immigrants, European, and crowded
    cities, 4
Imperialism (see also Expansion):
  Berlin General Act as entering
    wedge of, 56
  capitalist need for, 49-50
  condemned by Democratic party
    in 1900, 180
  economic factors in, 49-50
  as escapism, 221-222
  first stirrings of, 50-70
  jingoism as background of, 48-49
  moral issue fought by anti-imperial-
    ists, 168
  retreat from, 303
  righteousness of, 168
  submergence of, post-Civil War, 12
  termed "un-American" by Cleve-
    land, 221
  triumph of, 182-183
Indo-China, 44
Industrial production, rapid increase
    of, and overseas expansion, 39

Industrial unrest, Cleveland's second term, 88

Industry, expanding, 1880's, 5

Influence of Sea Power upon History, The, 42, 101; *see also* Mahan, Alfred Thayer

Inter-American Conference, 1904, 264

International affairs, complacency in, 14; *see also* Foreign affairs

International Conference on American Affairs, 1889, 57; 1904, 264

International politics:
increasing involvement in, 12
seen as preventive for business depressions, 39
U.S. ignorance of, 18, 313

International Red Cross, rejection of, on isolationist grounds, 13

Irish-American vote, vs. Anglophiles, 22-23

Isolationism:
abandonment of, 44, 108
effect of Midwest wheat crops on, 15
and International Red Cross, 13
need for abandonment of, 44
roots of, 16
traditional U.S., 6, 10, 12, 50

Italy:
friction with over New Orleans lynchings, 46
imperialism in Ethiopia, 44

James, William, 166

Japan:
American sympathy for, in Russo-Japanese War, 277
anti-American riots in, 276
enthusiastic welcome for U.S. fleet, 1908, 283
opening up of, 9
possibility of hostilities with, 267
prediction of 1941 war with, 307-308
protests annexation of Hawaii, 112
threat of war with, 1906-07, 278-279

Japanese, discriminatory treatment of, in U.S., 278

Jefferson, Thomas, 2, 6, 34

Jews, Russian persecution of, 227

Jingoism, 58, 80, 89, 99, 105, 109, 120, 126, 151-152, 255, 259, 280, 303
beginnings, 46
Chilean dispute, 58, 60
newspaper, 119
see also Yellow press; on possible war with Japan, 282
and Spanish-American War, 48
stimulated by Cleveland's stand on Venezuela dispute, 85

"Jingo Jim," epithet for Blaine, 51

Johnson, Andrew, 11

Jones Act, 194

Jordan, David Starr, 166, 311

Journal of Commerce, 152

Jusserand, Jean Jules, 237

Kaiser, *see* William II

Kalakaua, King, 64-65

Kansas City *Star,* 123

Katsura, Taro, Prince, 277

Kennan, George F., 230 *n.*

Kettle Hill, San Juan, 139

Kimball, William Wirt, 118

Kipling, Rudyard, 14, 35-36, 100

Korea, 269, 276

Labor strife, Cleveland's second term, 70

Ladrones (Marianas), 155-156

Laissez-faire:
under Cleveland, 2
under McKinley, 108

Latin America:
distrust of U.S., 264
interests in upheld by Cleveland, 16
as primary concern of Secretary Blaine, 56-62; *see also* Roosevelt, Theodore

Latin American policy and relations (*see also* Pan-American Union), 242-266
motives behind, 265

Law of Civilization and Decay, The, 93

Lawton, General H. W., 138

Lazear, Jesse W., 186

Leslie's Illustrated Newspaper, 60

Lesseps, Ferdinand de, 246

Liliuokalani, Queen:
agrees to amnesty, 76

Liliuokalani, Queen (*cont.*):
  opposed to foreign influence, 65
  permanent loss of throne, 78
  proclaims new constitution, 66
  proposed restoration of, 75-77
  seen as "barbarous," 62-63
  surrenders authority, 67
Lincoln, Abraham, 95
Lindsay, Vachel, 108
Lippmann, Walter, 230 *n.*, 311
Literary Digest, 85, 157, 208
Lodge, Henry Cabot, 14, 20, 36, 91, 103, 132, 172
  character and policies of, 96-99
  conversion to Anglo-American viewpoint, 291-292
  expansionist policies, 154
  partisanship, 97
  on Philippine annexation, 150
  praises jingoism of Cleveland, 80
  proclaims supremacy of Monroe Doctrine, 84
  supports annexation of Hawaii, 98
  supports Mahan's big-navy policy, 43
  urges annexation of Hawaii, 111
  urges peaceful solution to Cuban rebellion, 119
Louisiana Purchase, 7
Louisville *Courier-Journal*, 91

MacArthur, General Arthur, 191-192, 194
McKinley, William, 95, 98, 103, 105
  alarmed at Japanese threat of annexing Hawaii, 112-113
  approves Rockhill-Hippisley Open Door plan, 207
  asks Congress for authority to intervene in Cuba, 127-128
  assassination of, 219
  character and policies of, 109-110
  committed to Panama Canal, 244
  contrasted with Roosevelt on foreign policy, 238
  "conversion" to overseas expansion, 148-149
  debate on foreign policy, 165-183
  1st administration, 107 *ff.*
  growing expansionist policies, 155 *ff.*
  inaugural address, 1st., 109

McKinley, William (*cont.*):
  indecision on Philippines, 156-157
  laissez-faire economy, 108-109
  opposes war with Spain, 121
  Peace Commission, 159-161
  reelection of, 181
  rejection of Open Door policy, 202;
  sees moral obligation in Spanish-American War, 162
  sees U.S. expansion as divine mission, 159
  torn by desire for peace in Spanish-American War, 124-126
  on "uplifting and Christianizing" of Filipinos, 163
McKinley tariff, effect of, on annexation of Hawaii, 65
Mahan, Alfred Thayer, 47, 118, 169, 223, 231
  belief in Anglo-Saxon superiority, 43
  career as big-navy advocate, 42-43
  heralds end of isolation, 90-91
  influence on Theodore Roosevelt, 101
  on necessity of annexing Hawaii, 73
  on need for "accordant" relations with Great Britain, 290
  on need for naval supremacy, 40
  on positive foreign policy, 32
  urges annexation of Hawaii, 111
Maine, USS, 48, 113, 122, 124
Manchuria:
  Japanese attack on, 272
  Russian and Japanese rivalry in, 269
  Russian imperialism in, 45
  tightening of Russian hold on, 267
  U.S. recognition of Japanese control, 284-285
"Manifest Destiny," 170
  in Hawaiian annexation, 73
Marcy, William Learned, 10
Mariana Islands, 155, 196
Meade, Richard W., 24
Mercantile imperialism, 41-43
Merritt, General Wesley, 150
Mexican War, 8
Midway Island, title to, 11
Middle Border, monotony of life in, 38
Midwest, wheat crops in, 15
Miles, General Nelson Appleton, 136

Missionary movement, influence of, on expansionism, 9, 153
Monroe, James, 2, 6
Monroe Doctrine:
Bismarck's view on, 51
challenges to, 6
Cleveland defense of, 89
"defiant challenge" by British in Venezuelan dispute, 254-255
"mothball" flavor, 254
popular support for, 242
principles of, 87
Roosevelt Corollary, 259, 261
supremacy of, 84
"triumphant vindication" of, in Venezuelan dispute, 256
Moody, William Vaughn, 166, 178
Morgan, John Pierpont, 49, 143
Morgan, John T., 14, 105
"Most favored nation" clause, 199
Morocco:
conference on, 1906, 287-288
crisis of 1905, 292
of 1911, 301
independence recognized, 299
Open Door in, 293
Myth of the Garden, 15, 38

Nashville American, 20
Nation, The, 210, 222, 235
campaign against jingoism, 48
National honor, 62
bellicose attitude on, 47-50
in Chilean dispute, 60
Cleveland's views on, 89
in Philippine revolt, 163
in Venezuelan dispute, 82
National mission, idea of, 164
National self-assertiveness, 49-50
Natural resources, 2
Naval expansion, economic arguments for, 40
Naval Policy Board, 41, 43
Naval power, implications of, 169
Naval supremacy, U.S. need for, 40-41
Naval War College, 42
Navy, U.S., see United States Navy
New Orleans Times Democrat, 123
New Panama Canal Company, 246, 252
New York Evening Post, 160

New York Herald, 28, 136, 119
New York Journal, 119
urges war with Spain, 123
New York Peace Society, 232
New York Press, 285
New York Sun, 13-14, 60, 68, 85, 282
New York Times, 20, 29, 69, 71, 77, 135, 151, 157, 196, 208, 251, 256, 257, 269, 276, 282, 299
New York Tribune, 20, 60, 104, 196, 297
New York World, 30, 69, 86, 119, 309
sensational report on Boxer Rebellion, 212-213
Nicaraguan Canal Commission, 244
Nobel Peace Prize, 228
Noninterference policy, 6-7; see also Entangling alliances
Norfolk Virginian Pilot, 255
Norris, Frank, 38
Norris, George, 252
North American Review, 48
North Atlantic fisheries dispute, 17
North Atlantic Treaty Organization, 305

Ode in Time of Hesitation, 178
Okinawa, naval and air base at, 9
Olney, Richard, 74-75, 82, 90, 102, 308-309
Open Door policy:
China, 106, 198-219
history of, 199-201
Kaiser's imperialist policies and, 273
momentum and force of, 219
in Morocco, 293
as return to fundamental principles, 221
in Russo-Japanese War, 269, 271
safeguarding of by Root-Takahira agreement, 286
and U.S. involvement in world politics, 217
upholding of by force, 306
Opium War, 200
Oregon, boundary dispute with Great Britain, 7-8
Orient, new markets in, 8; see also Asia; China; Japan
Organic Act:
of 1900, 183

Organic Act (cont.):
of 1902, 194
Osgood, Robert E., 230 n.
Our Country, 33
Outlook, The, 252
Overland Monthly, The, 39
Otis, General Elwell S., 191

Pacific:
expansion into, 8, 152
new territories in, 79
U.S. importance in, 45
Page, Walter Hines, 104
Pago Pago:
American rights in, 195-196
discovery of, by Commodore
Wilkes, 24
establishment of U.S. naval station,
25
Pan-American Exposition, Buffalo, 219
Pan-American Union, 58
Panama:
independence of, 250
revolution in, timed with plans for
Panama Canal, 248
seizure of, 248-253
Panama Canal, 242-253
Blaine's belief in need for, 56
McKinley platform, 108
opened to commerce in 1914, 252
and revolution in Panama, 248-251
Roosevelt's reckless policy on, 227
route of, 246
yellow fever and, 187
Pauncefote, Lord Julian, 245
Peace movement, 1900's, 232-233
Pearl Harbor:
Japanese attack on, 278
naval station at, 64
Peking, siege of foreign legations in,
210
Perry, Commodore Oliver Hazard, 9,
10, 277
Philadelphia Inquirer, 69
Philadelphia Press, 61, 62, 151
Philadelphia Public Ledger, 157
Philadelphia Record, 151
Philippine Commission:
1st, 193
2nd, 179-180
Philippine Organic Act, 194

Philippines:
Henry Adams' views on acquisition
of, 94
annexation of, 150, 183-184
blockade of, 151
cession of, 162
constitutionality of annexing, 181-
182
expeditionary force to, 150
guerilla warfare in, 191-195
independence, 192
revolt of insurgents against U.S.
occupation, 174
self-government program, 191 ff.
treaty approved, 174
war in, 132
Phillips, William, 91
Pierce, Franklin, 8
Platt, Orville, 153, 189
Platt Amendment, 189
Populism, 38, 70
Portsmouth, N.H., peace conference,
274-276
Powers, H. H., 306
Proctor, Redfield, 105, 122
Puerto Rico, annexation of, 183-184
Pullman strike, 1894, 71, 82

Quesham, Walter Q., 71-72

Racial superiority, American concept
of, 49
Reconstruction, Southern, 11
Reed, Thomas B., 127
Reed, Walter, 186
Reid, Whitelaw, 104, 158
Republican party:
foreign policy, 109
imperialist platform, 180-181
Review of Reviews, The, 104
Rhodes, Cecil, 44
Richmond Times, 124
Rockefeller, John D., 4, 49
Rockhill, William W., 103-104, 216
and Open Door policy, 199, 203-
204
Rockhill-Hippisley plan for Chinese
Trade, 204-208
Roosevelt, Alice, 295
Roosevelt, Franklin Delano:
changed attitude toward Japan in
1940, 287

Roosevelt, Franklin Delano (*cont.*):
note on 1907 danger of war with Japan, 281
Roosevelt, Theodore, 97, 104-105
acceptance of Open Door in China, 267
acclaimed as peacemaker in Russo-Japanese War, 276
accused of exceeding constitutional powers in Morocco dispute, 300-301
admiration for Japanese, 270
arranges Gentlemen's Agreement with Japan, 280
assistant Secretary of Navy, 111
attack on San Juan Hill, 138
attempts treaty with Santo Domingo, 260
attitude toward "Dagoes" in Latin America, 243
belief in strong navy, 231-232
"big stick" policy, 241, 279
changed views on imperialism and expansion, 224
character and policies, 99-101
on Winston Churchill, 47
conduct of foreign affairs, 237 *ff.*
on consequences of American power, 231
controversy with President Eliot of Harvard, 100-101
Corollary to Monroe Doctrine, 259, 261
criticism of Brooks Adams, 93
decision to "go to extremes" with Russia, 268
defends policy in Panama, 252
delight in growth of Navy, 236
denounces fear of war, 235
dependence on Hay, 238-239
desire to aid Santo Domingo, 258
desire to mediate in Russo-Japanese War, 272
disclaims interest in Morocco, 293
faced with Cuban revolt, 262
fear of Japanese supremacy in Asia, 271
final significant moves, 302
first and second administrations, 219-241
foreign policies, 226 *ff.*
friendliness toward Kaiser, 238, 273

Roosevelt, Theodore (*cont.*):
idea of peace based on justice, 229
ignorance of German diplomacy, 273
important role in Spanish-American War, 131-132
incensed by Colombian government, 248
induces France to accept Moroccan conference with Kaiser, 294
influenced by Mahan, 101
intense nationalism, 304
involvement in Panama Canal, 243-253
Japanese-American relations and, 278
jingoism of, in Panama revolt, 252-253
on Kipling's call for American expansionist policy, 36
"League of Peace" idea, 228
martial fervor, 100
as mediator in Russo-Japanese War, 274-276
momentum of, toward imperialist expansion, 91
on Monroe Doctrine, 242-243
for more active role in Asia, 267
on need for strategic control of Caribbean, 264
Nobel Peace Prize award, 228, 302
opposed to annexing Cuba, 263
orders Dewey to take Philippines, 132
personal diplomacy in Morocco conference, 299
plight of Rough Riders, 146-147
popular support during Panama crisis, 253
and possibility of war with Japan, 267
president of American Peace Society, 234
pressure on Kaiser to accept arbitration in Venezuelan dispute, 255
"pro-Japanese" assertion, 277
reckless policy on Panama Canal, 227
recognizes common interests with Great Britain, 291
refusal to acknowledge foreign commitments, 304

Roosevelt, Theodore (cont.):
  retirement from presidency, 303
  role in instigating Panama revolu-
    tion, 250-251
  Rough Riders, 138-141
  scorn for Russian government, 270
  seen as "madman" by Hanna, 220
  sees Philippines as "heel of Achil-
    les," 224-225
  sends U.S. fleet on "demonstration"
    cruise in Pacific, 281-284
  singlehanded direction of foreign
    policy, 240
  strong nationalist views, 300
  supports Mahan's views on big
    navy, 43
  on "taking Canada" in Venezuelan
    dispute, 86
  threat of intervention in Latin
    America, 259
  urges war with Spain, 118, 121, 124
  uses personal influence in Califor-
    nia anti-Japanese violence, 280
Roosevelt Corollary, 259-261
Root, Elihu, 234, 259
  on American apathy toward expan-
    sion, 226
  character and policies of, 188-189
  as major architect of American
    policy in Philippines, 194
  on Roosevelt's role in Panama af-
    fair, 253
  tour of South America, 264
Root-Takahira Agreement, 284-285
Rough Riders, 138-141
Russia (see also Soviet Union):
  aggressive imperialist policy of, in
    Asia, 1900's, 267 ff.
  control of China predicted, 167
  diplomatic victory at Portsmouth,
    276
  imperialism in China and Japan, 45,
    267
  inevitable conflict with U.S., 306-
    307
  opens concession at Talienwan,
    Manchuria, 206
  peace conference sponsored by,
    1900, 233
  persecution of Jews, 227
  as protagonist of U.S., 92-93, 306-
    307

Russia (cont.):
  purchase of Alaska from, 11
  war with U.S. predicted, 308
Russian navy, defeat of, by Japan, 272
Russo-Japanese War, 266-276
Ryukyu Islands, 9

Sackville-West, Sir Lionel, 22-23, 27
Salisbury, Lord Robert Arthur, 83, 87,
    92
Samoa:
  American annexation of proposed,
    25
  continued problem of, 78-79
  dispute with Germany over, 17-18,
    23-30
  division of, between U.S., Germany
    and Great Britain, 196
  final settlement, 53-56
  revolt in, 27
  struck by hurricane, 30
  three-power protectorate, 52, 55,
    195
  U.S. imperialism in, 45
  Washington Conference on, 26-27
  Wilkes' discoveries in, 23-24
Sampson, Admiral William Thomas,
    134, 141-145
Sandwich Islands, see Hawaii
Santiago, capture of, 145-146
Santo Domingo:
  acquisition of, 11
  control of custom houses by U.S.,
    260-261
  guarantee of territorial integrity,
    260
  revolutions in, 258
Schley, Admiral Winfield Scott, 58
Schomburgk, Sir Robert, 80
Schurman, Jacob Gould, 191, 206
Schurz, Carl, 71, 73, 109, 178
Scruggs, William L., 81
"Semiprotectorate" idea, in Latin
    American policy, 266
Seward, William H., 9, 11
Shafter, General William R., 137, 145
Shaw, Albert, 104
Sherman, John, 156
Social revolt, 70
South America, threat of European
    intervention in, 44

Soviet Union (*see also* Russia):
concessions to, at Yalta, 272
defense against, 305
Spanish-American War, 38-39, 40, 108, 111, 113, 129-148
beginnings of, 116 *ff.*
Congressional appropriation following sinking of *Maine*, 124
as denial of republicanism, 198
destruction of Cervera's fleet, 141-145
Dewey's victory at Manila, 130-135
immediate cause of, 128
imperialist nature of, 117, 128
invasion of Cuba, 136-141
jingoism as background of, 48-49
malaria and dysentery in, 146
newspaper jingoism in, 119
outbreak of hostilities, 129 *ff.*
Rough Riders, 139-141
as "summer skirmish," 130
surrender of Spanish forces, 146
Treaty of 1898, 162
yellow fever epidemics, 147
yellow press atrocity stories, 121-122
Speer, Robert E., 153
Spencer, Herbert, 33
Springfield *Republican*, 84, 209
Spring-Rice, Sir Cecil Arthur, 15, 21, 60-61, 62, 92, 93, 97, 104, 237, 270
description of Samoan conference, 27
on possibilities of Chilean war, 46
Stegomyia mosquito, 186
State Department, U.S.:
imbecility and pusillanimity charged, 50
lack of experience in foreign affairs, 13
Steinberger, A. B., 24
Sternberg, Speck von, 237, 254, 258
Stevens, John L., 65
Stevenson, Robert Louis, 30
Story, Mansfield, 173
Strong, Josiah, 32-33, 39, 105
Suez Canal, 135, 246
Sullivan, John L., 4, 60
Sumner, William Graham, 166, 173
Sun Yat-Sen, 307

Taft, William Howard, 179-180, 224
aloofness in second Moroccan crisis, 301-302
Philippine Commissioner, 194
Secretary of War, 277
Taft-Katsura agreement, 277
Tardieu, André, 304
Tariff, Cleveland administration, 2
McKinley, 65
Technology, growth of, 3
Telephones, development of, 3
Teller, Henry Moore, 21
Teller Amendment, 128, 185
Territorial expansion, *see* Expansion
Texas, annexation of, 7
Theatrical road companies, 5
Tillman, Benjamin Ryan ("Pitchfork Ben"), 70
Togo, Admiral Heihachiro, 272
Transportation, improvements in, 3
Treaty of Washington, 200
Trevelyan, Sir George Otto, 240
Triple Alliance, 288
Triple Entente, 289
Tutuila, Samoan Islands, 196
Twain, Mark, 166; scorn for expansionism, 179
Tzu Hsi, Empress Dowager, 45, 211, 214

United States:
bellicose attitude of 1890's, 47 *ff.*
Department of Commerce, on need for international trade, 39
failure to develop coherent global policy, 313
idea of world leadership by, 34
obligations of, as world power, 313
United States Navy:
Cleveland's support of, 16
continued growth, 1890's, 41-42
damage by hurricane at Samoa, 30
decline of, 1870-1880, 14, 40
desire for war, 1892, 62
influence of Mahan on, 42-43
replacement of wooden ships with steel, 41
Theodore Roosevelt's support of, 231-232
seen as factor for peace, 236
seen as limited to continental defense, 16

United States Navy (*cont.*):
triumphal "demonstration" cruise
to Pacific, 281-284
United States Supreme Court, decision in Philippine annexation,
181-182

Valor of Ignorance, The, 307
Valparaiso (*see also* Chile), attack on
American sailors in, 58
Venezuela:
Anglo-German blockade of, 256
boundary dispute, 82-88, 242
defaulting on debts, 254
German bombardment of, 257
Vest, George B., 170
Virgin Islands, 225

Walker, Rear Admiral John G., 244
Wall St. Journal, 122, 152
War:
as "occasional excess," 47
readiness of Americans to resort to,
in 1890's, 47
romantic attitude toward, 47-48
Washington, George, 2, 6
Washington *Post*, 68, 84, 85, 94, 121,
151
Washington *Star*, 53, 151, 177, 280
Watterson, Henry, 91, 104, 154
Well being, era of, 3
Westward movement, 8, 12
discouragement at ending of, 38

Westward movement (*cont.*):
completion of, and overseas expansion, 37
Whaling ships, trading and, 9
Wheat crops, Midwest, and isolationist philosophy, 15
Wheeler, General Joseph, 138
White, Henry, 82, 150, 256, 291
character and policies of, 101-102
at Moroccan Conference, 294
successes at Algeciras, 298
White, William Allen, 36, 120, 310
"White Man's burden," 35-36
Whitney, William C., 41
Wilkes, Commodore Charles, 23-24
William II, German Kaiser, 87, 136
friendship with Theodore Roosevelt, 238
imperialist designs in Russo-Japanese War, 273
pressure brought by Roosevelt in
Venezuelan affair, 255
Willis, Albert S., 75
Wilson, Woodrow, 295, 312
Wood, General Leonard, 186
Woodford, Stewart L., 125
Woolsey, Theodore, 123
World peace, era of, 12
World's Work, 104, 182

Yellow fever, 147
Cuba, 186-187
Yellow press, 121-122
on threat of war with Japan in
1907, 282